MASTERING THE ART OF EXPERT WITNESS TESTIMONY

BRIAN PETER BRINIG, JD, CPA

ADJUNCT PROFESSOR, UNIVERSITY OF SAN DIEGO SCHOOL OF LAW
MANAGING DIRECTOR, CBIZ FORENSIC CONSULTING GROUP LLC

(www.brianbrinig.com + brinigb@gmail.com)

Published by Burlington Business Press
New York – Austin – San Diego

Printed and bound in the United States of America
ISBN
Hardback: 979-8-218-09825-4
Paperback: 979-8-218-06746-5
Ebook: 979-8-218-09826-1

Library of Congress Control Number: 2022920066

Other books by Brian Peter Brinig

Mastering Self-Discipline:
A Thoughtful Approach Gets Better Results
New York: Burlington Business Press, 2020

Finance & Accounting for Lawyers
2nd ed., 2020
Portland, OR: BVResources LLC

Finance & Accounting for Lawyers WORKBOOK
4th ed., 2020
Portland, OR: BVResources LLC

Developing and Managing a Litigation Services Practice
With Elena Gladson
San Diego, CA: Harcourt Professional Publishing, 1999

The CPA's Role in Litigation Support Services, coauthored
Dallas, TX: Practitioners Publishing Company, 2000

CONTENTS

Background and History

Managing the Forensic Consulting Practice

Expert Witness Testimony

Other Considerations

CHAPTER 1

INTRODUCTION

This book is the celebration of my forty-year career as a forensic consultant, specifically a financial one. When I began my niche career as a business appraiser in 1979, the word "forensic" wasn't even used as a descriptive term for a professional service. The formal definition of the word is "relating to or denoting the application of scientific methods and techniques to the investigation of crime." It also means "relating to courts of law."

I began my earlier, short-lived career in public accounting after college but soon became disillusioned with its monotony and tedium. Quickly abandoning that unfulfilling path, I embarked on a law school education, only to learn that the fate of an apprentice business lawyer was just as boring as that of a staff accountant. Those experiences led me to try my hand at business brokerage, which soon evolved to business appraisal, the professional service that became the basis of my forensic consulting career.

In the beginning, I didn't know that people only needed their businesses appraised if they were in some kind of dispute—usually a partnership split or a divorce—but I soon learned that business appraisal was litigation-related. The initial potential clients were almost all lawyers who needed business appraisers as experts in their cases to solve valuation disputes between their clients. Providing business valuations looked to be a service that I could elevate to a higher professional level rather than merely being a salesman of business opportunities. I was on my way to building a professional services firm.

One of my early business appraisals resulted in my first experience as an expert witness, and it was horrifying. I received a call from a panicked lawyer who was soon scheduled for trial in his case representing Suzie's Ice Creamery[1] against the landlord whom Suzie claimed had breached her lease in the idyllic commercial district of Coronado, California. A few hundred yards from the famous Hotel del Coronado, Suzie's had operated successfully until her landlord abruptly canceled the sublease that granted her occupancy of a small portion of his larger retail store on prosperous Orange Avenue, the tony commercial district of the quaint beach town. Suzie's lawyer had filed suit to recover the losses she sustained from losing her remaining three years of occupancy after finally achieving profitability and expecting to recover her early start-up losses. The justice of Suzie's case was compelling but, unfortunately, Suzie did not have the good fortune of being well-represented.

For me, the business appraiser, the first clue to problems with the case was the last-minute panic of Suzie's lawyer hiring me about ten days before the scheduled trial in San Diego Superior Court. In the beginning days of my litigation-related expert witness practice, I wasn't familiar with the norms of litigation, but I was still surprised at the late contact by the lawyer. Regardless of my concerns and for reasons I won't belabor here, I agreed to prepare a business appraisal of Suzie's Ice Creamery and testify in court to my findings. I quickly reviewed Suzie's financial performance, visited her abandoned premises, discussed the opera-

1. Not the real business name.

tions of the closed business with her, and did my market research to determine the fair market value of her abandoned business, assuming she would have been allowed to continue to operate.

The shocking part of this story was my appearance at the trial in Suzie's case. Because of my inexperience, I simply did what Suzie's very mediocre lawyer told me to do: show up at 9:30 on Thursday to testify on my findings. There was no advance plan or preparation; it was simply "Be there at 9:30." I didn't know any better, so I did what I was told to do. As soon as I was sworn into my first expert testimony, I immediately realized the difficulty of the situation both Suzie and I were in. Her lawyer didn't have a clue about how to conduct the direct examination of a witness, much less an expert witness who had performed a sophisticated analysis.

Forty years later, I am still incredulous at the fiasco that took place on my direct examination—not to mention a very effective cross-examination—and the poor result that was provided for the client. Suzie's lawyer wasn't prepared for conducting a trial and, candidly, I'm not sure he had the mental capacity to *ever* be prepared. One of the occasional sad realities of forensic consulting is being retained by a below-average lawyer who isn't capable of handling the trial of a sophisticated lawsuit. I will discuss strategies and techniques to overcome this infrequent situation in the pages of this book, but I'm sorry it has to be discussed at all.

In 1983 I left the employ of my second business brokerage firm, where I was doing exclusively business appraisal work, and formed my business appraisal firm, Brinig & Company Inc. At first, it was only me renting a month-to-month office in a downtown office building in San Diego. I used my downtown contacts and my bar association membership to meet lawyers, trying to find business appraisal cases. It didn't take long to be busy enough to be making rent and a couple of thousand dollars a month to take home. As I grew my appraisal practice, I added some young staff financial analysts and trained them to do support work and report drafting. A couple of years into the practice, I began getting calls to provide other types of forensic financial work, primarily personal economic loss analysis and business damages. Over the years, several other principals joined the firm, expanding our base into broader areas of financial consulting, but every area of our practice was forensic, meaning it was litigation related.

I won't continue the story through the stages of growth of Brinig & Company Inc.—it was a great ride—but by the time the firm was acquired in 2019 by CBIZ, a publicly traded financial services firm, we were a twenty-person organization with a prestigious reputation in Southern California as a valuation and forensic accounting firm. As I will discuss in subsequent chapters, I always considered it important for the firm to look and act like a consummate professional organization. Nice offices, professional dress code, no cheap advertising, and most importantly, the highest-quality work product possible.

In recent years, I have described myself as a "forensic accountant," and I think the term fits what I do. My practice has evolved to be about one-third business valuation, one-third personal economic loss analysis (for personal injury cases, wrongful death cases, and wrongful termination cases), and one-third business damages cases (usually lost profits from a breach of contract or business tort). I have tried to maintain a fairly balanced practice, meaning I am retained roughly equally by plaintiffs and defendants to provide services to them. I want the marketplace of lawyers and judges to perceive me as an honest economic expert, not one whose opinion can be bought and paid for.

At this stage of my career, I can candidly write the things I share in these pages, knowing that lawyers will no longer have the opportunity to distort them in arguments against me on cross-examination. I'll be busy teaching at the University of San Diego School of Law and writing my next books. My objective here is to share everything I know about this niche industry, and I believe these pages will help you develop your new or existing forensic consulting practice into a successful professional venture. Mine has been an enjoyable, successful career, and I can't think of anything I would rather have done professionally for the last forty years.

CHAPTER 2

THE OATH

"Do you solemnly swear that the testimony you are about to give in this matter will be the truth, the whole truth, and nothing but the truth, so help you God?"

If you answer "Yes" to this question, you are signed on for the professional ride of a lifetime. Testifying as an expert witness is one of the most exciting and hazardous forms of duty that professionals can be asked to perform. It is not for the weak or faint of heart, but it's a skill that can be studied and elevated to an art form. The same way a doctor, lawyer, or teacher learns to truly master her craft, the forensic expert can understand the subtleties of the skill of testifying in front of judges and juries and withstanding the attack of cross-examination in which opposing lawyers are trying to destroy the witness in a public forum. Becoming a competent expert witness is a talent that can be learned by an experienced professional who possesses a number of dynamic personality skills: intelligence, creativity, public presence, speaking and teaching ability, and confidence. If you are fortunate enough to possess these capabilities, opportunity awaits you in this exciting, expanding field.

In my forty years as a forensic economist and certified public accountant, I have testified in more than 200 jury trials across the country and given about 600 depositions. Providing expert witness testimony is a professional skill with a fairly steep learning curve, but an experienced, competent professional who possesses the right mix of personal and professional skills can add this area of practice to his or her other work. Expert witness testimony is a much-needed component of the American judicial system that contributes to the administration of justice and the resolution of civil (and criminal) disputes. It is also work that is challenging and exciting, and it continues to be a growing and lucrative area of professional services. If you're inclined to participate in this area of professional services, this book will take you through the strategies and tactics of expert witness work and help you elevate your practice to an art form.

During my career, I have lectured many times to groups of experts about strategies and tactics of expert testimony. (Full disclosure: I also speak to lawyers about how to examine and cross-examine expert witnesses.) Every time I speak to experts, I always share the following embarrassing story to remind the audience—and me—that I am still learning this craft after all these years.

In 1987, I had been working in the field of forensic accounting and damages analysis for about nine years and I was beginning to think I could present expert testimony quite effectively on direct examination and do an adequate job of withstanding cross-examination. That many years into my career, I was fortunate to be hired on some significant cases. One of my law school classmates, Scott Metzger, was a ten-year lawyer who was the litigation partner on a very substantial case involving a

Ponzi scheme perpetrated by a real estate con artist named Gary Newhart.[2] At the time, the Newhart litigation was a huge matter in Southern California that I had worked on for many months and, in conjunction with Scott and some other excellent trial lawyers, we had crafted very sophisticated expert testimony to address the complex financial issues of the case. Mr. Newhart had obtained about $85 million of investment money from scores of investors and, by the time the authorities had caught up with him, there was only about $4 million to be found. He had shuffled the money among thirty different real estate entities and, through the process, had skimmed much of it off the top to fund his extravagant lifestyle. My professional staff and I had invested hundreds of hours of time examining the flow of funds among the labyrinth of entities, identifying missing monies, and exposing the Ponzi scheme.

I had been testifying on direct exam for three-quarters of the first of two days of my expert testimony in the two-month trial that was being held in the largest courtroom available in San Diego. The audience was packed with victims of Newhart's scam, news media personnel, and representatives of other defendant abettors of Newhart's complex scheme. Halfway through the afternoon of my direct examination, the judge ordered the usual fifteen-minute break with instructions to the jurors not to discuss any aspect of the case among themselves until they heard all the evidence. The jurors filed out of the courtroom to take their well-deserved break from the trial, and different groups of the many lawyers present congregated to discuss their strategies.

2. I am using a pseudonym because the person's real name doesn't add anything to the story, and it would expose me to some liability that isn't worth risking.

I walked up to my former classmate, the second-chair trial counsel, to discuss the status of my testimony.[3] In my judgment, my direct examination was proceeding quite well. I said to my friend, Scott, "You know that lady in the middle of the first row of the jury? She's nodding her head and smiling at me—I think I've got her." Scott looked at me and smiled. "The Hispanic lady in the red dress?" "Yes," I said, "she's the one." Metzger look at me smugly. "You're doing great, Brian, but that's Mrs. Rodriguez and she hardly understands English!"

I have used that lesson for thirty years to remind myself of how fragile my knowledge is of the sophisticated art of expert witness testimony. I may think I know what I am doing, but there's always the problem of my own perception of reality and the fact that we each see the world through our own eyes. Keep that in mind as you begin to think that you're getting knowledgeable about this complex area of professional practice. I will try to maintain a genuine humility in sharing my knowledge and experiences with you because I am still learning this fascinating art form forty years into my career. I hope I continue to get better at it every day.

Sworn testimony is evidence given by a witness who has made a legally enforceable commitment to tell the truth. If the witness is later found to have lied while bound by the commitment, he or she can be charged with the crime of perjury, a serious criminal offense classified as a felony under federal and state laws and punishable by a prison sentence of up to five years. For this and many other reasons of professional integrity, the commitment of an expert witness—or any witness, for that matter—is a serious responsibility that is relied on by the entire judicial system.

---

3. In some jurisdictions, expert witnesses are prohibited from talking to their retaining lawyers from the moment they take the witness stand, but that is not a rule of court in California.

In my very early days as a business appraiser, I will never forget one of the first calls I received from a lawyer calling to retain me in a case. I can still hear him saying, "I represent the terminated partner in this case, so we're looking for a really high value for the business." I hadn't processed the comment at that point, but after I got off the phone, I thought to myself, "I don't really care what 'value' you are looking for; I need to appraise this business legitimately and come up with an opinion of fair market value that is the right answer to the question." I wasn't self-righteous about the issue at all; I had never thought about the reality that one side of a case might be looking for a biased conclusion in its favor. I subsequently called the lawyer back and politely told him that I couldn't accommodate his request for a high value, but if I was hired, it would be my intention to determine a supportable opinion of the true fair market value of the business.

Upon early reflection in my career, I concluded that my job as a valuation expert witness was to objectively determine the value of the subject business without concerning myself with the supposed needs of the lawyer's client. This story exemplifies the difference between the roles of the expert witness and those of the client's lawyer, discussed in detail in Chapter 3. The lawyer's job is to aggressively advance the client's interest through legal argument, while the expert's role is more nuanced. The expert's role, regardless of his or her[4] area of professional practice, is to objectively apply judgments and professional expertise to the subject matter and develop supportable opinions to present to the trier of fact. And this difference between experts and lawyers is one of the most important characteristics of the art of expert witness testimony.

4. I will try to be gender neutral in this book, routinely switching from "him" to "her" in my writing style. For the sake of clarity, however, I am not going to say "him or her" all the time.

My field of expertise is business valuation and economic damages analysis: in short, amounts of money measured by numbers. In my world, the bias in an analysis can easily be measured by "too high" or "too low." The larger field of forensic consulting and expert witness work spans many more disciplines than economics, but the general rules and notions of bias still come into play. Clients would like experts to agree with their views of the facts, but the expert's role isn't to *represent* clients and their arguments; the expert's role is to objectively analyze underlying facts and derive supportable opinions that can be testified to under penalty of perjury. Sometimes this is a difficult challenge, because clients and lawyers often challenge experts to see the world from their perspective. The competent forensic consultant must maintain objectivity and resist the temptation to yield to the client's frequent desire for a technical conclusion that favors his perception of the facts of the case.

In the following chapters, I will share the perspective of my four decades of expert witness work. I first testified as an expert at age 29, and I wasn't a very mature-looking 29-year-old. In one of those early court appearances, I even remember being asked my age by the cross-examining lawyer. Since that time, I have been retained in several thousand cases (they didn't all go to trial or deposition, of course), which have resulted in approximately 600 depositions, 200 jury trials, and about 100 bench trials. One of the reasons there isn't a trove of literature on being a good expert witness is that experts are cross-examined on every word they write, so candor is in short supply on the question of how to be a good expert witness. Also, there is a tendency for cross-examining lawyers to distort any statement written by an expert to gain argumentative advantage over the expert in a present case. A perfectly logical, written statement like "The expert should always meet with the lawyer to plan an effective direct examination at trial" will be taken out of context by the cross-examining lawyer. It will be fed back to the expert witness as, "So, you and Mr. Lawyer got together for three and a half hours to figure out how to craft your story of deception to put in front of this jury, right?" Welcome to the world of litigation—that's how it works.

I am close enough to the end of my professional road that I'm not worried about being questioned on my writings and I am committed to telling it like it is, complete with subtleties and nuances of the practice. I'm not afraid to throw some lawyers under the bus—anonymously, of course—and even a few judges. I will also be candid about relying on the litigation system to resolve financial disputes: it is a terribly expensive and inefficient process with a very unpredictable outcome. Clients should think twice before they jump into it, and they should continue to seek settlements during the process. I have never been afraid to tell anyone that, at any point in the process.

Testifying as an expert witness is among the highest callings of experienced professionals who have honed their craft to a level enabling them to provide opinions to courts and juries in the American judicial system. Testifying is truly an exciting and hazardous form of work, and the courtroom setting brings life to some otherwise mundane, technical analyses. Testifying is not for the apprehensive personality, but it is a studied art and there are strategies and tactics that elevate the practice to a sophisticated art form. You can learn to be highly skilled at it and bring value to the judicial process by helping triers of fact make informed decisions about issues that are beyond the common experience of the judges and juries who make factual determinations.

I will candidly share my knowledge and experience in these pages. I have also interviewed many of my experienced colleagues to obtain their perspectives on this challenging career.

CHAPTER 3

THE EXPERT'S ROLE VS. THE LAWYER'S ROLE AND THE RESPONSIBILITIES OF THE EXPERT WITNESS

The expert's role in the litigation process is to develop an objective opinion and to be an advocate for that opinion. The attorney's role is to advocate his or her client's position (claim or defense) within the ethical boundaries of the legal profession. Although the attorney may retain an expert to analyze a substantive issue, the expert is not an advocate for the client or the client's attorney.[5] A competent expert should never view her role as developing or advancing a biased position for the benefit of the client.

An argument is a set of components or reasons (facts, assumptions, rationale, substantive principles) underlying the logic of a supportable conclusion. For discussion, think of an argument as having two sides, although most arguments are multifaceted. The lawyer-advocate emphasizes the strengths of one side of an argument and minimizes the weaknesses of the other side of the argument. Although they often do, lawyers shouldn't ignore the weaknesses of their side of the argument, just minimize them. A skillful lawyer[6] will characterize the weaknesses in an argument as less important than the strengths of the argument, trying to persuade the fact finder to adopt his client's view of the issue.

A lawyer's advocacy on behalf of the client is not objective, by definition. It is adversarial. It is intended to advance the desired interests of the client by emphasizing the facts and law that support the position that best serves the interest of the client. It is expected that the adversarial argument advanced will be strenuously opposed by the other side(s) of the litigation. That's the adversary system: each side of a case puts forth the strongest argument for its position, and justice is assumed to come out somewhere on the spectrum between the extremes. And, the system generally works pretty well.

5. The ultimate "client" in a forensic consulting engagement is the person or entity involved in the litigation matter. Technically, the client's attorney is not usually the forensic consultant's client. But the consultant clearly has duties to both the client and the client's attorney, and I will frequently refer to either or both of them as "the client," and I do think of both of them as clients. When it is important to differentiate between them, I will refer to the attorney as the "attorney-client" and the client as the "ultimate client."

6. The terms "lawyer" and "attorney" are used interchangeably throughout the book.

The concept of argument extends to the work of the forensic expert. In contrast to the lawyer, the expert's job is to consider both the strengths and weaknesses of each component of the argument (facts, assumptions, and the reasoning informing a conclusion) and try to balance and weigh the underlying components to arrive at a supportable conclusion. The expert shouldn't ignore facts that go against her conclusion, but carefully weigh them and incorporate them into the conclusion.

Expert witness testimony is both a science and an art. The science is the technical precision of objectively applying the steps of the expert's substantive area to the facts of the case to develop a correct opinion that is credible and defensible. The art of expert testimony is an awareness of the strategies and tactics of litigation so the well-reasoned opinion can be successfully advanced in the process of dispute resolution.

The competent expert witness has an ethical obligation to properly apply the tenets of her substantive area of expertise to the facts of a particular case and draw reasonable conclusions and opinions from those facts. The duty of the expert is to be true to the substantive field, knowing that the expert opinion will be rendered under penalty of perjury and be relied on by the judicial system to help parties resolve disputes. Although the expert functions within the adversary system, the expert's responsibility is to rise above adversarial arguments and bring objectivity, integrity, and truth to the process. Just as a judge crafts a judicial decision, the expert evaluates the strengths and weaknesses of the particular substantive argument in her field and balances those strengths and weaknesses to derive the most objectively supportable conclusions from those underlying facts.

A judicial conclusion is a balanced position, often referred to as an argument, one that considers all underlying facts that go "either way" in arriving at the conclusion. Everything in legal reasoning is some form of argument, and few arguments are perfect. An example of a near-perfect argument is that water will always flow downhill, absent some scientific anomaly causing it not to. There is simply no reasonable fact, assumption, or principle that contradicts that conclusion. That position is still an "argument," albeit a nearly perfect one. (The only contradicting fact I can think of would be having a little model of a hill on a spinning circular platform like a Tilt-a-Whirl and, because of centrifugal force, the water would "roll" uphill. Ridiculous, I know, but I am trying to strain logic here for instructional purposes.) The point of the tangent is that the pull of gravity on water is a nearly perfect scientific argument.

The forensic consultant makes an argument—a balanced argument—with the facts and reasonable assumptions related to the substantive issue she is addressing. I characterize the consultant's argument as a "judicial" argument, focusing on the desired balance of the competing elements of rationale that support each step of the analysis. The competent consultant should not ignore weaknesses, but should consider them and incorporate them in the rationale that leads to the derived conclusion.

The art of mastering expert witness testimony elevates the practice of forensic expert witness work to a professional level, recognizing that the importance of the work goes beyond the immediate consultant-client relationship. The retention of an expert witness is not a pure commercial transaction like buying or selling a car or providing contracting services for a fee. The objective of the work goes beyond simply helping to advance the client's interest in an adversarial way, only focusing on the strengths of the client's position. The ethical expert witness understands her duty to objectively apply the tenets of her profession while rendering truthful and accurate opinions in the judicial process.

Chapter 3: The Expert's Role vs. the Lawyer's Role and The Responsibilities of the Expert Witness

The forensic expert plays an important role in every aspect of the litigation process. Many litigated issues are beyond the common experience of the fact finder, and the expert's analysis and opinion are necessary to properly adjudicate the question presented. The expert's contribution begins with helping the client identify and understand the substantive issue involved in the case. This contribution may initially include educating the lawyer on technical aspects of the issue and identifying documents to be produced by parties to the litigation. The expert's consultation will likely expand to involve a complete investigation of the technical issues, helping the client determine how best to present the issues to the trier of fact, or possibly educating the client that his position isn't as strong as was initially thought. On this last point, my personal experience includes having strenuous arguments with my own clients about the strength of their arguments and helping them understand where their positions are weak. In the big picture, the client's understanding the weaknesses in their position is as important as understanding the strengths. Sometimes, the client is overly focused on one aspect of the case, say liability, and not mindful of other important elements of the complete matter.

I recall a clear example of this shortsightedness in a matter in which I was involved about twenty years ago. I was contacted by a lawyer representing a catering firm that filed a lawsuit against two former managers who were claimed to have "stolen" a number of regular catering customers when they left the employment of the company. (Don't forget, there are always at least two sides to the story, and the expert is usually only privy to one of them.) The former managers had clearly breached their employment contract by converting the company's customers to their new business and the company management was understandably upset about the violation. As would often happen in my practice, the case had been going along for about eighteen months (motions, depositions, various preliminary hearings, etc.) before I was contacted to do an economic damages analysis. It didn't take long to figure out that the "stolen" customers amounted to $50,000 or $60,000 of annual revenue with a 20% gross profit margin, yielding a meager $10,000 to $12,000 of actual losses to the company. I also inquired if the company thought the defendant former managers had sufficient net worth to sustain any award of damages, and my clients didn't think the defendants had "a pot to pee in."

This is a classic example of the lawyer's putting the cart before the horse and wasting a lot of money and emotional energy on an economically worthless litigation claim.[7] I understand that the defendants might be bad guys who breached their covenant not to compete, but a smart initial analysis would consider the amount of damages resulting from the alleged "crime" as well as the financial strength of the target defendants to withstand a judgment. And one more comment: the anxious, less-experienced lawyer will be quick to point out that there is the possibility of punitive damages in a case such as this one. In my experience, punitive damages are only awarded in a very small percentage of cases where some egregious conduct has occurred, not the simple "theft" of a small number of clients in a free and competitive industry. Not to conclude that punitive damages couldn't be awarded here, but even if they were, could the defendants afford to pay a punitive damages award? They didn't appear to be financially strong enough for the catering company to spend a lot of time and energy going after them for

7. To an experienced lawyer or forensic consultant, a ten- or twelve-thousand-dollar claim is nearly worthless. As a practical matter, a party can't file a complaint and take a few depositions for less than $10,000.

either special[8] or punitive damages. This story is an example of the futility of litigation to resolve many business matters: it's expensive, emotionally draining, and very high risk as to its predictable result.

Expert witness testimony is very intelligent public speaking, with a highly educated heckler in the audience who's allowed to question the speaker. So, first and foremost, your speech has to be intelligent. That means you have to have carefully thought out your position; you have to have thought out the arguments against it; you have to understand that somebody is going to disagree with you (that's okay), and you have to effectively present your position. You have to have thick enough skin that you're not going to be personally offended when somebody attacks you in public. In fact, if they vociferously attack you in public, that's probably a good thing, because they might not have a better intellectual argument against you. But, if they calmly and carefully call you an idiot, you probably have more of a problem; you might have a serious weakness in your opinion and conclusion. So the bottom line as a competent expert witness is that you have to think, really think about the intellectual merit of your position.

As an expert, it helps somewhat to think like a lawyer, which means about half of the thinking you do about your position is "What's wrong with it?" At every step of the analysis that you're undertaking (I don't care if it's medical, architectural, engineering, accounting, vocational rehabilitation, etc.), you should be thinking, "Why am I interpreting these facts (at this point in the analysis) the way that I am interpreting them? What other ways could they be interpreted?" Because sure as you're sitting in the

8. Special damages are objectively measurable economic damages like lost profits, extra costs, and property losses. General damages are non-economic damages like pain and suffering and punitive damages.

witness chair, someone who doesn't like your opinion (and there will be that person) is going to come after you at every step in your analysis and say, "Why didn't you zig instead of zag?" And, you need to have a logical, defensible answer for the reason why you zagged instead of zigged.

STAND YOUR GROUND

The expert's duty is to the court and to the truth, not to the client who has hired him or her. In my practice, some of my strongest arguments are with my own clients who are trying to advance an untenable position with respect to the issue at hand (damages, in my case). I'm sure it's true in other areas of forensic expertise as well. The proudest days of my professional career were the ones when a client dismissed me (fired me, in fact) because I stood my ground and told them I couldn't say what they wanted me to say. Being an ethical expert witness (and there are many of us), I can look myself in the mirror every morning and know that I will only testify to things that are truthful, defensible, and credible. Yes, there have been a handful of times in my career when the facts have withered away under my opinions and I have had to testify on an issue that I felt wasn't as adequately supported as I would like, and those days didn't feel very good. The reality of forensic practice is that some days you have a grand slam position and other days the best you can do is get a single, or maybe only a bunt. Only you can make the professional judgment as to when the underpinnings of your opinion get so weak that you will tell your clients that you can't step up to the plate for them. I am a realist and that is a difficult situation to be in, but it happens.

I have two stories related to this point. The first is a case where a very notable plaintiff's lawyer retained me in a case where he represented two gentlemen who had designed a real estate course that they intended to present as a weekend-type seminar to wannabe house flippers and developers. They were prevented from providing the course by the wrongful conduct of a defendant who had fraudulently diverted potential customers from taking the course. As always, there were some problems with the plaintiffs' case (so what else is new?). The first problem, which was not my issue to be concerned about, was that it wasn't clear that the defendant's conduct prevented them from proceeding with their course. The second problem, which was my concern, was that they hadn't yet brought the course program to fruition to present it to students. All they had were some grandiose projections of how much money they hoped to make when their course got off the ground. In the world of damages calculations (and all expert testimony, for that matter), speculation is a problem.[9] To be recoverable, the fact of economic damages must be reasonably certain, although the precise amount of damages, while less certain, must still not be speculative.

The details of the damages analysis in this particular case may be a bit too granular for a general point about expert witness testimony, so I will generalize. My clients' lawyer wanted me to calculate the present value of the grandiose profit projections of the clients' business plan, resulting in millions of dollars of presumed losses to them. My argument to him was: How much would it cost

9. An expert's job is to look at the facts that occurred and render opinions as to why those facts happened (some problem, defect, negligence, or whatever). The expert will also assume what should have happened or what will happen if certain things had been different. So, much of expert analysis and opinion deals with assumptions, and assumptions can be well-grounded in science or logic, or they can be very speculative.

for them to simply reconstruct the course? All it consisted of was a couple of hundred pages of workbook showing students how to look for real estate opportunities, find them, acquire them, fix them up, and sell them for a profit. It seemed to me that it would take about 100 hours of work to replace the course workbook, and the plaintiffs would be in the exact same position they were in with the thwarted course, meaning they could advertise it, attract students, and present the program. The lawyer was outraged at me because this calculation of replacement cost wouldn't produce anywhere near the millions of dollars of damages he was seeking for his clients.

This matter happened about thirty-five years ago when my forensic practice was embryonic, and I remember the panic I experienced arguing with this senior plaintiff attorney, worrying about my substantial unpaid fees as a backdrop to the conversation but, of course, not making any mention of them. The argument was simply a matter of my professional judgment: I was not willing to testify to a calculation that I believed was speculative and did not fairly represent the loss to the plaintiffs. I'll never forget his parting words in our last phone call. He simply said, "Well, if you can't say that [several million dollars in damages], I can't use you," and hung up the phone. Aside from the sickening feeling that I would not get paid for the substantial work I had done, upon quick reflection, that was one of the proudest days of my career. I stood up for the integrity of my position in the face of strong pressure to compromise myself. And, ironically, through a fluke of some weird insurance coverage that included compensation to experts for their professional fees,[10] I was subsequently

10. It would not be unusual for the defense lawyers and experts—often paid by insurance companies—to be paid under all circumstances, but it would likely be more difficult to be paid by a plaintiff who was abandoned by his expert.

paid the entire balance of the fees I had accrued, something in the neighborhood of $9,000, an enormous fee in the early days of my forensic accounting practice.

STAY IN YOUR LANE

The second story I will share makes a completely different point, but an important one nevertheless. Sitting in my office about twenty years ago, I received a call from two lawyers on a new matter, one of whom I knew slightly from a previous case. There were two issues they wanted me to address in an important matter they were handling. The first was a calculation of damages suffered by their business client as the result of the breach of the client's lease in a major shopping center. The client operated a very successful "beer-and-burger" restaurant and there was an exclusivity clause in the lease restricting the landlord from leasing to a similar type of business. After the closing of an ethnic chain restaurant in the front corner of the shopping center property, the landlord leased the freestanding restaurant building to TGI Fridays. In the litigation by the beer-and-burger restaurant against the landlord, the landlord claimed that TGI Fridays was not *similar* to the client's beer-and-burger restaurant, and furthermore, it was not "*in the shopping center*" because it was a freestanding building at the front corner of the parking lot of the shopping center. So far, I was comfortable with the proposed assignment: calculating economic damages from the breach of a lease. That would simply be an exercise of comparing the reduced profits of the restaurant after TGI Fridays opened to a reasonable projection of the profits assuming Fridays hadn't opened. Now, the conversation continued to the second opinion the lawyers wanted me to address. To succeed in the litigation, the lawyers had to establish the similarity of their client's restaurant to the TGI Fridays restaurant, and they also had to establish that the freestanding building in the front corner of the parking lot was part of "the shopping center," as described in the lease. Surely, they argued to me, I could testify on those two ancillary issues, couldn't I?

One of the unwritten rules of expert witness work is to know what you know and know what you don't know. What issues do you have sufficient background, education, and experience to qualify to testify about? I have always been very careful to stay "on the page" of my expertise or "stay in my lane." All you have to do is stretch your expertise a little bit and you'll quickly find out how little you know about X, Y, or Z issue that you are pretending to be expert on. This was one of those situations. The lawyers wanted me to become a leasing expert and/or restaurant expert and testify about similarities in types of restaurants and provisions in leases relating to the definition of "shopping center." If we were having a conversation at a cocktail party about whether a TGI Fridays is a beer-and-burger joint, I might have an opinion, but I certainly don't have sufficient background, education, and experience to testify to that issue in a court of law. So the conversation with the two lawyers proceeded to a fairly strong argument where they were pushing me to include these "very simple" issues in my proposed testimony, and I continued to resist them, saying that I was not qualified to include them and I was not comfortable testifying to them. I finally prevailed in the conversation and I didn't agree to include the non-damages issues in my expert designation which, of course, was due within a day or two of the conversation. (Lawyers always seem to be in some emergency situation, often because of their own poor planning.)

But, the icing on the cake of this story happened about six months later. I ran into the lawyer from the conversation whom I had previously worked with and he told me that the two lawyers had a bet. My friend bet that I wouldn't agree to the "stretch" opinion designation and the other lawyer bet that I would. My friend won the bet, and I was gratified to hear that the lawyer I knew had confidence in me that I would stay on my page, although he didn't have any problem trying to push me off the page for the benefit of his client. Thankfully, I didn't go there.

Stretching your opinions beyond your true expertise has several drawbacks even though it feels good in the moment because you are acceding to your client's wishes. The obvious drawback is that the court might prohibit you from testifying to the opinion because of insufficient qualifications. You further run the risk of creating a permanent record of disqualification that will be used against you in future matters, even if the disqualification isn't related to the precise issues you are testifying on in the future. Beyond that, you are exposed to strong cross-examination on your qualifications in the "stretch" area and also risk tainting yourself for the opinion you are qualified to render. Other than the superficial, immediate gratification that you are satisfying the poorly-thought-out request of your client's lawyer, there is little benefit to stretching your expertise. Stay on your page.

Before leaving the subject of staying in your lane, I will mention my occasional statement that "Your client's lawyer is not your friend." I don't mean that negatively, but the forensic consultant must remember that the lawyer's responsibility and loyalty is to the client, not the expert witness. The lawyer will often push the expert to the limits of his comfort zone—or beyond—for the benefit of the client. Keep that in mind when dealing with your retaining lawyer.

PERCEPTION OF ADVOCACY

Another reality of forensic expert work is dealing with the perception of advocacy.[11] The fact of the matter is that the trier of fact, whether it's a judge or a jury, has a perception that the expert witness is an advocate for his client and he has some bias. If not, the expert would not be sitting where he sits making the case for that lawyer and that client. So the question is not whether there is a presumption of bias or advocacy—it's there—the question is how does the expert deal with it. Like any difficult situation, the answer is to acknowledge it, accept it, own it and deal with it, and not pretend that it's not true.

There are two ways to deal with it. One is candor. Tell the trier of fact, "Look, this is how I get from fact to inference to opinions. Yes, other people may do it differently. This is how I do it, and this is why." The other aspect of dealing with the presumption of advocacy is that there are uncertainties in any process stepping from fact to inference to opinion—you're going through a level of abstractions and, by definition, abstractions contain some uncertainty. Own the uncertainty.

Owning the uncertainty is a subtle and fairly advanced expert witness technique. In any assumption made by an expert witness, any of the steps going from hard fact to inference to opinion will include some factors that are uncertain. And lawyers are going to ask, "Isn't it true you don't know this?" "Isn't it true you can't quantify that?" "Isn't it true that you're not absolutely certain of

11. The next few paragraphs are summaries of continuing education programs I have conducted with attorney and mediator Dirk T. Metzger, a colleague of mine for many years. Mr. Metzger brings a unique perspective to the subject of expert witness testimony and I credit him for some of the ideas presented here.

that?" By owning the uncertainty, the expert says, "Yes, that's true… I don't know that"; "Yes, I can't perfectly quantify that…." That gives the expert the opportunity—and this is the subtle point—to say, "That's not certain, but what's also true is that's not important. It won't affect my opinion; it won't affect the outcome of my analysis, and here's why…." That way the jury says, "Yes, he's not perfectly sure about that," but they can also say, "I can still trust him. I can still follow him because he's acknowledged that he's uncertain or unsure about some aspect of it, but he's also satisfied my desire for confidence in our decision by saying it's not going to affect my final opinion."

TWO TASKS OF THE EXPERT

The expert witness has two real jobs: making meaning and creating context. Remember that the trier of fact has heard hundreds of seemingly unconnected facts, and these people are looking for a pathway through this maze; they're looking for someone they can trust. And it is the expert's role in her particular area to take all of those facts and bring them together in a meaningful way to say what all this means, and, in terms of creating context, saying why it meant it. "Creating context" means going from fact, to inference, to opinions. The bridge between those steps is the assumption, and the assumption is how you create context. Example: When we go from the fact that the business made a million dollars last year to the assumption that the business is going to continue to be profitable, our assumption is based on the fact that the business has been operating for six years, that it's always made a profit, and there has been a steady uptick. The assumption bridge between those historical facts and the opinion that the business is worth $5 million is we're projecting that out for five years and we're basing that on the fact that the economy is going to be strong, we believe borrowing will be available, we believe the market will expand, and we believe the customer base will expand. It is these assumptions, and the reasonableness of them, that enable you to go from fact to inference to opinion, and that's the context you use to create the meaning in your testimony.

UNDERSTAND THE AUDIENCE

The most important aspect of the expert's role as a testifier is to understand your audience. If you're testifying to a sophisticated arbitration panel of experts, for example, it would be insulting to talk down to those people and to translate too much in that context. You can go ahead and use sophisticated terms of art because you're saying "one peer to another, this is how this works and we all understand that..." The expert is engaging the audience at that level. If the expert is talking to a jury, again, he cannot talk down to them, but he has to have much more of a translator function because the expert is dealing with twelve people from all walks of life, all levels of understanding, and the task is to reach them all.

At the end of the trial, your job as an expert is to make the jury want to choose you. One of the unfortunate realities of testifying as an expert is that rather than make a hard decision, a hard choice between experts, sometimes the trier of fact will just let the experts cancel each other out. So, if you want to be the expert that the trier of fact chooses, you have to do something a little different. In a sense, make them want to choose your opinion over the opinion of the other expert. There are two areas that help the expert in that department. One is of substance and one is of presentation. In terms of substance, you certainly have to be thorough, competent, and accurate. That's the minimum to establish the baseline of trustworthiness. In terms of presentation, it's a little more subtle. Consider being understated in your presentation. Let the jury go the last mile to connect the dots. And finally, they have to like you. So you have to be likable. That means being authentic, owning any difficulties that you have; it means not overstating; it means behaving in a way that they can look at you and say, "This is a regular fellow or regular woman. … I would trust him or her with this decision."

UNDERSTAND YOUR LAWYER-CLIENT: "AVERAGE," "BELOW AVERAGE" AND "GOOD" LAWYERS

I use the characterization of "average" and "good" lawyers throughout this book. One of the realities of building a forensic consulting practice is that about 80% of the lawyers who are going to come through the door are "average" lawyers, at least with respect to their litigation experience. I don't make this point to denigrate the legal profession; the reality is that the typical general practitioner only goes to trial occasionally. In fact, most experienced forensic consultants will have been to trial (and possibly expert deposition) more times than their retaining lawyers. I use this somewhat unfair characterization, the "average" lawyer, to make the point that frequently, the expert witness has to lead the average lawyer through the expert's substantive analysis, report drafting, deposition preparation, and trial testimony (along with assisting the average lawyer with cross-examination). The simple fact is that the experienced forensic consultant probably has significantly more actual litigation experience than the "average" lawyer-client.

Then there's the "below average" lawyer, who I really don't talk about, except briefly here. What can I say? These are the ones that you can't even lead through the process. Unfortunately, they do exist, and in the early days of your practice, they seem to constitute about 20% of the calls that come in. Over time, you can figure out how to screen these folks out of your client base, and most of us would agree that it can't happen soon enough.

Then there's the remaining 15%–20% (☺) constituting the "good" lawyers, the ones who are regularly experienced in litigation and who know how to supervise a litigation matter, "conduct the orchestra" to properly tell a story on direct examination, work with experts and cross-examine opponents. These are the lawyers you want to be working with, but it takes a few years to build your practice to this level. If you are fortunate enough to be working with a good lawyer, you still need to understand the strategies and tactics of effective expert witness testimony, but you can probably defer to the lawyer to be the trusted quarterback of the litigation.

The good lawyer will also be able to work with you to jointly prepare for deposition and direct examination as well as effectively cross-examine the opposing expert witness. A good lawyer can point out weaknesses in the other expert's analysis, and, even if there are only a few weaknesses in the opposition's case, use effective cross-examination to create doubt in the minds of the trier of fact as to the validity/accuracy of the opposition's conclusions. (See Chapter 12, page 229 for preparation between expert and lawyer for direct examination.)

So it is with apologies to my lawyer brothers and sisters (I do happen to be a member of the bar) that I create these somewhat unfair characterizations of litigation attorneys for the benefit of my expert witness readers, those trying to elevate their forensic practices to a higher, artistic level.

DIRTY LITTLE SECRET

Before I conclude the differences between the lawyer's role and the expert's role in the litigation process, I will share a fact that contributes to the economic benefit of both groups. One secret of litigation and forensic consulting practices is the profusion of continuances and delays during the course of a case. The economic value of these inefficiencies is immense to the lawyers and experts, and clients should be mindful of this boondoggle in their evaluation of the litigation process. I have never tried to quantify it, but I would estimate that 20% to 25% of the revenues I have generated from forensic consulting over the years have been the result of the perpetual delays in the process.

Litigation is a committee activity, and most people understand the inefficiencies of decisions by committees. At the very least, simply scheduling committee activities is very difficult, particularly when dealing with a bureaucratic judicial system. Every litigation date requires the agreement of at least two lawyers, two clients, a judicial officer, and a handful of experts who are consulting to different aspects of the litigation. Those scheduling problems, coupled with interminable delays in the legal system, result in the can being kicked down the road time and time again before any meaningful decision is made.

Every time a lawyer or forensic consultant puts down a file for several months, restarting the matter is an inefficient, expensive proposition. It takes time to get back up to speed. Because experts bill their professional time, they have to bill time to their clients again. It is a sad fact that one of the most profitable areas of a forensic consulting practice (and a law practice, I am sure) is the inefficient delay of the process. Buyers beware.

CONCLUSION

Lawyers and experts have dramatically different roles in the litigation process, but they work in tandem to help their clients succeed. The lawyer focuses on the strengths of the client's overall position and minimizes the weaknesses. The expert must investigate and understand each detail of the forensic analysis and develop an objective, supportable conclusion in the substantive area. The expert must be mindful of the strategies and tactics of the litigation process so her opinion can be presented effectively to the trier of fact, whether it be a judge, jury, or arbitration panel.

CHAPTER 4

THE BUSINESS OF EXPERT WITNESSING

This chapter deals with the business of expert witnessing in an overview fashion because the details of each area are dealt with in other chapters of the book.

Offering your services to the public as an expert witness is not merely a business endeavor that seeks to sell services in the marketplace for a profit. It is a professional activity with duties and responsibilities that extend beyond the purchaser of the services. It requires knowledge of the ethics and standards of the expert's specific business or profession as well as the responsibility of one who is sworn to present evidence in a court of law. The expert's ultimate responsibility is to render objectively truthful testimony under penalty of perjury in a court of law or other dispute resolution tribunal.

In commercial business transactions, the vendor has legal and/or ethical responsibilities to the customer to provide a quality product or service in exchange for fair compensation. The vendor's business activity may be licensed by the state with requirements for performance standards to safeguard the public. In many cases, the vendor may also be a member of a business or professional association that has standards of performance that apply to its members. Regardless of the regulatory authority, the duties of the vendor extend to the customer or client, and usually no further.

When the vendor does a quality job for the customer, the vendor's responsibility is met.

A forensic consultant's duties are greater than those of a commercial seller of services; they extend beyond the purchaser of the services. The forensic consultant must uphold the ethics of his or her profession as well as render unbiased, objective analysis that results in truthful, objective expert testimony before the courts. Forensic consulting services span professional, scientific, and technical areas, but individual professions have been slow to create codes of conduct and professional standards for forensic experts working in those particular fields. I have found pronouncements on litigation services in the fields of accounting, appraisal, and forensic economics, but I am not aware of litigation guidance in other scientific and technical areas that are often the subjects of litigated matters. Review the professional literature in your field to become familiar with any litigation-related standards.

To pursue a forensic consulting practice, identify areas of your business or profession that interact with the judicial system or, specifically, civil or criminal disputes. Over the last 50 or 75 years, it seems that many issues in litigation have become "expertized," meaning they have fallen within the province of experts to analyze and opine on. It is not unusual for trials to become high-priced battles of the experts, and the experts are those seasoned professionals who have marketed themselves to the legal community to address technical substantive issues.

Ask yourself if you have sufficient background, education, and experience to meet the legal qualification to testify as an expert on the issue you focus on. Don't be intimidated or overwhelmed by this requirement. Be confident that you can obtain a threshold of knowledge and experience to meet the minimum qualification to testify in a court of law. You can enhance your present experience by taking professional education courses dedicated to your substantive field and/or expert witness courses related to your field. As I indicate in Chapter 8, Marketing a Forensic Consulting Practice, you can do some writing or speaking in your field, and those activities enhance your reputation in the relevant community. Yes, you have to have enough experience to give potential clients confidence that you can handle their problem, but be mindful that judges are inclined to allow experts to testify, particularly in smaller cases, the types that a newer expert would typically be retained in. Identify the target market for your services, which in my experience is usually the legal community. There is also a defined market in the insurance industry because those companies are constantly involved in dispute resolution with customers and/or litigation on their behalf.

I want to be careful not to dissuade the competent professional from expanding into the forensic consulting arena, but I do want to caution you not to simply put an advertisement in a lawyer's magazine or on the internet to get your first expert witness case. As discussed in detail in the management and marketing chapters of this book, forensic experts must make considerations that are different from those made in your regular professional practice. The primary difference is the reality that the opposing side of the case is arguing against both you and your analysis at every step. The argument against you may not occur until late in the litigation process (at deposition or trial), but by that time, it is too late to clean up the record that you may have already established during your work.

The mere realization that lawyers are arguing against your entire analysis should be enough to make the novice forensic consultant cautious in his or her approach to an assignment. A second difference in forensic consulting practice is that nothing you do during the course of your work is shielded from exposure to the other side. Nothing—not your communications, your writings, preliminary drafts of your analyses, or your billing records.[12] During discovery, the opposition has the right to explore the record of all your activities during the case, and they use any information they can find to show bias, predisposition to conclusion, or mistakes in your analysis. Finally, the opposing counsel will likely hire a highly qualified expert to analyze your work with the objective of showing that your work is flawed, wrong, or unreliable. The litigation environment is a hostile workplace in which you may be uncomfortable working.

Lawyers are often duplicitous in their interactions with forensic consultants, whether they're on the same side of the case or the opposing side of the case. The lawyers on your side of the case have their client's interest as their primary concern, not their forensic consultant's. Consequently, the consultant's own lawyer will sometimes "hang him out to dry" in the interest of loyalty to the client. The opposing lawyers are trying to defeat the expert's position in the case at any cost. Opposing lawyers will often make representations such as "I'm just trying to understand what you did here" when, in fact, they're really trying to learn anything they can about you or your analysis that will undermine it. So, the representation that "I'm just trying to understand what you did" is only partially true, and the experienced forensic consultant realizes this.

As you build a forensic consulting practice, recognize that your major asset is and will be your reputation in the legal and judi-

12. There is one exception to this blanket statement for some draft reports under the Federal Rules of Civil Procedure. See Chapter 14.

cial communities. We all know how challenging it is to build a reputation and how easy it is to lose one. Damaging your reputation can occur at the very beginning of your career, and that can include "stepping in it" before you even fully understand what "it" is. Pay attention to the details in the marketing and management chapters before you embark on your first assignment.

The substantive areas that litigation is about are endless, and forensic consultants bring value to the litigation process from beginning to end. Litigation attorneys are specialists in the art of argument (evidence, depositions, trial strategy and cross-examination), but they are not expert in many of the technical fields that make up the issues in litigation. The lawyers are focused on the legal aspects of the case—investigating facts, researching theories of liability, pursuing discovery, and preparing for trials—but the forensic consultant's input about her substantive area is vital.

While the objective of forensic consulting services is always the reality that the matter may proceed to trial and the opposition will argue against you, most cases settle before trial, and the expert's contribution to that settlement can be instrumental. The forensic consultant brings value to the litigation process from the beginning stages of the case. Initially, the consultant will educate counsel about the expert's technical area and help with document requests and technical strategies. As the case proceeds, the expert's guidance will help structure the direction of discovery and deposition strategies. The competent expert can add value to the litigation matter at virtually every step of the process. However, the expert and the lawyer must be mindful of the lack of privilege applicable to the expert's participation in many jurisdictions and limit the expert's involvement to his or her substantive area. See

Chapter 14 for a critically important discussion of the legal privileges applicable (or not!) to expert witnesses.

CONCLUSION

Subsequent chapters of this book address the details of case management and other issues in forensic consulting engagements. Those are the details that elevate the practice of providing expert witness services to an art form.

CHAPTER 5

THE HISTORY OF EXPERT TESTIMONY AND THE LAW OF OPINION EVIDENCE

Expert witnessing—the act of rendering sworn opinion testimony by a person with sufficient background, education, and experience to legally qualify as an expert

INTRODUCTION

As a general rule, witnesses are only permitted to testify about facts they have observed, and not their opinions or conclusions about the consequences of the facts. Subject to two exceptions, the opinions of witnesses are considered to be irrelevant and therefore not admissible. The attorneys will make arguments about the meaning and significance of the proven facts of the case and ask the jury to make findings of fact and conclusions based on their findings, but witnesses may only testify about the facts. Generally, witnesses may not testify about their beliefs, impressions, opinions or conclusions about the facts.

The two exceptions to the prohibition of opinion testimony are (1) non-expert opinion testimony about subjects that are matters of common daily experience and (2) expert evidence. A lay witness is allowed to give opinions and testify about matters that are within the common experience of people. Examples of admissible areas of non-expert opinions are estimates of speed or distance, the emotional state of a person (upset, agitated, angry), or other everyday estimates (size, weight, etc.). Lay opinion testimony of this sort is allowable where the witness has personal knowledge of the facts, the witness's conclusion conveys a definite conception of the facts, and the conclusion is one that people in general are capable of drawing. This exception is rationalized as a way to get necessary facts to the jury from a witness whose knowledge cannot otherwise be articulated.

Opinion testimony is also admissible in situations where the testimony will assist the trier of fact in understanding an issue that is beyond the common knowledge of lay persons, and it is provided by a person of sufficient background, education, and experience to qualify as an expert in the eyes of the court. This is the general definition of expert witness testimony, and it can be based on facts or data that were not personally observed or facts presented outside of court. The facts and data relied on need not be admissible, so long as experts in the same field would reasonably rely on the facts in forming an opinion on the subject.[13]

---

13. Branch, D., Brown, P. and Damji, S., "The Admission of Expert Testimony: *Daubert* and Related Issues," *Lost Profits Damages,* 2nd ed. (2020), Harry, E.P. & Kinrich, J.H., eds., Valuation Products and Services, LLC, Ventnor City, NJ, p. 755.

HISTORY OF EXPERT TESTIMONY

The use of individuals with specialized knowledge of facts and information dates back to ancient times in tribunals to resolve disputes. Midwives were called upon to give their opinions as to conditions of pregnancy, virginity, or fertility, and Roman tribunals recognized the expertise of midwives, handwriting experts, and land surveyors as legal experts. Over the centuries, the legal system developed three procedural options to deploy such sciences in the courtroom by experts who, from their special training and experience, could instruct the court or a jury in regard to the disputed facts.[14] The first option was to call experts as jurors.[15] The second was for the court to nominate experts as consultants whose advice the court or the jury could adopt as they pleased.[16] A third option was for parties to call experts as witnesses testifying on their behalf, although there was no special procedure to define such witnesses as experts.

The codified use of expert witnesses and the admissibility of their testimony has developed over the last 250 years.[17] In the seventeenth and eighteenth centuries, the English courts were absolutely ruled by judges. In criminal proceedings, defendants were

14. Golan, Tal, *Revisiting the History of Scientific Expert Testimony*, 73 Brook, L. Rev. (2008). Available at https://brooklynworks.brooklaw.edu/blr/vol73/iss3/3. Professor Golan's article is a brilliant summary of the history of the expert witness. I have relied heavily on it in my summary here.

15. Golan, *Ibid.*, footnoting J. H. Beuscher, *The Use of Experts by the Courts*, 54 Harv. L. Rev. 1105, 1108–10 (1941); Learned Hand, *Historical and Practical Considerations Regarding Expert Testimony*, 15 Harv. L. Rev. 40, 40–43 (1902); see also 4 Thomas Roger Forbes, *Surgeons at the Bailey* (1985).

16. Golan, *Ibid.*, footnoting James C. Oldham, *The Origins of the Special Jury*, 50 U. Chi. L. Rev. 137, 173–75 (1983).

17. Milroy, Christopher M. "A Brief History of the Expert Witness," *Academic Forensic Pathology: The Official Publication of the National Association of Medical Examiners* [Canada], vol. 7, issue 4 (December 2017), p. 517.

brought before the court and witnesses were examined by judges, not by the lawyers. Because the judge was the questioner, he (and it was always a "he") could control the testimony of witnesses, limiting their testimony to the facts they had observed. If a trial involved areas of technical expertise that were beyond the judge's experience, he would do one of two things: he would empanel a jury of specialists having knowledge of the scientific or technical issues before the court (the trades, commerce, medicine, etc.), or he would appoint a special consultant to advise him on technical matters (effectively the court's expert).

Because the judge was asking the questions of the witnesses and was completely in charge of the proceeding, the formal rules of evidence were only in their embryonic stages. As the lawyers' roles expanded to include examining and cross-examining witnesses and the judge became more of an observer, the rules of evidence evolved to limit hearsay testimony and matters of opinion. "By the end of the eighteenth century, [the lawyers'] evidentiary battles had produced two powerful legal doctrines: the hearsay doctrine, which attempted to limit testimony to information based solely on personal observation, and the opinion doctrine, which sought to control the form in which witnesses communicated their perceptions to the jury, requiring them not to use inferences where the subject matter is susceptible to factual statements."[18] By the late eighteenth century, the use of subject-matter experts to assist the court was a well-established practice. However, the rules of evidence at the time did not allow for witnesses—including

18. Golan, *op. cit.*, footnoting Landsman, *The Rise of the Contentious Spirit: Adversary Procedures in Eighteenth Century England*, 75 Cornell Law Rev., 572; Gallanis, *The Rise of Modern Evidence Law*, 84 Iowa L. Rev. 499 (1999), 530–37; Hand, *Historical and Practical Considerations Regarding Expert Testimony*, 15 Harv. L. Rev. 40, 44–45 (1902); Wigmore, *The History of the Hearsay Rule*, 17 Harv. L. Rev., 437, 448 (1904).

experts—to provide opinion evidence.[19] In summary, under the evolving rules of evidence, witnesses were only allowed to testify to facts that they personally observed, and they were not permitted to testify to inferences (opinions) from those facts.

Wells-next-the-Sea, Norfolk County, England

The first record of a partisan expert (or a party-retained expert witness) is the case of *Folkes v. Chadd,*[20] a 1781–1783 case involving long-term changes to the tidal harbor[21] located in Wells-next-the-Sea, England, a seaside city on the North Norfolk coast about 120 miles north of London. In the 1720s, Wells Harbour began to show signs of decay,[22] with parts of the harbor becoming increasingly clogged. By mid-century, the town's piers had become inaccessible to shipping, and the greater part of the cargo

19. Milroy, Christopher M., *op. cit.*, pp. 516–526.
20. *Folkes v. Chadd*, 99 Eng. Rep.; (1782) 3 Doug, K.B. 340.
21. A tidal harbor is one whose level is affected by the tides, as opposed to a harbor in which the water level is maintained by inflowing rivers.
22. Golan, *op. cit.*, p. 889 (citations omitted).

had to be carried to and from the town by flat-bottomed barges. In 1758, adjacent landowners erected embankments at the edges of the harbor, and the harbor continued to decay because of silting.[23] The harbor commissioners and townspeople believed that the embankments were the cause of the harbor's decay and the landowners alleged that the clogging was from natural causes. Litigation ensued between the harbor commissioners and large landowners who had erected embankments reclaiming land, encroaching on the harbor. The court was considering whether to allow the continuation of the alleged nuisance from the harbor embankments or require their demolition.

The first trial took place over two days in the county of Norwich in August 1781 with the question before the jury whether the said embankments harmed the harbor and whether the harm justified the removal of the embankments. During the first day, the commissioners' lawyers presented a long line of traditional witnesses who testified from their personal experience to the rapid deterioration of the harbor following the construction of the embankments. They were testifying to what they personally observed and implicitly to their belief of the reasons for the deterioration. On the second day, it was the landlord's lawyers' turn. They presented one expert, Robert Mylne, Fellow of the Royal Society and the owner of a thriving London-based architecture-engineering practice. After visiting the harbor, he concluded that the troubles of the harbor could not be attributed to Folkes's embankment or to any other embankment. The opposing witnesses, fact witnesses, Mylne explained to the jury, had been misled by their perceptions.[24]

23. Silting is the process of becoming filled or blocked with silt.
24. Golan, *op. cit.*, pp. 889–90.

"The authoritative testimony of the famous engineer and Fellow of the Royal Society, who had made a special study of the cause of the trial, made a strong impression on the jurors, who, we are told, 'relying on the weight of Mr. Mylne's abilities of knowledge, and not having the least doubt of the truth of his evidence, found a verdict for the Folkes.'"[25] The commissioners' lawyers moved for a new trial "on the ground that the defendants were surprised by the doctrine and reasoning of Mr. Mylne."[26] A new trial was granted and was promptly set for the following summer term of the Norfolk assizes[27] in July 1782.

Prior to the second trial, the royal judges of the King's Bench directed the parties to exchange written opinions of the experts whom they intended to produce "so that both sides might be prepared to answer them."[28] The landowners retained a leading civil engineer, John Smeaton, to provide his written opinion based on undisputed facts (the situation of banks, the course of tides and winds, and the shifting of sands). Like Mylne before him, Smeaton also concluded that the decay of Wells Harbour was not caused by the hand of man, but by the hidden hand of nature. At the trial, Smeaton's testimony was objected to by the opposition on the grounds that it was not based on the facts of the case. Rather, the opposition argued, it was based on a high-minded hypothesis about natural processes, imperceptible to anyone but Smeaton, and it could not be measured, tested, or otherwise verified. The trial judge, Chief Justice Gould, did not permit Smeaton to address the jury from the witness stand. With Smeaton out of the way, the jury gave a verdict for the commission-

25. Golan, *id.*
26. *Folkes*, 3 Doug. at 157, 99 Eng. Rep. at 589.
27. Assizes are the courts that formerly sat at intervals in each county of England and Wales to administer the civil and criminal law.
28. *Folkes*, 3 Doug. at 157.

ers, allowing them to cut the embankments that allegedly choked their harbor. Folkes's lawyers immediately asked for a new trial on the grounds that their expert was improperly silenced.

The plaintiffs appealed, and the appellate court, with opinion written by Lord Mansfield, concluded as follows: The court "cannot believe that where the question is, whether a defect arises from a natural or an artificial cause, the opinions of men of science are not to be received. … Therefore we are of opinion that his [Smeaton's] judgment, formed on facts, was very proper evidence."[29] The decision by the English court to allow for an expert to provide opinion testimony, formed on facts, is often cited as the foundation of modern rules on expert testimony, paving the way for the partisan expert.

Wells Harbour at low tide

29. *Folkes,* 3 Doug. at 158–59, 99 Eng. Rep. at 590.

The result of this evidentiary evolution was the indirect creation of the expert witness—the only remaining witness who did not have to personally observe facts and could pronounce opinions based on them in court. "Traditionally, experts, whether as part of the jury or as court advisors, were summoned and controlled by the court, which conferred on these experts a large degree of impartiality."[30] During the nineteenth century, after *Folkes v. Chadd* laid the groundwork for allowing expert opinion testimony, the practice of expert witness testimony appears to have evolved into party-retained real and so-called experts providing testimony that generally supported their client's positions, without objective scientific or technical support. No rules were in place in the United States to determine who was a competent expert, and expert testimony was seen as highly partisan and unreliable.[31]

"During the early nineteenth century, among the crowd of experts who were allowed into the witness stand, besides the traditional figures of the physician, the merchant, and the sea captain, we find the growing presence of men of science—chemists, microscopists, geologists, engineers, mechanists, etc. These experts untangled for the court and the jury the complexities of the growing number of cases involving science, in fields ranging from insurance, mining, and energy to toxicology, patents, and even regulation."[32] By the end of the nineteenth century, it was stated in the leading U.S. textbook on evidence that there was no specific rule admitting opinions or inference when made by one class of persons—experts—and excluding

30. Golan, *op. cit.*, p. 885.
31. Branch, Brown & Damji, *op. cit.*, p. 758.
32. Golan, *op. cit.*, p. 904–5.

them when made by another class—laymen; but there is a rule excluding them whenever they are superfluous and admitting them when they are not.[33] "The tremendous nineteenth century expansion of science and technology into industry and other public sectors quickly established the scientific expert witness as a pivotal figure in the courtroom and turned partisan expert testimony into an acrimonious and persistent thorn in the side of Common Law."[34]

LAW OF OPINION EVIDENCE

District of Columbia Court of Appeals

33. Milroy, *op. cit.*, footnoting *A Treatise on the Law of Evidence* by Simon Greenleaf, 16th ed. Boston: Little Brown and Company, 1899, p. 440–1.
34. Golan, *op. cit.*, p. 904.

The modern era of the law of opinion evidence began in 1923 with the District of Columbia Court of Appeals case, *Frye v. United States,* 293 F. 1013 (D.C. Cir. 1923). Frye was convicted of second degree murder and appealed his conviction because he was prevented from offering expert testimony at his trial. The single issue on appeal was whether Mr. Frye's expert witness should have been allowed to testify to the results of a systolic blood pressure test—the examination that came to be known as a "lie detector" test—administered and interpreted by the expert.

The offer of expert testimony was objected to by counsel for the government, and the trial court sustained the objection. The rule of evidence at the time was that the opinions of experts were admissible as evidence in cases in which the matter of inquiry was such that inexperienced persons were unlikely to prove capable of forming a correct judgment upon it. When the question involved did not lie within the range of common experience or common knowledge, but required special experience or special knowledge, then the opinions of witnesses skilled in that particular science, art, or trade to which the question related were admissible in evidence.

On appeal, the opinion of Justice Van Orsdel noted that "courts will go a long way in admitting expert testimony deduced from well-recognized scientific principle or discovery, but the thing from which the deduction is made must be sufficiently established to have gained general acceptance in the particular field in which it belongs."[35] Concluding that the systolic blood pressure deception test had not yet gained such standing and scientific rec-

35. *Frye v. United States*, 293 F. 1013 (D.C. Cir 1923).

ognition among physiological and psychological authorities, the Court of Appeals affirmed the lower court's holding to exclude the expert testimony.

Frye's "general acceptance" test, as it came to be known, became the standard for the admission of expert testimony for the next seventy years. Courts struggled to determine whether *Frye* applied to all experts and whether it applied to both civil and criminal cases. Many had trouble interpreting "general acceptance" in a clear and consistent manner.

In 1975, Congress issued the Federal Rules of Evidence (FRE). FRE 702 provided a standard for expert witness testimony that answered some of the stickiest questions related to Frye. The rule specified that it applied to "scientific, technical, or other specialized knowledge," it listed potential qualifications as an expert in terms of "knowledge, skill, experience, training, or education," and it clearly applied to civil cases. The 1975 rule:

> Rule 702: Testimony by Expert Witnesses. If scientific, technical, or other specialized knowledge will assist the trier of fact to understand the evidence or to determine a fact in issue, a witness qualified as an expert by knowledge, skill, experience, training, or education, may testify thereto in the form of opinion or otherwise.

"Since the FRE did not state an explicit intent to abandon the Frye rule, some federal and almost all state courts remained committed to the 'general acceptance' criterion as an absolute prerequisite to the admissibility of scientific evidence."[36]

36. Golan, *op. cit.*, quoting Gianelli and Imwinkelried, p. 932–933.

THE DAUBERT TRILOGY

United States Supreme Court

The next significant development in the evolution of the law of opinion testimony is the 1993 case of *Daubert v. Merrell Dow Pharmaceuticals, Inc.*[37] The plaintiffs in *Daubert* were children born with serious birth defects that they alleged were caused by their mothers' ingestion of Bendectin, a prescription anti-nausea drug marketed by Merrell Dow Pharmaceuticals and taken during their pregnancies. At trial, the plaintiffs intended to present experts who had concluded that Bendectin could cause birth defects, based on animal-cell studies, live-animal studies, chemical-structure analysis, and "reanalysis" of previously pub-

37. *Daubert v. Merrell Dow Pharmaceuticals, Inc.*, 727 F. Supp. 570, 571 (1989), *aff'd*, 951 F.2d 1128 (9th Cir. 1991), *vacated*, 509 U.S. 579 (1993), 113 S.Ct. 2786.

lished epidemiological studies that had found no link to birth defects. The lower court found that "given the vast body of epidemiological data concerning Bendectin, ... expert opinion which is not based on epidemiological evidence is not admissible to establish causation." Thus, the expert testimony based on animal studies and chemical analysis was not considered to be based on methods sufficiently established to have general acceptance in the field to which they belong. While epidemiological evidence was considered to have general acceptance, the plaintiffs' "reanalysis" of previous studies was also considered inadmissible because it had not been published or subjected to peer review. Consequently, the trial court granted summary judgment for the defendants. The plaintiffs appealed the decision but it was affirmed by the appellate court. The case was then appealed to the Supreme Court, with plaintiffs arguing that the *Frye* test of general acceptance had been superseded by the FRE, particularly FRE 702. The Supreme Court granted certiorari "in light of the sharp divisions among the courts regarding the proper standard for the admission of expert testimony."[38]

The Supreme Court agreed that FRE 702, which does not reference general acceptance, had superseded the *Frye* test. It declared that "that austere standard, absent from, and incompatible with, the [FRE], should not be applied in federal trials."[39] Importantly, the court noted that this did not mean the FRE placed no limits on admissibility of scientific evidence nor that a trial judge is precluded from screening this evidence. The court parsed FRE 702 as only permitting expert testimony if it is relevant and reliable and provided by a qualified expert, as follows:

38. This summary is substantially quoted from Branch, Brown & Damji, *op. cit.*, p. 760.
39. *Daubert*, p. 2794.

> If scientific ***[reliability]***, technical, or other specialized knowledge will assist the trier of fact to understand the evidence or to determine a fact in issue ***[relevance]***, a witness qualified as an expert by knowledge, skill, experience, training, or education ***[qualification]***, may testify thereto in the form of opinion or otherwise.[40] [Emphasis in original article, not in statute.]

As part of its opinion, the Court laid out the following criteria that could be considered by a trier of fact in evaluating whether scientific expert testimony was reliable:[41]

- Whether the theory or technique can be and has been tested;
- Whether the theory or technique has been subjected to peer review and publication (noting that publication is considered a relevant but not dispositive consideration);
- The known or potential rate of error of the technique and the existence and maintenance of standards controlling the technique's operation;
- Whether the theory or technique has general acceptance within the relevant scientific community. Importantly, general acceptance is a consideration, not a requirement, although a technique that has only minimal support within the community "may properly be viewed with skepticism."

The *Daubert* decision provided guiding principles to judges to assist them in performing their gatekeeping role for scientific expert testimony and moved federal courts away from the uncom-

40. Branch, Brown & Damji, *op. cit.*, p. 760 citing Fed.Rul.Evid.702, *"Testimony by Expert Witness,"* https://www.law.cornell.edu/rules/fre/rule_702.
41. Branch, Brown & Damji, *ibid.*, p. 760.

promising general acceptance test under *Frye*. After *Daubert*, the trial judge is to be the gatekeeper of expert testimony, evaluating the expert's analysis and opinions in light of the criteria enumerated in the case.

Kumho Tire Co. v. Carmichael (1999).[42] While *Daubert* addressed the admissibility of scientific expert testimony, its applicability to non-scientific experts was not resolved until 1999 in *Kumho*. In *Kumho*, plaintiffs were the owners of a minivan that suffered a tire blowout; one passenger died and others were severely injured. The plaintiffs sued the tire manufacturer, claiming the tire was defective. The plaintiffs intended to offer the testimony of an expert in tire failure analysis, but the testimony was excluded (and summary judgment granted) based on the trial court's application of the *Daubert* factors to the expert's analysis. On appeal, the 11th Circuit reversed, holding that "the Supreme Court in *Daubert* **explicitly** limited its holding to cover only the 'scientific context,'" adding that "a *Daubert* analysis applies only where an expert relies on the application of scientific principles" rather than "on skill- or experienced-based observation." It concluded that [the expert's] testimony, which it viewed as relying on experience, falls outside the scope of *Daubert*."[43]

The defendant petitioned the Supreme Court, which granted certiorari and concluded "that *Daubert's* general holding—setting forth the trial judge's general 'gatekeeping' obligation—applies not only to testimony based on 'scientific' knowledge, but also to testimony based on 'technical' and 'other specialized' knowledge."[44]

42. *Kumho Tire Co. v. Carmichael*, 526 U.S. 137, 119 S. Ct. 1167 (1999).
43. *Kumho*, p. 1173.
44. *Kumho*, p. 1167.

GE v. Joiner (1997).[45] *Daubert* established the factors to be considered by a trial court when it evaluates the admission of expert testimony. In *GE v. Joiner*, decided December 1997, the Supreme Court established the proper standard for appellate review of decisions by trial courts to exclude evidence. *Joiner* establishes that trial court rulings will be difficult to overturn on appeal, leaving great discretion in the trial courts.

In *Joiner*, the plaintiff proffered an expert to testify that the plaintiff's exposure to certain chemicals used by the defendants was likely responsible for plaintiff's cancer. The trial court ruled this testimony inadmissible because it failed to show a link between the chemical exposure and cancer and "did not rise above a subjective belief or unsupported speculation."[46] The 11th Circuit Court of Appeals reversed the trial court, holding that "[b]ecause the Federal Rules of Evidence governing expert testimony display a preference for admissibility, we apply a particularly stringent standard of review to the trial judge's exclusion of expert testimony."[47] Upon review by the Supreme Court, the Court stated that questions of admissibility of expert evidence are reviewable under the same standard—abuse of discretion—as are other decisions regarding evidentiary issues and are not subject to a more stringent standard of review.

AMENDING THE FEDERAL RULES OF EVIDENCE

Rule 702 was amended in 2000 in response to *Daubert* and to the many cases applying *Daubert*, including *Kumho*. In *Daubert*,

45. *GE v. Joiner*, 522 U.S. 136, 118 S. Dt. 512 (1997).
46. Branch, Brown & Damji, *op. cit.*, p. 761.
47. 118 S. Ct. at 516, citing 78 F.3d 524, 529 (11th Cir. 1996).

the Court charged trial judges with the responsibility of acting as gatekeepers to exclude unreliable expert testimony, and the Court in *Kumho* clarified that this gatekeeper function applies to all expert testimony, not just testimony based in science.[48] The amendment affirms the trial court's role as gatekeeper and provides some general standards that the trial court must use to assess the reliability and helpfulness of proffered expert testimony. Consistent with *Kumho*, the Rule as amended provides that all types of expert testimony present questions of admissibility for the trial court in deciding whether the evidence is reliable and helpful. Rule 702, as amended in 2000:

> Rule 702: Testimony by Expert Witnesses. A witness who is qualified as an expert by knowledge, skill, experience, training, or education may testify in the form of an opinion or otherwise if:
>
> (a) the expert's scientific, technical, or other specialized knowledge will help the trier of fact to understand the evidence or to determine a fact in issue;
> (b) the testimony is based on sufficient facts or data;
> (c) the testimony is the product of reliable principles and methods; and
> (d) the expert has reliably applied the principles and methods to the facts of the case.

As of the date of this writing (March 2022), the following minor amendments are proposed to FRE 702:

> Rule 702: Testimony by Expert Witnesses. A witness who is qualified as an expert by knowledge, skill, experience, training,

48. FRE 702, *Committee Notes on Rules—2000 Amendment.*

or education may testify in the form of an opinion or otherwise if the proponent has demonstrated by a preponderance of the evidence that:

(a) the expert's scientific, technical, or other specialized knowledge will help the trier of fact to understand the evidence or to determine a fact in issue;
(b) the testimony is based on sufficient facts or data;
(c) the testimony is the product of reliable principles and methods; and
(d) the expert's opinion reflects a reliable application of the principles and methods to the facts of the case.

The first change introduces an explicit burden of proof as to the reliability, and thus the admissibility, of expert testimony—a preponderance of the evidence—and makes clear that the burden is on the proponent of the evidence. The second change emphasizes the judge's gatekeeper role in determining whether the expert's ultimate opinion is within bounds based on a reliable application of the expert's methodology to the facts of the case. The intended effect is to clear up any lingering judicial misapprehension that the reliability of an expert's ultimate opinion is merely a question of weight for the fact finder to decide.[49]

OTHER JURISDICTIONS

Over time, most states gradually embraced *Daubert*, although the California Supreme Court quickly made it clear that it

49. American Bar Association, *"Ensuring Intellectual Rigor: Three reasons for Amending the Expert Admissibility Standard,"* https://www.americanbar.org/groups/litigation/committees/mass-torts/articles/2021/fall2021-ensuring-intellectual-rigor-three-reasons-for-amending-the-expert-admissibility-standard/

did not intend to shift to *Daubert's* empirical validation/reliability standard.[50] In 2012, however, a *Daubert*-like issue presented itself to the California courts in *Sargon Enterprises, Inc. vs. University of Southern California.*[51] In that case, a trial court excluded the expert testimony of a CPA who compared a small dental manufacturing company to six major international companies. The court concluded that the comparison was too attenuated and resulted in speculative expert testimony. "In a unanimous opinion citing not only *Daubert* but also its progeny, *General Electric Co. v. Joiner,* 522 U.S. 136 (1997) as well as *Kumho Tire Co. v. Carmichael,* 526 U.S. 137 (1999), the [California] Supreme Court upheld the trial judge's ruling. Echoing *Daubert,* Justice Chin emphasized that a California trial judge has a 'gatekeeping' responsibility to exclude 'unreliable' expert testimony."[52] After *Sargon*, it appears that California is closely aligning itself with *Daubert.*

In summary, state courts generally follow the federal rules, although there are numerous subtle differences that should be considered in particular jurisdictions. In California, testimony of expert witnesses is governed by California Evidence Code §§720-723 and §§801-805. California and federal statutes are generally similar and confer upon the trial judge broad discretion in ruling on the admissibility of expert testimony. The forensic consultant is advised to be familiar with the evidentiary rules governing the admission of opinion testimony in the jurisdiction in which he or she testifies.

---

50. Imwinkelried, E.J. & Faigman, D.L., "*Sargon Enterprises v. U.S.C.*—A Different Perspective," U.C. Davis Legal Studies Research Paper Series No. 376, 4/14, https://papers.ssrn.com/sol3/papers.cfm?abstract_id=2427497
51. 55 Cal.4th 747, 149 Cal.Rptr. 614.
52. Imwinkelried, *op. cit.*, p. 2.

THE DAUBERT CHALLENGE

The *Daubert* trilogy of cases and the expansion of FRE 702 has given rise to the legal strategy known as the *Daubert* challenge. Given the trial judge's function as a gatekeeper to control the admissibility of expert testimony, the requirements of the *Daubert* decision and FRE 702 are used as hurdles to challenge the admissibility of expert testimony. A *Daubert* challenge is entirely a legal strategy, but the expert must be prepared to meet it.

A *Daubert* challenge to the admissibility of expert witness testimony can be focused on any prong of the trial judge's gatekeeper function: the expert's qualifications, sufficiency of underlying data, reliability of methodology, and/or the relevance of the expert's opinion. If successful, a *Daubert* challenge can limit (exclude) all or part of an expert's proposed testimony.

Procedurally, a *Daubert* challenge can be raised before, during, or after trial, but it is usually used before trial to exclude all or part of an expert's testimony. The trial judge may require a hearing on the *Daubert* motion (to exclude testimony) or simply rule on the question of admissibility based on the expert report and the lawyers' arguments.

Every aspect of the expert's testimony is exposed to a *Daubert* challenge, but the most important part of the expert's work is the reliability and applicability of the methods of the expert's analysis. Assuming the expert is qualified to render the opinion and she has sufficient relevant data on which to base the opinion, the expert must use reliable scientific or technical methods to support the opinion to be rendered. The expert cannot simply draw a conclusion without competent underlying analysis.

In federal cases, and in states that follow the Federal Rules of Evidence, the *Daubert* challenge has become a routine pre-trial strategy to oppose expert testimony. The competent expert witness must be aware of this procedure and expect that it will be used against him, and prepare the analysis and opinion with this threat in mind.

CONCLUSION

The law of opinion evidence has evolved from allowing the general philosopher-expert to state unsupported opinions based on subjective beliefs to a more rigid standard requiring the expert's analysis and opinions to be based on sufficient facts and data and be the product of reliable principles and methods. The expert will only qualify to testify if he or she has sufficient background, education, and experience, and the expert's specialized knowledge will help the trier of fact to understand the evidence or determine a fact in issue. By following the guidance set forth in Chapter 9, Developing the Expert Opinion, the forensic consultant will find it much easier to successfully advance a scientific or technical opinion through the litigation process.

CHAPTER 6

MANAGING A FORENSIC CONSULTING PRACTICE: PRACTICE MANAGEMENT CONSIDERATIONS

INTRODUCTION

Managing a forensic consulting practice[53] is unlike the management of any other kind of professional consulting practice. The operating environment of a forensic practice centers around the legal system, which in addition to being adversarial, has its own set of unique procedures, customs, and practices. Although a forensic expert operates within this adversarial environment, the practitioner does not function as an adversary.[54] Therefore, the management of a forensic practice must be tailored to working within the legal environment while also maintaining the goal of objectivity in the substantive work of the firm. There are many practice management considerations that do not typically arise in the operation of a traditional professional services practice.

53. The term "forensic consulting practice" is synonymous with "litigation services practice," "litigation practice," and "forensic practice."

54. A forensic consultant who is not designated as an expert witness may provide consulting support for an adversarial argument, but one who is designated as an expert witness is ethically obligated to provide unbiased, objective opinions to the trier of fact.

CONFLICTS OF INTEREST

Dealing with real and potential conflicts of interest is a major administrative issue in managing a forensic practice. In substance, a conflict of interest exists when a professional's ability to objectively evaluate and present an issue for a client may be impaired by current, prior, or possible future relationships with another party to the litigation. In simple terms, a conflict may exist if the expert (or her firm) has had any prior relationship with a client who is presently adverse to the current client of the expert. The simple definition seems straightforward enough, but administering conflicts of interest in a litigation practice is a formidable task, especially as the practice expands.

As a general proposition, the forensic consultant cannot accept an assignment adverse to a present or former client.[55] Most cases have multiple parties—particularly defendants—and the forensic professional must keep track of the parties and co-parties who have retained him or her in the past, and the consultant must also track the parties to whom he or she has been adverse in the past. This problem quickly multiplies into one that can only be managed by an appropriate computer database. There are many software programs available to track conflicts of interest, and these programs are generally marketed to the legal community.

The issue of conflicts of interest arises immediately with any communication from a potential client in the marketplace. The forensic professional must be keenly aware of the problem and undertake

55. The exception to this generalization occurs when a waiver of conflict is obtained, or the accepted practice of government entities or companies may be to allow lawyers and/or experts to accept completely unrelated matters both for and against the entity concurrently. The expert should clear this potential issue with counsel.

management practices to protect herself from it. Typically, and under normal business practices outside of litigation, a potential client or potential patient would call the professional's office to inquire about the professional's availability to perform a particular service. During the introductory conversation, the potential client would usually share some preliminary facts about the situation and the professional (or her staff) would discuss her ability, willingness, and availability to perform some services. Normally, this type of conversation would be routine, the call would end, there may be some exchange of written information, and the client might retain the professional to perform services.

In the environment of litigation, as soon as the professional (or her staff) receives any substantive information from a potential client, the information can be said to be confidential and the professional can be prevented from accepting an assignment adverse to that potential client under the theory of conflict of interest.[56] It is important to note that the amount of confidential information that is required to create this problem is minimal. In fact, according to one significant legal case relevant to the issue, there is no clear definition as to how much confidential information needs to be in the possession of an accountant to prohibit him or her from working against a client.

The conflict of interest issue raises two significant practice management considerations. First, it is imperative to have clear procedures in place for communications with potential new clients.

56. Even a communication with a potential client can subsequently disqualify a lawyer or a forensic consultant under the theory of conflict of interest. In *Shadow Traffic Network v. The Superior Court of Los Angeles County* (1994) 24 Cal.App. 4th 1067, a one-hour meeting between a CPA firm and plaintiff's lawyers to discuss the possible retention of the CPA firm as an expert witness for the plaintiff led to the disqualification of the defendant's lawyers when the CPA firm was later retained by the defendant as an expert witness.

Second, your firm must meticulously track past and present clients, adverse parties, and co-parties to litigation matters, as well as regular clients of the firm.[57] These management procedures are essential to competently run a forensic consulting practice.

> **Practice Tip:** It is best practice to not even accept a telephone call from a potential new client without formally clearing conflicts. Initial calls are routinely transferred to a senior administrative person who is trained to obtain the information that is necessary to perform a conflicts check. (Name of case, legal case number, all parties and their counsel, adverse parties and their counsel.) Only after conflicts are cleared does the forensic professional communicate with the potential client. This practice ensures that you can accept the present assignment without fear that you will later be "conflicted out" of the case because of some past communication or employment by you or other members of your firm.

The initial telephone conversation procedures merit additional discussion here. When the expert receives a telephone inquiry from a potential client, the expert should immediately take control of the conversation, advise the potential client that the expert does not consider herself retained, and ask the potential client to limit this initial conversation to administrative details described in the above practice tip. The expert's proffered reason for deferring a substantive discussion is to "check conflicts," and that is a true statement. At this point, the expert cannot be certain that she or her firm has not had previous conversations or performed services for the other side of the dispute; in short, a conflict may already exist, preventing the consultant from being retained by the potential client, or even discussing the case.

57. A conflict-tracking system should also include the lawyers representing clients and adverse lawyers as well. Whether these law firms create conflict of interests is discussed in the text.

The details of the initial telephone conversation must be limited to case name, parties, opposing counsel, litigation schedule, a brief description of the nature of the case (i.e., contract dispute, wrongful termination, personal injury, patent infringement, etc.), and the particular need for expert consulting services (economics, engineering, medical opinion, standard of care, etc.). It is also advisable to have the potential client email a pleading caption[58] sheet so that a formal conflict check can be made. Absolutely no substantive discussion of the facts or strategies of the case should be undertaken in this initial telephone call. Advise the potential client that you will "clear conflicts" and return the phone call as soon as possible.

If this practice management procedure is not undertaken with respect to initial telephone conversations, three problems can occur. First, you may find yourself engaged in a substantive conversation about facts of a particular case only to learn that you or one of your partners has already been retained by the other side or performed some services for the other side. If this happens, the likely remedy will be completely withdrawing from the matter and possibly returning all fees that have been paid to date. Second, if you engage in a substantive conversation about a case in an initial telephone conversation and the potential client chooses not to contact you again, you will find yourself "conflicted" from ever accepting work in this matter from the other side. (It only takes one five-minute conversation that precludes you from a potential subsequent $15,000 professional fee to learn this lesson. Regrettably, I have made this mistake several times over the years.) The third problem that arises from loosely engaging in an initial telephone conversation is that you lose control of your ability to choose the cases and clients that you want.

58. A pleading caption sheet lists the formal case name, case number, court of jurisdiction and attorney(s) representing the party.

One of the advantages to limiting the initial conversation to a brief, non-substantive outline of the case is that it enables you to step back and consider whether you want to work for this client, this attorney, or on this matter. By removing yourself from the initial phone conversation to "clear conflicts," not only will you truly clear conflicts, but you will also have the opportunity to pause and consider whether you want to accept this assignment. Your subsequent telephone call with the attorney will be much more organized and you will be managing your litigation practice proactively, not reactively.

> **Practice Tip.** Develop a checklist for gathering information during initial telephone calls and follow the list scrupulously. Consider including a written outline of the admonition that you routinely give the potential new client so you can read it from your notes every time. Include a space on the checklist to indicate (by initialing) that the admonition was given so your own file will be clear that the inquirer was advised not to disclose any confidential information during the phone call. (See exhibit 6.1: Sample File Intake Sheet)

> **Example:** "Hey, Bill ... don't give me any substantive information about this case until I have the opportunity to run conflicts. I don't think I'm conflicted, but I never really know until we run it through our system. Let me get enough information to run a conflict check and I'll get back to you shortly." *[Attorneys understand this procedure and will have no problem with it.]*

The second major practice management consideration regarding conflicts is the actual conflict management program that you implement. Any significant litigation practice will require a computer database program to manage its conflicts. In the database, all parties, co-parties, adverse parties, and adverse co-parties are entered at a minimum. It is also helpful to enter client lawyers and adverse lawyers in your conflict management system for future reference. Finally, if you choose to engage in substantive conversations with potential clients (which is not recommended, per the preceding paragraphs), the names of these potential clients must be entered in your conflicts database at the time of the initial discussions. Assuming substantive information has been exchanged, you are now effectively conflicted from ever working for the other side of this initial-phone-call case.

When a potential client requests your services, you must review the historical conflicts database to determine if any adverse parties in the potential new matter have ever been client parties in a previous matter, or if a potential client in the new matter has ever been an adverse party in a previous matter. This knowledge is critical to determine whether or not to accept the potential new assignment.

> **Practice Tip.** It is impossible to track conflicts informally. If your litigation services practice grows to any meaningful size (meaning more than one or two cases per year), conflicts must be tracked by a computer database management system.

In the context of conflicts, much has been discussed about substantive information exchanged in a preliminary telephone call or meeting with a potential client. Many times, this substantive information is truly innocuous and has no meaningful effect on the case and, as a practical matter, it should have no effect on the expert's ability to perform services for the opposing side. In fact, the superficiality of this information is irrelevant. If a conflict issue later arises and it has not been handled properly by the forensic practitioner, when the allegation is made that the expert is in possession of confidential information that can be used against an adverse side to the litigation matter, it's too late to talk about how superficial the information was. It is almost a black-or-white proposition; if the expert has ever received any *arguably* confidential information, the expert will be precluded from working against a party in a litigation matter. And remember, the only reason the possible conflict issue is arising later in a case is that somebody wants to get you thrown off the case because they don't like your opinion or your expected opinion. Consequently, the arguments about how significant an earlier communication was will be distorted and the expert will be in a no-win defensive position. There is a good chance that your side's own lawyers and clients will not want to fight to keep you involved. It's usually not worth it; they can more easily find someone else, or worse, your client is left without an expert and it's your fault because you failed to properly disclose a conflict. Good luck with your malpractice carrier.

Practice Tip. Consider implementing the following procedure: If, after an initial inquiry, you are not recontacted by the potential client within a reasonable time period, send a perfunctory letter or email acknowledging that you received only administrative information about the case. In the written communication, reiterate that you advised the potential client not to disclose any confidential information and that none was disclosed. Advise the potential client that you do not consider yourself retained in the matter and you are not in possession of any confidential information regarding the case. (This written disclosure will allow you to later consider accepting a forensic assignment from a party on the other side of the case.)

The short answer to this complicated dilemma is to implement practice management procedures within your firm. There is no way around the issue; conflicts are a serious matter in a forensic consulting practice and must be competently dealt with.

An unfortunate final point regarding conflicts of interest is that some lawyers or clients have a practice of contacting experts at the outset of a case simply to conflict those experts from being retained by the other side of the litigation. Although this practice borders on unethical, it is certainly undertaken and it has happened to me more than once over the years. Very tight initial communication procedures will help the forensic consultant defend against this improper conduct on the part of some unscrupulous lawyers.

WAIVER OF CONFLICT

If, at the initial stage of a possible retention, a potential conflict presents itself, the consultant has the opportunity to seek a waiver of conflict of interest from the adverse party. Obviously, some discretion must be exercised in seeking a waiver, but the alternative is to simply reject the possible assignment. First, the consultant has to disclose the potential conflict to the attorney and client who seek to retain the consultant, asking whether they would still want the expert on board, knowing that the expert has had some past involvement with the opposing side of the litigation. (Often, the past involvement is completely innocuous—perhaps the opposing side of the present matter was a co-party in a previous matter, or there was some distant previous relationship by another member of the expert's firm.) But, the potential conflict must be disclosed if the expert is going to try to proceed with the retention. Assuming the retaining clients want to proceed, the opposing side must be contacted, and this is usually done by the potential lawyer-client in the present matter. Sometimes it's a big deal, and other times it's not. The opposing side may be indifferent to having the consultant adverse to them in the present matter, or they may be happy to have a quality forensic consultant in opposition to them presently.

Of course, the opposition may simply say they don't want to waive conflict, and that's the end of it.

> **Practice Tip.** The following language should be considered in a "Waiver of Possible Conflict of Interest" agreement with the opposing side of the litigation. (In fact, both sides to the present dispute should be asked to agree to the waiver of conflict, although it is the opposing side that has the direct claim of conflict of interest against the forensic consultant.) "Forensic Consultants Inc. is presently retained to provide vocational rehabilitation [or any type of] litigation consulting services to Plaintiff John C. Doe in the present litigation, Doe v. Burns, et al., Case No. 1234567. Forensic Consultants Inc. was previously retained by defendant Bill Burns in connection with his marital dissolution in 2019 to provide vocational rehabilitation consulting services related to the employability of Betty Burns. Forensic Consultants Inc. is not in possession of any information from the previous retention by Burns that would affect any services it expects to perform in the present matter. Burns agrees he will not raise possible conflict of interest claims against Forensic Consultants Inc. in the matter of Doe v. Burns."

You can see how difficult it is to cover all the bases to get an opposing client to waive a conflict of interest. Why should they? But, the result of not trying is to preclude yourself from being able to render any services in the case.

Interestingly, after an initial telephone call in which the expert (or her staff member) only obtains administrative information, the expert might advise the potential client of conflict of interest and the inability to accept the assignment. At this point, there is nothing technically preventing the expert from accepting the assignment from the other party, although this is obviously a situation that should be handled very tactfully. There are a lot of delicate moving parts here. Just make sure you don't end up doing a lot of work in a case and learning that you missed a conflict problem.

MANAGING THE WORKFLOW

A system for tracking work in process is imperative in a large litigation practice. The system can be as simple as a computer spreadsheet, updated weekly or biweekly, that includes case name, type of case, retaining attorney, total budget, percentage completed, deadlines, responsible staff person, and work remaining. This type of system is also very effective for managing staff time as well as assessing your work-in-process backlog.

The work-in-process schedule should be the basis of a weekly or biweekly meeting with senior litigation staff to assess the status of current projects in process and can also be used as the basis for near-term staff scheduling. These regular planning meetings are an invaluable tool in overall practice management and are essential for ongoing case management and staff scheduling efficiency. Be mindful, however, of the consequences of retaining detailed notes of these meetings as part of the case file. If they are part of the file, they will be produced to opposing counsel during the discovery phase of the litigation.

Litigation services work is non-recurring and unpredictable as to timing. The uncertainties of the legal system create timing problems; a large case may settle, ending all work, or the litigation schedule may be continued, deferring work to some vague date in the future. These scheduling issues are a simple fact of litigation and must be incorporated into your overall practice management strategy.

Good practice management procedures can bring some control to the continuity of the workflow in a forensic consulting practice. In some cases, the workflow crisis is exacerbated by poor planning on the part of an attorney or client in the litigation matter. The forensic professional should make it clear to the client in the engagement letter that there are minimum time requirements for certain aspects of the forensic analysis required for the litigation. (See Chapter 16, Engagement Letters.) It is simply not possible for the expert to perform a competent, thorough analysis if documents are provided three or four days prior to a deposition, for example.

Practice Tip. Consider the following provision in your engagement letter: "It is imperative that documents be provided at least 30 (45?, 60?, 90?) days prior to the date that our analysis is expected to be completed or deposition testimony is required."

BILLING AND COLLECTIONS

Litigation matters are unpredictable in the scope, amount, and timing of the work required. Also, because they are non-recurring projects (among other reasons), they tend to be somewhat inefficient and, as a result, litigation matters tend to be very expensive.

First and foremost, the client must be advised that the expert's fees are not contingent in any way on the outcome of the litigation. Many professions have prohibitions against members charging contingent fees, but whether or not it is professionally prohibited, a contingent fee arrangement would affect the bias of a witness in that he would have a financial interest in the outcome of the matter. Contingent fees are unacceptable for designated expert witnesses, and the client must be keenly aware of this fact from the outset of the litigation. A consulting expert, one not designated as an expert witness and not testifying, could ethically provide services under a contingent fee arrangement, but the consultant should be mindful of tainting the overall nature of the practice. In a subsequent unrelated case, I would not want to answer the following question: "Have you ever worked on a contingent fee basis in a litigation matter?"

Forensic consulting services are generally performed for non-recurring clients, and this fact should impact the professional's billing and collection practices. There will likely be no required future services such as recurring tax preparation by a CPA or needed engineering drawings update by the engineer expert to use as leverage for the payment of a previously unpaid fee. When the litigation matter is resolved, the client may very well be gone forever. For billing purposes, it is very important to use the deadlines imposed by the litigation process as benchmarks for the timing of the payment of fees. For instance, a report due date or a deposition date will require substantial effort on the part of the forensic expert. These are obvious dates to require that past invoices be brought current.

Practice Tip. Consider a provision in your engagement letter that states "Fees are due within 30 days of statement date and are all due and payable prior to the issuance of our final report or the time expert testimony is required."

"Forensic Consultants Inc. reserves the right to withdraw from this matter if fees have not been paid as agreed in this engagement agreement."

It is a sad reality that a client may be dissatisfied with the overall litigation process. In general, the process often consumes more financial resources than the client intended and the outcome is less desirable than the client's original expectation. (This is often true because a client may have an unrealistic emotional expectation of the result of a litigation that is not borne out by the reality of the process.) Nevertheless, the forensic expert's professional fees are not dependent on the client's satisfaction with the outcome. As long as the forensic expert is careful to point out the business and financial risks of the litigation during the process and the client knowingly undertakes the litigation, the expert should not be reluctant to demand payment for the full value of services rendered. The expert is only one part of the entire litigation process; if the work was competently performed under the terms of an engagement agreement, the expert should be paid for the services.

On an emotional level, a client who has fully paid his bill is less likely to complain about the quality of your services. Psychologically, a client who owes a substantial balance to a provider of services will look more critically at the performance of those services. And remember, paying last year's expert witness is not a high priority in the mind of a client.

In the final analysis, the best method of billing and collections for a litigation service is simply good, basic business practices. Be clear about the terms of your retention; you bill an hourly rate for your time and demand payment on normal business terms. You are not in the business of financing a client's litigation matter; pursuing litigation is your client's business decision. You should expect your financial terms to be met during the course of the engagement, and if they are not, you should enforce the consequences. Generally, the primary problems in billings and collections are negligent or poor business practices on the part of the forensic services provider. Apply basic business principles to your engagement letters and your procedures during the process and you will have little difficulty with billings and collections.

Practice Tip. Attorneys often have different billing cycles than you do. Include a transmittal letter with your invoice requesting the attorney to forward your invoice to the ultimate client with a recommendation for payment. Alternatively, you can ask for and deal directly with the client's accounts payable contact.

Practice Tip. Consider the use of a "rolling retainer." This is a fee arrangement in which the retainer is constantly being replenished and the expert is always billing against a positive retainer balance. Another common practice is the "evergreen retainer," one which is requested at the outset of the engagement but is clearly defined to be applied to the final balance of the bill, and not a retainer that is to be "worked off" during the course of the engagement.

BILLING RATES AND FORMATS

Your firm's billing rates for litigation services work should be given careful consideration. Of course, they are subject to discovery as all other aspects of your engagement are. The first question is whether to use the same billing rates for your services in a litigation matter as you do in non-litigation matters. (I will shortly explain why I think the rates should be the same.) This is a matter of judgment for the forensic professional; some practitioners believe that litigation work is more stressful and demanding than general professional services and believe that a premium for this type of work should be charged. Whatever your conclusion is to this question, it is important to be prepared to explain the rationale for any billing rate differential to the opposing side of the case. If you choose to use higher billing rates for litigation services work, the opposing side may try to draw some negative inference from this fact.

Within the litigation services work that is performed, some experts charge a premium for expert testimony in depositions and in trial. Those practitioners generally believe that the act of rendering expert testimony is more difficult and complex than the rest of the litigation services that are performed and, therefore, expert testimony services demand a premium hourly rate. The rationale for this "hazardous duty premium" may be justified, but the consequences of this policy are generally not worth the benefits. First of all, the number of hours that the forensic expert actually spends rendering expert testimony in depositions and trials is not that great a percentage of the expert's overall billable time, so the aggregate dollar amount of the premium charged is not that significant. When an expert charges a premium for his or her testimony, the opposition will often cross-examine the expert on that point, insinuating that the testimony is bought and paid for at an extra high rate. In the minds of typical jurors, the rates that professionals charge are very high in relation to average wages, so increasing an already high retail billing rate for an additional premium can be made to sound greedy. In the opinion of this author, the aggregate benefit of this policy does not outweigh the cost (in the form of argument) against the credibility of the expert.

Practice Tip. Be sure to familiarize yourself with the jurisdiction's rules about payment for expert testimony in depositions. Most jurisdictions require the deposing party to pay the opposing expert's time in a deposition. Be familiar with your jurisdiction's rules regarding minimum fees for depositions, rounding practices (i.e., up to the next hour, for instance), travel time, and waiting time. Be sure that your billing practices conform to the rules of your jurisdiction.

A noteworthy final suggestion related to billing is the format and level of detail of the forensic consultant's invoice. Most professional service firms are pleased to provide clients with detailed descriptions of the work performed during the statement period. This practice notifies the client of the thoroughness of the professional's services and also presents an affirmative defense to the amount of time charged to the project.

In a forensic practice, detailed billing is ill-advised because it provides the opposition with a roadmap to the twists and turns of the consultant's process of solving the case, including avenues contemplated but abandoned. The subtle details of preliminarily "investigating X," or preliminarily "researching Y," or "discussing Z with counsel" provide the opposition with myriad unproductive questions for cross-examination in deposition and trial. Detailed billing enables the opposition to undermine the forensic's quality work by argumentatively distorting the contemplated or uncompleted steps of the process.

Simply stated, the categories of services shown on the forensic's invoices should be general, not specific. In my field, I have limited my billing categories to generalized descriptions such as "economic analysis," "review of records," "research," "client meeting," "site visit," "telephone call," "report draft," "deposition preparation," and "trial preparation." This isn't a complete list, but it conveys the general nature of the categories I suggest using. In my experience, it is a mistake to present detailed billing description of every step of the analysis that you and your staff undertake. These details—especially the uncompleted ones—will be taken out of context and used to discredit your position later in the case. You may find it helpful to advise the client orally that your bills will only include a generalized description of your services, and this practice is ultimately for the client's benefit.

PROFESSIONAL STAFFING

Finding and developing competent professional staff is one of the most difficult practice management problems in a forensic consulting practice. Litigation projects are the antithesis of routine or repetitive work, and professional staff members handling these engagements must be intelligent and creative. Staff people who are comfortable in the more routine aspects of public accounting, engineering, architecture, or other professions sometimes find it very difficult to transfer to the creative area of litigation consulting.

There seems to be no way to ensure the successful recruiting of new professional staff. If your forensic consulting practice is part of a larger firm, you may have success recruiting the "best and brightest" of professional staff from other departments. Some practitioners have successfully recruited students with more broadly based degrees than the technical sciences (engineering, accounting, or finance), in the hopes that a stronger liberal arts background will aid in the employees' research, writing, and creative skills. No matter what the recruiting process, when a competent staff person is found, however, intensive training in substantive and procedural areas related to litigation support services should be undertaken. (The subjects covered in this book are a good place to start.) Quality continuing education courses are available through many state and national professional organizations, and using legal continuing education programs designed for lawyers dealing with experts can be a great resource for staff training as well.

Some litigation practitioners have been successful using contract support staff for litigation matters. In large cases, the work can be divided into two types: creative litigation analysis work and more routine data-entry work. Contract support staff from temporary personnel agencies can often be used for the less sophisticated data-entry work. It is unlikely that staff from temporary agencies can be used effectively for the creative aspects of litigation services projects.

Practice Tip. One way to test the effectiveness of new staff is to hire part-time graduate students in your professional field. Although it is difficult to use these individuals as senior litigation support staff, they can be very effective entry-level staff. A part-time internship gives the litigation practitioner the opportunity to review the work of these individuals before offering full-time employment.

RESEARCH MATERIALS

Opinions rendered in litigation services engagements are heavily dependent on competent underlying research. It is critical for the forensic expert to develop extensive resources to support the litigation services practice. When you are advancing an opinion in an adversarial environment, the opposition will extensively cross-examine the details of your research. It is important to have valid, reliable supporting research for every sub-opinion that you render or rely on as part of your ultimate expert witness opinion.

One of the weaknesses that can often be exposed in an expert's analysis is the failure to perform adequate and complete research. Examples of inadequate research include using the following:

- Outdated surveys or studies that relate to periods different from the particular analysis;
- Studies or surveys of industries that are different from the industry under consideration;
- Statistical research that is not directly relevant to the questions at hand;
- Research data that is not competent on its face because it is from too small a sample or from a biased source.

It is important to develop a complete resource library or obtain access to resources directly or through the internet. Many of the types of studies that are used in a forensic consulting practice are very expensive because they are published by trade associations and independent research firms. Nevertheless, these types of studies that address very specific sub-issues in litigation services engagements (professionals' wage rates, profit ratios for niche industries, cost of capital analyses, engineering studies, medical research studies, labor and employment studies, etc.) are essential for developing and supporting the expert's opinion. The practitioner must allocate a sufficient budget to obtain these resources (with annual updates, if appropriate) and catalog the resources in a library format so they can be easily accessed when needed. It is often reasonable to charge the cost of unique studies directly to the case they are being acquired for.

In recent years, the research available on the internet has eliminated the need for development of "hard copy" library resources. It is important that the practitioner have the ability and knowledge to access the wealth of resources available in her professional area related to the expert's analysis and opinion. As with any specialized area of practice, an investment in a relevant library is an absolute necessity so that you have adequate resources to complete your forensic engagements.

Practice Tip. Many consultants specialize in performing internet research on a contract basis. Given the complexity and pace of change in this growing area, it may be beneficial to use independent consultants for this work.

MALPRACTICE INSURANCE

In the opinion of most underwriters, a litigation practice is not a high-risk area for malpractice claims. Notwithstanding this fact, it is still important to maintain an errors and omissions policy and also to advise your insurance carrier that you perform litigation services.

With respect to potential malpractice claims, three areas merit additional discussion. First, fee disputes are often the primary triggers of malpractice claims. When a forensic expert sues a client for unpaid fees, it is almost automatic that the client will counterclaim some form of negligence on the part of the forensic witness. This fact is so commonplace that one major national accountants' malpractice carrier, CAMICO, includes a specific provision in its insurance policies that excludes professional malpractice coverage for lawsuits that arise from fee disputes. The insurance carrier adopts the policy of counseling its customers to maintain strong business relationships with their clients, suggesting the requirement of payment of professional fees on an ongoing basis and avoiding the accumulation of significant past due balances. This is good advice for any forensic practitioner and sometimes difficult to follow because litigation matters become very expensive and clients often find themselves behind the curve in planning for the financial commitment that litigation requires. The forensic consultant should also include a provision in the engagement letter that clearly requires fee payment at significant benchmarks during the litigation process (i.e., a report due date or deposition date). The most extreme protection against this problem is requiring a "true" retainer, also called an "evergreen retainer," described earlier in this chapter.

A second concern with respect to potential malpractice claims arises when an attorney sues a client for unpaid fees, and in response, the client sues the attorney for performing incompetent work. Although this dispute does not directly involve the forensic expert, when a client countersues the lawyer for negligence, it is possible that the client will name all of the professionals associated with the original lawsuit. While there is no way to completely protect against this possibility, it is advisable that the litigation services practitioner remain cautious about the attorneys for whom he or she works. I also recommend provisions in the engagement letter (Chapter 16) limiting the liability of the forensic consultant, although these attempted limitations may be difficult to enforce.

Finally, in cases in which a client chooses to accept an early settlement, the forensic consultant should advise the client, in writing, that had the case proceeded, more work would have been performed, and the result of this additional work might have been the discovery of facts that would have changed the client's settlement position. As part and parcel of the settlement, the client is consciously choosing not to proceed with the litigation and therefore not to continue the expert's work related to the matter. Sending this letter will aid the forensic consultant if the client should later have second thoughts about settling the case.

LOCATION

The choice of the forensic expert's office location is a minor practice management consideration that can have some effect on the professional's ability to develop business and perform litigation consulting services. Since clients are often referred by their lawyers, it is helpful to consider a location that is convenient to the legal community and that maintains the visibility of the forensic professional within that community. A successful practice will also involve a lot of deposition testimony and expert testimony at trial, so it is helpful to be situated near courts and the concentration of lawyers in your area.

If you are establishing a new litigation services practice that is not simply augmenting an existing professional practice, you may want to consider locating in a professional suite arrangement where some lawyers practice. A typical professional suite arrangement is a month-to-month rental of office space in an established professional office with multiuse tenants. If the professional suite is in the heart of the legal community in your city, many of the other tenants may be lawyers. This association becomes an excellent basis for building a litigation services practice.

> **Practice Tip.** One advantage to a professional suite arrangement is that, generally, additional office space can be obtained on a month-to-month basis. If the practitioner obtains a large engagement that will require extra staff and extra space, the location can be expanded on a variable cost basis. At the end of the project, the extra space can be abandoned with no fixed overhead consequences.

Another alternative for the new litigation services practice is an office sharing arrangement or subletting of office space from an existing law firm.[59] Again, the proximity to and relationships with lawyers is invaluable in developing the practice.

CONCLUSION

The adversarial operating environment gives rise to practice management considerations that are unique to a litigation services practice. Non-litigation professional practices don't need to be con-

59. This arrangement would likely preclude the expert from being retained in a matter handled by that law firm; the relationship would be argued to be "too close" for independent, unbiased analysis.

cerned with conflict of interest issues, nor do they fear every aspect of their work being scrutinized by an opposing party. Structuring the management of the practice to address these considerations will help contribute to the forensic consultant's success as a litigation services practitioner.

Exhibit 6.1

FORENSIC CONSULTANTS INC.
FILE INTAKE SHEET
CONFLICT CHECK

Date:____________________

Contact: ______________________________

Case Name: ______________________________ Case No:. ________________

CONFLICT CLEARED: ________
(Initial)

Client Party: ______________________

Phone: ______________________

Client Atty: ______________________

Phone: ______________________

Nature of Case: ____

Assignment Requested: ____

Opposing Party: ______________________

Opposing Atty: ______________________

Phone: ______________________

Critical Dates:

Expert Desig. Date: ________________

Discovery Cutoff: ________________

Report Due Date: ________________

Trial Date: ________________

Other Deadline Date: ________________

"PLEASE DON'T GIVE ME ANY 'SUBSTANTIVE INFORMATION UNTIL I HAVE BEEN ABLE TO CHECK' CONFLICTS ON THIS MATTER"

Confirm: No Substantive Information Discussed: ______________________
(Initial) (Date)

CHAPTER 7

MANAGING A FORENSIC CONSULTING PRACTICE: CASE MANAGEMENT CONSIDERATIONS

An expert witness engagement is multifaceted, and the forensic consultant has a complex set of responsibilities during the process. During the engagement, the expert has responsibilities to the client, to the client's attorney, to the opposition, to the court, and to himself or herself. The responsibilities include providing high-level professional services, an awareness of the adversarial process, objectivity, and truthfulness. There are unique case management considerations that must be made if the forensic expert is to accomplish the task successfully. This chapter discusses these considerations.

ENGAGEMENT ACCEPTANCE ISSUES

Conflicts of interest. The first question is: Can you take the case? This is primarily a question of conflict of interest, and it has been discussed procedurally in Chapter 6. In addition to a possible substantive conflict of interest, a related concern at the engagement acceptance stage is the "business" conflict possibility. Even though you might not be substantively conflicted from providing services to this particular client, will you be putting yourself in an adversarial position with respect to a law firm or company whom you do not want to go against? Might there be future business from this law firm or other ramifications from taking this case? These are practical business questions which the forensic expert must answer at the engagement acceptance stage.

Practice Tip. Some lawyers are very sensitive to your taking cases both "for" and "against" their law firms; others view lawyers and experts as detached consulting professionals with no vested interest in the case and, therefore, no reason not to be on both sides of the same law firm in different cases. In fact, it is probably not a professional conflict to be "for" and "against" the same law firm in different cases at the same time. The business conflict of this situation may be somewhat sensitive, however, and any potential problem should be discussed with the lawyer. It is probably wise to err on the side of conservatism on this issue. Why risk a potential long-term client relationship for the sake of one engagement?

Another consideration: If you have worked on several cases for a law firm and expect to continue to do so, it is wise to work on a case against that firm at some point in time.

Merits of the case. Before accepting an assignment, ask yourself if you want to work for this lawyer and this client and whether or not you are comfortable with the position they appear to be taking in the litigation. Unfortunately, some lawyers and clients are looking for the expert who will testify to an unreasonable position, and these are not the kinds of cases in which a competent forensic professional wants to be involved. Also, some experts are concerned about the balance of their practices between plaintiff work and defense work. Even though the side that hires you should not affect the outcome of your opinion, some practitioners are concerned about the appearance of consistently working for plaintiffs versus consistently working for defendants. If your practice is biased to one side or the other, be prepared to answer questions about this alleged bias.

Area of expertise. After the possible conflicts have been cleared, in the initial substantive discussion with the lawyer, the forensic expert will be asked if he or she is able to testify on certain issues. This is the time for the practitioner to critically evaluate her background, education, and experience to decide whether the issue in this case falls within her area of expertise. In the litigation services environment, it is important for the practitioner to know what she is expert at and what she isn't expert at.

There is a tendency on the part of many lawyers to expand the role of a competent expert in the case. The lawyer and client would rather hire one professional—for instance, a financial professional—to deal with all financial aspects of the case, rather than hire two or three professionals. The potential client may think that because you have some expertise in a generally related area, you are expert in all aspects relating to the general field of your expertise. In reality, no one is qualified to testify on a range of broad issues; if you attempt to cover too many areas with your expert testimony, you will be rigorously cross-examined and you run the risk of being discredited in a minor area that will affect the primary area of your expert testimony. Before accepting the assignment, be sure that you have sufficient background, education, and experience to qualify to give expert testimony and to withstand foundational cross-examination in the area.

> **Practice Tip.** Remember, the more critical an issue is, the more heavily it will be cross-examined. If there is a seemingly insignificant side issue that can be incorporated into the forensic expert's testimony, then it is probably reasonable to do additional research and render the opinion in that area. For instance, as it relates to economic testimony, maybe some item of demographic information would be helpful, such as population growth, traffic count, or consumer spending habits in a particular area. If the forensic economic expert perceives that this issue will be relatively insignificant, some additional research may be sufficient to incorporate it into the expert's analysis. On the other hand, if traffic counts, for instance, are going to be a significant issue in the litigation, the forensic economist who expands the expert testimony to include this issue will find out how little experience he has in the area of traffic counts on cross-examination. Be mindful of the tendency of lawyers and clients to stretch the forensic expert's areas of expertise. Stay in your lane.

Background, education, and experience. The issue of the expert's qualifications is a major question in a litigated matter. By definition, the other side of the case is adverse to your side; the other side will try to discredit you and your opinion in any way that it can. If it can be shown that the expert does not have sufficient background, education, and experience to qualify on the particular question at hand, the case is over on that issue. The other side wins. Don't think for a minute that, when the stakes are high, the opposing side will not push the issue of the expert's qualifications.

How much background, education, and experience on a particular issue is needed before a forensic expert can qualify to render an opinion in a court of law? Of course, there is no empirical test to answer that question, but the forensic expert should approach this issue carefully. Generally, by virtue of the fact that an individual is licensed in his or her profession, he or she will probably pass the minimum foundational threshold to qualify as an expert witness on most issues related to that profession. As already noted, the more important the issue in the case, the more scrutiny the issue (and the expert) will have.

Whether or not an individual possesses sufficient background, education, and experience to qualify as an expert witness is a legal question, reserved for the judge. If a minimum legal foundation is met to qualify the expert, the depth of the expert's specific background, education, and experience for the question at hand will be considered to go to the weight of the expert's opinion. When a question or concern goes to the weight of the evidence, it becomes a factual question, not a legal question. The trier of fact can give more or less weight to the expert's opinion, depending on how it feels about the strength of the expert's qualifications and analysis.

As a practical matter, the forensic expert should limit his expertise to selected areas in which he can truly become an expert and not be subject to foundational cross-examination on *voir dire*. *Voir dire* is a cross-examination process at the beginning of the expert's testimony undertaken by the opposition to attack an expert's qualifications to render an opinion on a particular question. If a forensic expert allows his or her areas of expertise to be continually expanding (accounting, finance, economics, valuation, management, marketing, pricing, competitive practices, leases, etc.), the possible success of the opposition's *voir dire* is increased.

In summary, know the areas in which you are truly experienced; study them, learn them, and practice them. Guard against the tendency of clients to try to expand your areas of expertise to suit their needs in particular cases. You run the risk of being embarrassed, discredited, and possibly disqualified from rendering your opinion. Also refer to Chapter 5, The History of Expert Testimony and the Law of Opinion Evidence, to understand the importance of *Daubert v. Merrell Dow Pharmaceuticals* on the court's gatekeeping function to limit expert testimony to legitimate methodologies.

Time period and budget. Your engagement acceptance criteria must include a reasonable time period and budget to perform the services that you deem necessary to reach a defensible opinion on the issues in the litigation. It is essential that adequate documents be made available in a timely fashion so your work can be competently planned and executed prior to preparing a report or testifying in a deposition. Sometimes lawyers will contact you at the last minute, when their case is in shambles, and expect an expert witness to perform miracles and rescue them from an impossible situation. However, poor planning on the lawyer's part should not create an emergency on the expert's part.

Lawyer clients will frequently ask the forensic consultant to prepare a budget for anticipated services in the assignment. Budgeting is a difficult challenge because the expert is at the beginning of an uncertain journey that is being explained to him by a person who is often unfamiliar with the substance being discussed. In addition, the availability and quality of documents is unclear and access to information is uncertain. Finally, the entire process is in litigation and it is difficult to predict the level of the fight that is about to take place. Parties and counsel may be reasonable or unreasonable, and the difference translates to the amount of preparation time the forensic consultant will expend.

So, how can the consultant reasonably prepare a budget for the client? Very carefully. The budget must be characterized as "Preliminary and based on information available as of [current date]." It also must be presented as a range of high and low estimates of professional time (and fees) to be expended. I suggest that the forensic consultant break the anticipated project into both detailed steps and phases and assign high and low staff hour time estimates to each step, multiplied by the appropriate billing rate at each phase of the project.

> **Practice Tip.** Provide a budget for your proposed work in phases, initially showing details for phase one, because the initial phase of the work is more predictable than later phases. At the conclusion of phase one, inform the client that phase two will then be more precisely defined and budgeted. This process will be repeated until the work is completed, providing a more informed budget about the work needed to be done and the intensity and changing strategies of the journey from start to finish.

The final aspect of the forensic consultant's budget will be the actual litigation process, meaning the deposition, trial preparation, and trial. Initial consultation with counsel about anticipated deposition, trial preparation, and location of the events will help inform the time estimates required for that stage of the work. In the final analysis, however, be certain that your budget does not limit the amount of work you must do to meet your obligation to do quality, professional work sufficient to form the basis for your opinion. And remember, the budget is discoverable.

CASE PLANNING PHASE

Planning the litigation engagement is different from most professional assignments because facts and strategies change continuously during the course of the project. Concurrent with the forensic professional's work, the client's attorneys will be pursuing discovery techniques and continuous strategic planning to maximize the client's position in the litigation. This constantly changing environment and discoverability of all the professional's work product are significant factors in dictating how the engagement must be planned.

After retention has been secured by means of a signed engagement letter (Chapter 16), the forensic professional should schedule an initial planning meeting with counsel and the client. At this meeting, the following things should be discussed:

1. Summary of the claims being litigated and a discussion of the substantive theories relating to each claim. Where does the particular expert's substantive field fit into the overall litigation theme?
2. Will a written report of expert testimony be required?
3. Timetable of the litigation, including expert witness designation date, discovery cutoff, (possible) mediation date, report due date, and trial date. If known, it is helpful to know deposition dates of key witnesses and the opposing expert.

4. Documents available, from both the client's side and the opposition.
5. If relevant, the timing and ability to investigate other aspects of the matter (site visits, interviews/examination of the appropriate party, ability to examine items of evidence, etc.).
6. The specific statement of the expert witness designation. (After all, it is imperative that the witness be aware of and agree to the expert witness designation.)

Sorry for the repetition, but it is critical to be aware that any planning memoranda, memos to other staff people, or procedural programs relating to your work in the forensic consulting matter will undoubtedly be discovered by the other side. These documents are ripe for misinterpretation by the opposition and must be prepared with extreme caution. Because facts and assignments are constantly changing and every step of your work is discoverable, it is critically important that the steps you undertake are well thought out at the time they are performed and that they are concurrently documented.

If the forensic expert has early memos that discuss major aspects of an analysis that was never undertaken, those memos can be misused by the opposition in trial. The forensic witness will be vigorously cross-examined on steps that were planned but never done. The obsessive desire to plan an engagement and meticulously document every possible step that was contemplated is a major pitfall for the forensic consultant in litigation services.

Always be mindful of future discovery problems. It is extremely helpful to plot out your understanding of the issues involved and the timing of pertinent factual events by creating a timeline early in the assignment, which will continually serve as a reference document. Multiple business entities and complex relationships must be identified and understood, and a preliminary graphic representation of the situation can be very helpful. If you undertake this graphic exercise early in a case, you may be amazed at how similar your final trial graphics are to your preliminary sketches. But remember, all retained documents must be produced during the discovery phase, so the clarity that your preliminary graphics provide may also benefit the other side.

The expert witness designation. Most jurisdictions require a party (through their counsel) to formally "designate" an individual as an expert in the present litigation. The "expert witness designation" is a formal statement of the name, qualifications, hourly rate, and anticipated testimony of the expert and the representation that the expert will be available for a meaningful deposition in the litigation proceeding. The expert should be involved in the drafting of her expert witness designation because, after all, it is the expert who is going to be held to the limitations of the document, meaning that the designation can be used to subsequently limit the expert's testimony. I suggest that the expert witness designation be a broad statement of the expert's anticipated testimony without being specific as to the expected details of the testimony. The designation is usually made before the expert has completed the investigation and the analysis, and it is simply unwise to attempt to state the expert's anticipated testimony in detailed fashion at this early stage of the process.

Practice Tip. I have created a generic "expert designation" form that I routinely share with my lawyer-clients, along with my professional résumé. In all the cases I am retained in, an expert witness designation by the lawyer is required, and it's easier for the lawyer if I (strongly) suggest what should be said on my behalf. Here's a copy of my proposed designation I share with lawyer-clients:

Sample Expert Witness Designation

General Information:

Brian P. Brinig specializes in the determination of economic damages (business and personal), forensic accounting matters, and the valuation of going business concerns and professional practices. **Mr. Brinig** is a Certified Public Accountant, an accredited senior member of the American Society of Appraisers and Past President of the Financial Analysts Society of San Diego Inc. He is an Adjunct Professor (Finance & Accounting) at the University of San Diego School of Law. He holds a BSBA (Accounting) from Georgetown University (1973) and a Juris Doctor from the University of San Diego School of Law (1979).

Mr. Brinig has been involved in the calculation of economic damages on more than one thousand occasions in business litigation, intellectual property issues, personal injury matters, wrongful death matters, and wrongful termination matters. He has qualified as an expert witness on the damages issues of lost profits, loss of personal earnings and earnings capacity, diminution in value, excess costs, relocation analyses, wage & hour litigation, contract disputes, and construction defect matters.

Mr. Brinig's business valuation experience includes the valuation of hundreds of businesses in San Diego County (and elsewhere) for purchase, sale, tax matters, litigation matters, and community property matters.

Mr. Brinig's specific experience is set forth in his résumé, which is included in the firm's company profile.

Mr. Brinig's hourly rate for deposition testimony is $XXX per hour, with no minimum fee.

Examples of specific language that may be appropriate for expert designations:

Mr. Brinig will estimate the possible loss of earnings and benefits experienced by the plaintiff as a result of the claim of (injury, termination)….

Mr. Brinig will estimate the lost profits experienced by ________ resulting from __________ as well as the additional costs incurred related to _________.

Mr. Brinig will render an opinion of the value of ABC Company Inc., the subject of the dispute in this matter.

Mr. Brinig will review and respond, if appropriate, to the damages analysis provided by ________.

I don't suggest that everything in my proposed designation be included in every formal expert witness designation, but I find it beneficial to provide helpful suggestions to the lawyer. I suggest that the description be as general as possible so it doesn't create any limitations to my anticipated analysis and opinion.

THE ORGANIZATION PHASE

Identify objectives. An initial step in planning the engagement is to identify the objectives of the assignment. This is accomplished through discussions with the attorney and the review of case and background materials. When the objectives are identified, they must be communicated to the professional staff who will assist you in the case. It is understood that changes in facts and strategies will occur, and these changes must also be adequately communicated. If staff members do not know the objectives of the engagement, they can overlook important information and will be unable to assist you efficiently.

Facilitate factual development of the case. At the onset of the engagement, the practitioner must have systems in place that facilitate the identification, development, and proper recording of a large number of complex facts. This task is undertaken by the systematic organization of the documents that are initially provided. It is critically important to begin the organizational phase as soon as any initial documents are made available. There is a tendency on the part of many practitioners to wait until all documents are available to begin to organize them, but that practice will impede the process of both the factual development of the case and the conceptual development of the case (discussed later).

Index all documents. It is advisable to begin the organization phase by indexing all of the documents provided initially. Documents should be organized in some order that will facilitate the litigation process. It is sometimes helpful to organize documents chronologically; other times it is helpful to organize them by issue. Regardless of what system you establish, begin the document organization process immediately.

It is important to develop an indexing system that is flexible, allows for expansion of document production, and facilitates the quick retrieval of documents. Although a discussion of the actual indexing system may seem trivial, in a large case it is important to design an effective system from the beginning. If documents are simply chronologically Bates stamped as they are produced, the indexing system will not add value to your work in the case. It is inevitable that documents will be produced in clusters, and it is helpful to integrate relevant groups of documents into the overall document organization system. An indexing system that allows for the integration of later-produced documents is beneficial.

One of the realities of a litigation assignment is that the facts are never perfect; they are usually not even complete. One of the best ways to deal with this reality is to analyze incomplete facts proactively. In one small way, this is accomplished by aggressively dealing with documents as they are produced. Upon production, the immediate organization and indexing of documents facilitates the factual development of the case by forcing you to think about the available documents, a logical organization for them, what documents are missing, and what documents would be helpful to provide a perfect factual background for the case. In short, aggressive document management is extremely helpful to the successful forensic consulting practitioner.

Create a document management system. Many high-technology methods of document retrieval are discussed in modern-day continuing education programs within the context of database management systems. These include scanning, database creation, and word recognition retrieval capabilities. These technologies can be extremely helpful in large document cases. However, those cases are the exception rather than the rule in the typical litigation services practice. In cases with tens of thousands of documents, it is essential to use high-technology document management systems, but those cases typically have the financial resources to allow for the hiring of document-management professionals. Those systems, while extremely valuable, are not the subject of the discussion here.

Your document management system must ensure that the documents are retrievable and accessible at a moment's notice.

In the typical litigation services assignment, document retrievability is as simple as organizing, indexing, cross-referencing, and cataloging documents in a table of contents. In fact, there is no magic here; it's the basic elbow grease of being a good paralegal or staff accountant. You have to be disciplined about document management. I have often observed that about 40% of the time spent in meetings with lawyers and clients is taken up by somebody looking for "that document." In one litigation case in which I was personally involved, I organized all the underlying documents in about fifteen binders, tabbed and cross-referenced every document, and provided a complete color copy to every lawyer, consultant, and party to the action. I frequently advise clients to do the same because the effort will streamline the process.

Litigation is a very inefficient way to solve a dispute. Two clients—regular people who aren't schooled in the legal process or the various substantive areas of expertise that will ultimately be needed—are locked in a form of combat. The combat does not conform to business principles; it is extremely expensive; it requires a significant commitment of time and resources; and it has a completely unpredictable outcome. What part of that makes sense? It is true that our society has tried alternative dispute resolution mechanisms, and they certainly have value, although they have become much like litigation themselves. Clients should be advised of the inefficiency of the process and the need for settlement of disputes. I never shy away from telling clients that settlement, even at an amount significantly different from what they think is fair, is much more efficient than litigating. I also sarcastically tell them that the "fair" is at the county fairgrounds once a year and that nothing that happens in litigation is fair.

Review individual documents. The final step to facilitate the factual development of the case is to direct your staff to review individual documents aggressively and thoroughly. This is a procedure in which a staff person is encouraged to identify and highlight as much relevant information as possible on a particular document. It is important for staff not to make editorial or opinion-type comments on underlying documents, but they should be encouraged to thoroughly review and factually annotate them. Specifically, elaborate cross-referencing is very helpful, and there is no exposure on cross-examination to simple cross-referencing. Numbers or facts on documents should be cross-referenced to as many other places as they can be found in the file. (See Chapter 10, Documenting the Expert Opinion.)

Secondly, the highlighting of relevant facts in documents is helpful, and there is little downside to the practice. Yes, opposing counsel will ask, "Why was this item highlighted?" That question is really not difficult; it was simply factual information that was more important or more relevant than the other information on the document. Finally, staff should be encouraged to write explanatory comments on complex documents to assist the reviewer (and ultimately you, the expert witness) in understanding the meaning and significance of items on the document. Simple explanatory comments are not concerning to the expert in terms of discovery, but opinionated or conclusionary comments by staff are a problem, particularly when the junior staff person isn't competent to make conclusionary findings. If editorial comments are to be made by other team members on documents, they should probably be made on informal Post-it notes that are considered very preliminary and not part of the final file, and removed prior to production of the file.

Frequently, cases are made up of hundreds of relevant, complicated documents that must be reviewed by the expert witness prior to deposition testimony. If there are no explanatory comments on complex documents, it can take 15 to 20 minutes to figure out the importance of any one document. When a staff member takes the time to do this, the staff person's thought process should be annotated on the document. Again, the comments should not include any argument or opinion on the part of the staff person; the comments should simply be explanatory and relating to an understanding of the relevant facts set forth on the document. This staff annotation would also include a notation that certain information was not used or not considered relevant in the analysis.

CONCEPTUAL DEVELOPMENT OF THE CASE

Development. One of the great challenges in a litigation services project is to develop a theoretically sound substantive opinion that embraces all of the facts, adopts reasonable assumptions when necessary, and applies sound rationale to derive its conclusion. To accomplish this lofty goal, the theoretical concepts of the case must be aggressively developed and repeatedly challenged during the analysis phase. In layman's terms, this process is an attempt to make the most out of what you have while recognizing you will never have all of what you need to do it. To some extent, every expert opinion is an argument that makes the most defensible position out of the available, underlying facts. The reason the case is in litigation is because the facts and the argument aren't perfect, and someone disagrees with your client's perspective on things. Hopefully, your piece of the overall puzzle is a strong one, but I have worked in the real world for forty years and I don't always get to kick the field goal from the ten-yard line with the wind at my back. Welcome to the land of the expert witness.

In order to develop the concepts of your part of the case aggressively, you must initially posit a substantive theory based on the facts as you know them and/or facts you expect to learn. So, the conceptual development of your part of the case begins with a plausible scientific or technical theory of the expert's substantive issue (damages, valuation, fraud scheme, vocational rehabilitation plan, construction defect, medical malpractice, legal malpractice, etc.). At the early stages of the expert's involvement in the case, there will rarely be sufficient facts or documents to fill in all the gaps of the theory of the case. To compensate for this problem and to advance the conceptual development of the case, it is essential to use temporary assumptions to fill in the missing facts. As the case develops, documents are produced, and additional facts are uncovered, the temporary assumptions will be replaced with facts. It is far better to develop conclusions with holes in the information initially than it is to wait for information to become complete. In most cases, "complete" information will never happen, and to whatever degree it does happen, it will often be late in the development of the case.

There is great benefit to developing the concepts of the case aggressively while waiting for the ultimate facts to unfold. Ultimately, the theoretical soundness of the expert's opinion depends upon the strengths and weaknesses of the logic underlying the opinion. And the strengths and weaknesses can only be evaluated when the opinion has been formed, even if only preliminarily formed. Consequently, it is very beneficial to use preliminary facts and many assumptions to fill the gaps in order to form preliminary opinions. It is also beneficial to force the development of the preliminary opinion early in the case, subject to constant revision by later discovered facts or strengths or weaknesses that emerge in the process. Also, an early attempt to finalize the argument in theory forces the expert to address strengths and weaknesses, and it also forces staff members to be alert to significant new facts that enhance or detract from the ultimate opinion.

Pulling it all together. Every litigation project proceeds on at least three tracks. First, the case is constantly developing and changing with respect to the facts; second, the concepts (financial theories, case theories, scientific/technical approaches, etc.) are evolving concurrently with the ongoing factual development; and third, the legal theories may be constantly changing as the case progresses as well. The analytic thought process of the entire case is tri-linear and, while it is ultimately presented as a sequential analytic process, it is not developed sequentially. Because of the sporadic way that facts unfold and theories evolve, the analytic thought process of a litigation project cannot be developed serially; it must be developed in response to the evolution of the case. So, the analytic thought processes used by the forensic expert are clearly different from the processes and order of the analysis used in the expert's day-to-day, non-litigation work.

The people involved in the project should be constantly challenging the validity and reliability of the facts and concepts with a view toward identifying weaknesses or alternative theories in the case. No one should be afraid of weaknesses—every case has them. These should be identified and incorporated into the analysis. The only fear should be not uncovering the weaknesses and dealing with them.

Quality control and review. As the work proceeds, your internal process of quality control and review will be implemented for every aspect of the litigation services project. It is a certainty that the opposition will pore over every fact, document, calculation and concept that you deal with in a litigation services project. There is no reason to let the opposition find the mistakes; you might as well do it first!

As in any professional assignment, a thorough review process simply requires that every step of the project be reviewed in an organized orderly fashion so that the correctness of every aspect of the project is assured. In litigation the importance of the review process is heightened because every detail of the project will be looked at by the opposition. After all, part of the litigation process from the attorney's perspective is to focus on strengths and minimize weaknesses; even a slight error in your analysis will be viewed as a strength by the other side and it will be exaggerated in the argument against your opinion.

If your internal reviewer has a practice of creating review notes, the disposition of the reviewer's "to-do" notes is different in litigation from that of a traditional professional services firm. In most professional services firms, a reviewer's notes would be maintained as part of a file to show the thoroughness of the professional firm's work. In forensic consulting, review notes will be used by the opposition (and argumentatively distorted) to show errors or weaknesses in the analysis. Consequently, it is important to adopt a consistent procedure of discarding review notes after they are used. Review notes should not be considered part of the analysis and opinion; they are simply internal communications to help achieve a better analysis and opinion. When the review is complete, the review notes are discarded.

FIRM POLICIES

Because the litigation process is argumentative and discovery procedures can be expansive, it is important to adopt policies that cover certain procedures relating to work on forensic consulting projects. The procedures generally relate to the creation, control, and disposition of various writings that relate to your work in a litigation project. It is important to adopt these policies consistently from case to case and follow them scrupulously.

In many professional service firms, the practitioners have a policy of writing extensive memos to the file about every aspect of the work on a particular project. In a forensic consulting assignment, these types of memos generally should not be written. Since all retained writings that relate to a case will be discoverable, the practitioner must be mindful of what documents to create and, if documents are created, it's logical that they should be maintained as part of the work file. If they are disposed of, there had better be a logical reason for their disposition (and I am hard-pressed to think of a good reason, other than trying to hide them from the opposite side of the litigation).

At an early stage, a memo to the file is necessarily incomplete. It must be based on preliminary facts and strategies that have not been adequately developed in the case. If the forensic consultant's preliminary thinking process is reduced to a writing at an early stage of the case, that writing may later be used to cross-examine the consultant in litigation. By definition, later-developed facts and concepts will have superseded the preliminary memo to the file. If such a document exists, it will later be taken out of context by the opposition. The clear message here is don't write memos about the evolution of the work.

Any final expert analysis or opinion is usually the result of numerous drafts of the analysis. It is critically important that the litigation services practitioner adopts a policy of discarding drafts of the analysis after they are reiterated. This policy must be extended to electronic data as well as hard copy drafts. Frequently, a document request will ask for the existing drafts of the expert's analysis. If the drafts exist, they must be produced, of course. If the consultant has a consistent policy of discarding and/or overwriting drafts as they are reiterated, these useless, historical documents will not exist and cannot be produced. Arguably, there is no benefit to retaining these earlier drafts; they are not part of your present analysis and opinion.

At the time of document production, all existing notes in the consultant's possession must be produced.[60] These notes include notes of meetings, telephone conversations, and review notes. Some unsophisticated lawyers may believe that their communications with experts are privileged communications[61] and the notes of those communications do not have to be produced. Clearly, the authority is to the contrary; attorney-expert communications are not privileged, and any notes of those conversations must be produced. (See Chapter 14, Legal Privileges Relating to Expert Witnesses.) Obviously, the notes of any meeting that are taken by the consultant must be carefully written and accurate.

The forensic consultant should be aware that neither the communications nor the notes are privileged and, if an attorney or client begins to strategize about non-expert aspects of the case during a meeting, the consultant should refocus the conversation to the relevant aspects of the case. Sometimes, the forensic consultant will have staff members attend a client or attorney meeting. Consideration should be given to adopting a firm policy that the senior person at the meeting is the only person

60. See Chapter 14, Legal Privileges Relating to Expert Witnesses, for a more complete discussion of the discoverability of the expert's file. In jurisdictions following the Federal Rules of Civil Procedure, draft reports and certain communications from lawyers to experts are shielded from discovery.

61. As described in Chapter 14, some communications may not be discoverable.

who takes and retains notes of the meeting. Otherwise, there could be duplicative inconsistent notes from meetings that are part of the expert's file. There is no perfect answer to this issue; I suggest the practitioner should consider the ramifications of multiple copies of notes of meetings and set a policy that only the senior person's notes are retained. But if you do follow this practice, you can't be discarding the junior staff's notes the night before your deposition; that procedure must be undertaken contemporaneously with client meetings.

The forensic expert should carefully consider the advisability of sending preliminary drafts of the analysis to lawyers or clients. If the expert believes that a preliminary draft is an insignificant iteration of the final opinion, why is the draft being sent to the lawyer for review? Also, if a draft is sent to a lawyer or client, it would be difficult to later suggest that a copy of the draft should not be retained in the expert's file. Be sure to consider all of the ramifications of sending these drafts. (As noted in Chapter 14, the Federal Rules of Civil Procedure permit report drafts to be privileged, but state rules are generally to the contrary.)

Regarding an attorney-client's review of the expert's preliminary work product, current technology allows for screen share through Zoom, Teams, or other virtual meeting platforms. Allowing a retaining lawyer to review a preliminary draft document with the expert using that technology avoids the problem of the expert having "sent" the draft to the lawyer and keeping a file copy of the communication for later production. By using screen share, the expert can later honestly say that "we [the lawyer and I] looked at a preliminary draft together and I sought the lawyer's input to make sure my facts and assumptions were correct." This is far better than having a hard copy of an early, preliminary draft retained in the expert's file that the opposing lawyer can later take out of context and use as a basis of strong cross-examination of the expert in deposition or at trial.

CONCLUSION

Because of the adversarial nature of litigation, there are case management considerations that are unique to professionals who function as forensic consultants. All professionals practicing in the litigation services arena will recognize their ultimate duty as an expert witness to tell the truth, the whole truth, and nothing but the truth. None of the issues discussed in this chapter are intended to undermine the expert's responsibility in the least. The obligation for complete and absolute truthfulness in the legal system is paramount, and no forensic expert should ever consider anything but complete and unequivocal truthfulness.

The considerations discussed in this chapter acknowledge the adversarial nature of the litigation process. In an adversarial system, the opposition will exaggerate any procedural or substantive weakness in the expert's analysis or opinion. Understandably, the opposition will take facts and assumptions out of context if the opportunity arises. A good opposing lawyer will try to have the expert's testimony excluded altogether on the grounds that the expert might not be qualified to render the testimony, or the expert is biased in reaching his conclusion. The case management considerations set forth in this chapter are presented to help the forensic professional perform competently and ethically within the legal system.

The competent forensic expert has an obligation to be aware of the strategies and tactics necessary to successfully advance his or her professional opinion in litigation. If the expert doesn't employ these techniques, the well-conceived truthful opinion will be undermined—and possibly even excluded—by adversarial arguments on the other side of the case. The forensic consulting expert needs to elevate her game to the art of expert witness testimony, and the strategies and tactics discussed in this chapter help to do that.

CHAPTER 8

MARKETING A FORENSIC CONSULTING PRACTICE

Most forensic consulting services are sold 90% to lawyers and 10% to others such as insurance carriers, claims adjusters, ultimate clients and other referral sources. Even if one of the other target markets is the buyer of your services, a lawyer will usually have some involvement in the purchase decision, so it makes sense to target lawyers in your primary marketing focus. My clients are primarily lawyers, so marketing to them is the strategy with which I am most familiar, and the one on which I will focus here.

The beauty of having the legal community as your target market is that it is very identifiable and the group is quite accessible. From the outside, the legal profession may appear to be a closed community, but it is easily reached. Lawyers are all members of the bar association, they attend required continuing education courses, they read the same professional journals, and they socially congregate at charitable and professional events. They talk to each other, they talk about their cases, they always "win" their cases, and they talk about who they have used as experts in their cases. There are easy techniques for penetrating the legal market, and once you have accomplished that, your marketing efforts as a forensic consultant will grow organically.

EARLY CAREER STAGES

At the initial stages of marketing your services, it is important to be mindful of the perception of the target market population. Few potential clients are inclined to use the person who "wants to be" an expert witness; the market wants to use an individual who is perceived as a seasoned, experienced expert. Now there is no single way to initially create the perception of yourself as a seasoned expert, but I will suggest a few different approaches, some or all of which may work, particularly for the experienced non-forensic professional who wants to evolve her practice into a litigation services practice.

Your professional résumé needs to look like an expert's résumé, not a job-interview résumé. The focus should be on your area of professional expertise and your relevant background, education, and experience as a court-qualified expert, if possible. Every phrase of the résumé will be cross-examined, so it must be absolutely true and any puffing must be factually based. There is no need to include the kinds of things one would include in an employment résumé, such as extracurricular activities in college, personal information, hobbies, or even volunteer work. To the extent you can tacitly include references to litigation matters in which you have been involved, that is a helpful addition.

Within your profession, be sure to be accumulating the requisite credentials that set you apart from the pack. They may be as simple as participation in local organizations of your peers and trying to obtain leadership roles in those organizations to be able to say you were the vice president of the local chapter of the American Institute of Architects, or the Orange County

Society of Certified Public Accountants. Every profession has additional certifications and credentials that can be acquired by the upwardly mobile professional that add to a résumé. Some of the credentials may not initially be perceived as being particularly special but, over time, many of these secondary credentials seem to gain credibility and prestige. Of course, be careful not to join organizations that are just selling "credentials," but the right mix of additional differentiators can be a meaningful distinction to potential clients. You will be building a professional résumé that will be the basis of your retentions in the future, and it's amazing how quickly these accomplishments add up.

Within your profession, it is usually possible to find speaking opportunities to small groups who have an interest in your substantive field, such as colleges, civic organizations, business associations, and even high schools for career-oriented presentations. Admittedly, this is a fairly introductory step, but these types of speaking engagements are also résumé-building and truly enhance your experience in forensic consulting by honing your public speaking and presentation skills.

An interesting irony of giving speaking presentations is the level of perceived expertise that accumulates from these presentations. I once reluctantly gave a talk about real estate appraisal—a topic I know little about—to a group of attorneys at the desperate request of a lawyer-friend of mine who was in charge of a luncheon meeting whose speaker had canceled. I initially declined his request to speak, but I eventually relented because of his persistence. As a result of my giving a very basic, forty-minute luncheon presentation, I received a number of requests for real estate appraisal assignments over the next few years, all of which I declined because I am simply not an expert in real estate appraisal.

The point of the story is that speaking on a subject creates a somewhat exaggerated perception of the expertise of the speaker and, over time, speaking on a topic that you actually know something about helps build your reputation.

Writing articles is an effective way to market your services to the legal community. I'm not talking about high-level scholarly articles in your profession, although if you are able to write those types of articles, you are well on your way to truly establishing your expertise. At the entry level, however, I am suggesting more basic articles of 300 to 750 words that are suitable for publication in community newspapers, local trade journals or local legal journals. The objective of these types of writings is to move you away from the "rank and file" architect, accountant, engineer, or other technical professional and expand your reputation into the larger community, particularly the legal community. In this area, however, you must remember that you will likely be cross-examined on anything you reduce to writing, so the forensic expert must be careful about making dogmatic, opinionated statements in articles that will eventually be scoured by opposing lawyers seeking to discredit you. Those statements will come back to haunt the expert in subsequent litigation.

I will share a brief, embarrassing story about writing and the problems it exposed me to without my knowing it would happen. I wrote my first book in 1999, *Developing and Managing a Litigation Services Practice* (Harcourt Professional Publishing, New York). In my experience writing articles and books, the authors and publishers are always behind the curve regarding deadlines, just like lawyers and experts in litigation. At the end of the editing process in 1999, the publisher never gave me the chance to review the book's cover and, to my great chagrin, they took the liberty of printing "Learn how to make huge profits in litigation support services" as one of the bullet points on the back cover. Now the publisher isn't in the business of getting cross-examined on every word it prints, but I am. And I definitely heard that quote for several years in depositions and it carried over to a few trials, to my great embarrassment. The message: review every word that goes out under your name—those words will come back to haunt you.

One of the most fertile areas of marketing I ever pursued was a closer relationship to the local bar associations through attendance at continuing legal education programs relating to my field. Attendance at those events gives rise to the opportunity to directly meet attorneys who are involved in areas which you seek to serve. Attorneys are required to obtain continuing professional education hours, and there are many programs for them to obtain those hours. Most of those programs are some form of "for-profit" (if only an admission fee to help defray costs), and most of those programs welcome related professionals who are willing to pay the admission fee. It's not difficult to find those programs through the local bar association, and attendance at such programs has the combined value of providing valuable substantive information in the expert's field (and the lawyer's perspective on the expert's area) as well as putting 50 or 100 members of your target market in one room for a few hours, enabling you to meet and greet potential clients. You don't need me to tell you that you can't be a wallflower at these events, but lawyers tend to be a fairly chatty group and I have always found them relatively easy to introduce myself to and talk to.

I will apologize for sharing an embarrassingly simple marketing tip that has served me extremely well over the years of my career. I intend this volume to be a high-level book about the art of expert witness testimony and not a sales "self-help" book, but I have used this personal tactic at professional education events for my entire career and it really works. I call it the "1½-second rule." Here it is: when you are within the personal space of another person, you have 1½ seconds to comfortably introduce yourself. If you do that, you will be part of a conversation with that person or those people. If you don't take advantage of the first 1½ seconds, you will find yourself standing or sitting there, alone, and not part of the conversation. This is such a big deal, I am going to write about it for a few more sentences in the hopes that I get some percent of readers to adopt it (and they will be glad they did). First of all, implementing the 1½-second rule does not feel comfortable—you have to force yourself to do it, because nobody likes to butt into a conversation. But I promise you that you will learn to get comfortable with it. Here are two situations that exemplify it. The first is the proverbial rubber chicken luncheon where there are round tables of eight, and three people are sitting there chatting when you walk up and sit down. You don't want to be rude, so you politely sit there quietly and wait for a break in the conversation to introduce yourself. And, it never comes! You end up sitting there by yourself until, hopefully, somebody else comes and sits down. So, here's what you should do. Immediately when you sit down, applying the 1½-second rule, you boldly interrupt the threesome and introduce yourself. You will instantly find yourself invited into their conversation and be part of the group.

I have learned to implement the 1½-second rule in every professional and personal situation I am in. If I am standing at the coffee station (or the bar line) at a lawyer's continuing education program, I stick my hand out and introduce myself to the lawyer who is within my personal space. Voila!! Now I am in a conversation. I won't keep preaching about this simple technique. You have to be smart enough to figure out how to continue the conversation, but my 1½-second rule will get you started.

Direct advertising of your services to the legal community is a proposition that requires thoughtful consideration. Part of marketing yourself as a qualified forensic expert is nurturing the perception of your esteemed professional reputation. By way of crude analogy, no prospective patient wants to go to the neurosurgeon who is offering a 25% discount for neurosurgery services during the once-a-year Christmas sale. The patient wants to go to the neurosurgeon who is acclaimed by the community and/or the one who is difficult to get an appointment with. So, advertising your expert witness services is a proposition that should be undertaken carefully.

One method to get your name in front of the crowd is to provide sponsorships for bar association or other professional organization events. Many of these programs seek sponsors to defray costs and they provide a tasteful opportunity to place an "advertisement" of sorts in professional programs or print advertising related to the event. Care should be taken to not have the insertion be "Hire me as your expert witness," but the opportunity exists for a tasteful presentation of your name, credentials, and some mention of your professional availability for services. Frequently, a distinguished lawyer or judge will be honored at these functions, and there is opportunity to insert a "Congratulations" into the event program. Not to overstate the effectiveness of this type of professional "advertising," but over time, the effects of advertising are cumulative and your reputation begins to build. Remember, you will later be asked in depositions to provide copies of any advertising you or your firm has undertaken in the last three or five years, so be prepared to be cross-examined on everything that appears in print. You don't want to be defending the "We-can-help-you-win-your-case" advertisement that appeared last year in the local law journal.

Some continuing legal education programs allow exhibitors and/or sponsors, most of whom are trying to sell their services to members of the bar, so you want to be careful to differentiate yourself from the companies who are selling some "lesser" services such as copy services, process serving services, and other legal support services that may be viewed at a lower level than forensic architecture, medical expert witness services, or economic damages analysis. There's no question that it's challenging to get your name in front of the crowd, but it can be done in a thoughtful, professional way that will help develop your reputation over a reasonable period of time while you hone your skills as an expert and obtain your first few cases.

Finally, I will mention the necessity of looking and acting the part. At least until COVID, lawyers tended to work in professional offices in business districts. If they are litigators (the majority of your lawyer-clients), they are used to going to court formally dressed, and they logically expect an expert who would be retained in one of their cases to look the part. Of course, there is some room for interpretation here too. If you're a construction defect expert or a land surveyor, you may decide that the right "look" for you is appropriate dress for that job description. A construction supervisor might look out of place in a Brooks Brothers suit, whereas a physician or banking expert would look inappropriate in a field shirt and work boots. Looking the part is subject to proper interpretation, but I always believed that my forensic accounting firm should look more like a law firm than a corner real estate office, and the professional staff in my firm should dress like professionals. Of course, the etiquette of professional dress changes with the times, but the forensic consultant should think about staying in front of the professional fashion curve.

INTERMEDIATE LEVEL OF FORENSIC PRACTICE

At a more intermediate level, as you develop a "book" of attorney clients and obtain some experience testifying as an expert witness, it is appropriate to build your reputation through speaking engagements, writing some relevant journal articles, sponsoring bar-related events, and discreetly promoting yourself as an experienced, successful forensic consultant. You want to evolve into the expert who the lawyers are talking about among themselves, not the expert who's groveling for the next big project. In an ironic way, if you can achieve the former, the latter will take care of itself.

Create the perception that you have plenty of work (you're busy, but never too busy to care for this new client); the subtle ability to discreetly say you've worked on "this" case or "that" case for others (without misrepresenting or breaching any confidences); and you're involved in "this or that" particular litigation project that is important, but so confidential—of course—that you can't discuss the names or details. These marketing techniques involve a bit of puffing, but they are a subtle building of your reputation. They amount to an understated building of your reputation while not *appearing* to be trying to build your reputation. It's a restrained art form that the professional marketing people are probably better to advise at, but I can at least identify some techniques for you to consider, and the ones that have worked for me over the years.

One of the things I have learned about public speaking is that almost any audience appreciates an intelligent overview of the basics of the subject matter. As an expert witness, you have to be able to be a speaker, and speaking to professional groups—particularly lawyers—is one of the most productive marketing activities you can undertake. You don't have to have a Ph.D. in your subject to intelligently review some fundamentals of the subject, make it interesting, and ask some smart questions about the concepts. The teacher doesn't have to have all the answers to everything and, importantly, good teachers absolutely know when to say, "I don't know the answer to that—that's a really good question."

I have designed a number of relatively simple presentations for lawyers and financial experts that I have used dozens of times to speak to professional groups. Whatever your substantive field, you can speak to lawyers about the basics of your field and, alternatively, you can speak to colleagues about how to interact with lawyers in the forensic application of your area of expertise. Either way, those speaking activities enhance your reputation in both communities and serve to build your forensic practice.

A litigation attorney's professional goal is to learn enough about a subject to be able to ask questions about it and prod for weaknesses (or subjective judgments) in a proffered analysis. One of my standard speaking techniques is to teach lawyers about the areas of judgment in my field so they are able to cross-examine witnesses trying to advance financial opinions in litigation. They are always eager to learn how to take depositions of financial experts or cross-examine them at trial. I assume this is also true for other areas of expertise. Teaching lawyers to do this puts you in demand as a professional speaker and enhances your reputation in your community.

The message here is a marketing message. The ability to speak is a shortcut to distinction[62] and the power of public speaking and teaching in the arena of professional marketing is incredible. Both teaching and speaking are learnable skills if you are not naturally good at them, and you have to be competent at them to be a good expert witness. Yes, first and foremost, you have to have something to say, but isn't that a given with respect to planning to be an expert witness? You have to have a subject in which you have sufficient background, education, and experience or one in which you're getting up to speed pretty quickly. If you're not comfortable with speaking, take a toastmaster's class and/or read a couple of books on effective presentations, because speaking is one of the most effective ways to advance your forensic career.

Don't half-step anything in developing your professional image and career as a forensic expert. Don't put a cheesy little classified ad in the back of some lawyer's journal. Don't have a cut-rate hourly billing rate. Don't work out of your house (at least have the façade of a professional office somewhere). Don't have cheap professional marketing materials (business cards, marketing materials, brochures). Don't have a low-rent website; spend the advertising money to create a professional image.

There's an interesting, counterintuitive concept in professional marketing that I learned when I was in law school. I was a part-time law clerk at a prestigious law firm in San Diego, California. This was in the mid-1970s, and this law firm had a practice of providing a car leasing allowance to its partners of a whopping $350 per month, an exorbitant amount for such an apparent luxury in those days. The firm's parking lot was filled with Porsches, Jaguars, a Rolls-Royce, and

62. Carnegie, Dale, *How to Win Friends and Influence People*, Epilogue, New York: Simon & Schuster, 1936.

my Volkswagen beetle. As a second-year law student clerk at this firm, my naïve observation was questioning why a client would want to use the services of a law firm that charged fees high enough to spend them on extravagant car leases, but as I reflected on the practice, I came to realize that reasonable extravagance works to establish a perception of success in the minds of the observers of it. Contrary to the logic of frugality, the perception of extraordinary success creates an impression of excellence in the mind of the observer and a desire to be associated with (or use) the successful professional service provider. Perhaps the analogy is that everyone wants to go to the outrageously expensive plastic surgeon rather than the reasonably priced one.

The benefit of writing articles was discussed previously. I have never been a fan of newsletters, but many forensic experts use them. From my perspective, the negatives outweigh the positives. Since the communication is likely directed to the legal community, it has to include fresh, current information and be at a high level. Producing such a document is a relentless, arduous commitment that takes away from your billing time. Everything you put in print is potential fodder for cross-examination and it is difficult to say something substantive, but not controversial, on a regular basis. There are services that produce newsletters for various professions, but I was never willing to trust those services to be knowledgeable about cross-examination and the subtleties of writing in a way that is argument-proof. The only advantage I see to a newsletter is keeping your name in front of the relevant community, probably lawyers, and I don't think the reward outweighs the risk and effort. Get your name in front of the legal community by doing good quality work, having a number of well-written reports circulating among lawyers, and being reported in the legal journals as the testifying expert in cases.

I am definitely not the person to educate forensic consultants on marketing techniques using social media, but there is no question that younger lawyers are often the ones charged with finding qualified experts for their law firm's cases. They are more familiar with social media and internet research to solve their professional problems. Recognize that these social media-savvy lawyers are often the first ones searching for the experts and be mindful of creating a social media presence.

Qualified by the disclaimer that I have never been a social media creature, I think the benefit of social media advertising is trying to reach young lawyers who may be considering hiring you, not reaching the ultimate clients. Over the years, I have occasionally been contacted by a non-lawyer who found me on the internet, but I have never obtained any work from that source. The only place I consistently get my cases is from lawyers, and they are the ones I want to target, not the ultimate clients. In fact, I am reluctant to take a litigation matter from an individual who is not represented by counsel, and I rarely do.

Somewhat similar to paying attention to the younger lawyers in law firms as a way to get to the senior partners who are the primary trial lawyers, the secretaries and paralegals often hold the keys to access to the bigwigs. And, sometimes the secretaries and paralegals are the de facto decision-makers themselves. Pay close attention to these folks and don't hesitate to invest time and energy cultivating relationships with them. Things like thank-you notes, gift cards, or event tickets given to those who aren't used to being thanked for their recommendations go a very long way toward developing long-standing business relationships.

At the risk of sounding too pedestrian, I will walk you through my technique if I meet a lawyer at a conference and I am on the marketing make. I will first use the 1½-second rule to meet the person I am standing near so I have the opportunity to converse with him or her. As

I begin the conversation, I will ask what type of law he practices and/or where his office is located. (Being more candid than I need to be here, I really don't care where his office is located, and I only care about the type of law he practices so I can see if it's compatible with the types of expert services he might need.) I will continue to explore the types of practice he's involved in, again really only fishing for opportunities to understand if he might have any need for my forensic expert services. At some point in this conversation (as I am feigning genuine interest in his law practice and the types of work he might be looking for), I will ask him for a business card. Importantly, don't ever directly offer to give your business card to someone—it's too much like groveling for work. After you ask for theirs, they will certainly ask for yours. Only then should you provide it; otherwise you look like you are pushing your services on them. In most of these conversations, I eventually get up the nerve to directly ask who they use for economic expert work. No harm, no foul... whoever they say they use, I will always give that person some level of compliment—genuine if it's deserved and tacit if the expert is at the other end of the spectrum. I have completed my real-time marketing strategy with this lawyer and I may choose to follow up with some emailed marketing communication with him after our original meet and greet. If appropriate, I may end the conversation with, "Let's do some work together next year," or a similar invitation.

Another thing I could have done better in my years of practice is kept a detailed "Rolodex" (or modern equivalent) of all these lawyer contacts. By this time in my career, I have encountered thousands of lawyers and I could have categorized them much better than I did. As I move toward retirement and want to stay in touch with these thousands of lawyers, my own marketing resource is a little bare. Don't make the same mistake I did: maintain a retrievable database of contacts you make during the course of your career.

VARIOUS OTHER MARKETING TECHNIQUES

Expert witness referral services. I don't believe there's anything wrong with them, I have just never needed to use one. My practice evolved before those kinds of firms existed, and by the time they started to spring up, I was busy enough not to use them. Most of the concerns I have about them are just basic litigation concerns. You will be cross-examined on where this particular case came from (there may be nothing wrong with the fact that it came from an expert referral service, but think about your answer to the question in advance so you have an appropriate response). Is there any concern about how referral fees are paid? If you are receiving fees from a client and paying a referral fee, it will be suggested that you are "paying" for this case, and that will not play well in front of a jury. Again, just be mindful of the fee arrangement and have a prepared response to the argument against you. If the referral service is paying you a net fee for your services (after the override for them), are you "working for them"? Who are they? Have you worked for them before? And, how much of their overall program do you have to adopt as yours? For instance, they might have a very aggressive marketing program that will be used to taint you. I don't have answers to these questions, and I am not suggesting that these services aren't worthwhile for some experts. I just know that the forensic consultant needs to think through the arrangement and be prepared to defend against any attack on the situation.

Close attorney relationships. Be careful of establishing too cozy a relationship with a lawyer or law firm, or even the perception of too cozy a relationship. Even though it may not be improper, the fact of a close or regular relationship will be used against you in litigation. This isn't an absolute reason not to do it, but it is a reason to think through the answer to the challenging question inferring that you are too close to the lawyer or law firm for whom you're working. Remember that opposing lawyers will use anything they can against you, and it's how you spin the argument against you that matters. In deposition, you may be asked if you have ever socialized with your lawyer-client or been invited to the other's home. Again, there is nothing wrong with these types of associations, but they will be blown out of proportion by your opposition.

Developing a practice. There are at least two lawyers in every case, and that fact creates an interesting marketing opportunity to expose your capabilities to a relevant audience. Even though the opposing lawyer is on the other side of your client in the present matter, you have the opportunity to show off your professional capabilities and expand your circle of influence. The best lawyers approach their cases professionally, not personally, and the fact that a forensic expert is on the other side of a case is no big deal, and it's only temporary. Another case will come along and, assuming the consultant did a competent and professional job, the expert on the opposite side of the last case is definitely in the mix of consideration to be retained in the next case.

You succeed at taking advantage of the marketing opportunity by doing the following things:

a. Present a very competent analysis and opinion in the present matter;
b. Not emotionally engaging in the litigation fight; you're just doing a professional job of advancing your well-developed opinion;
c. Act professionally and respectfully to opposing counsel in every encounter;

d. By doing good work, you subtly convey the availability of your professional services to the legal community in other matters;
e. If you see the former opposing lawyer in some quasi-professional setting (a professional education program, a luncheon), do not hesitate to be professionally friendly and complimentary of the lawyer's skills in representing his/her client in the previous matter;
f. You can always find a way to be complimentary. "You did a good job examining me in that case." If you "beat him," compliment his skills by saying something like, "Yeah, you just didn't have good facts in that one," or something to that effect. If he/she kicked your butt, compliment them for their good skill. It will come back to you manifold.

Think of the opposing attorney as your likely next best client. In the present case, you have the ability to demonstrate your professional strengths as a highly qualified, competent expert witness. Do not alienate your potential next best client by being emotionally invested in the outcome of the matter. Stay above the fray; you are a professional doing a job in the present situation. You are willing and able to do another professional job for this lawyer's client if you are retained on the next case.

Price sensitivity. Be careful about your personal preconceptions about price because they might not apply in the world of litigation consulting and expert witnessing. As I said before, no one wants to go to the lowest-priced neurosurgeon; why would anyone want the cheapest expert? I suggest you take stock of the rates charged by medium- to high-level lawyers in your community and, given your level of experience, place yourself a little below "comparable" level attorneys in your marketplace. That seems about the right place to fit in. One of the beautiful aspects of expert witness work is that you can resist giving a client a "deal" for your services on the theory that you will be cross-examined on your fee arrangement and there is no basis to give any one lawyer a better "rate" than anyone else. I won't suggest there aren't ways to work around this issue, but you have a very good argument for not "dealing" on fees and also not paying referral fees for a litigation matter. A referral fee suggests you are "paying" for a case, and that is simply inappropriate. Also, many professions simply prohibit paying referral fees. Finally, there is no place in the litigation arena for contingent fee arrangements for expert witnesses. It is a given that a contingent fee creates the fact of bias in an expert opinion and it is simply unethical to participate in such an arrangement.

CONCLUSION

There are many workable strategies for marketing yourself (and your firm) as a qualified expert witness to the legal community. Lawyers are identifiable and reachable. The tactical considerations should include building your reputation and résumé while not creating material for cross-examination by opponents of your present and future clients. The seasoned expert will employ sophisticated marketing tactics that are worthy of the status of a court-qualified expert witness, and not merely retail advertising.

CHAPTER 9

DEVELOPING THE EXPERT OPINION

INTRODUCTION

One of the great challenges in an expert witness project is to develop a theoretically sound expert opinion that embraces all of the facts, adopts reasonable assumptions when necessary, and applies sound rationale to derive a conclusion. In order to accomplish this lofty goal, the forensic consultant must aggressively develop and repeatedly challenge the underlying facts and theoretical concepts of the case during the analysis phase. In litigation, every step of an analysis will eventually be challenged, and the expert's job is to practice rebutting those challenges during the course of developing the opinion. Another reality of the imperfect world of forensic analysis is that the expert will have to make the most out of what she has while recognizing that she will rarely have everything she needs.

Advancing a substantive opinion in litigation requires a blending of technical and legal theory. Neither one is sufficient to carry the day; competent practice requires a thorough knowledge of your substantive field and its intersection with legal principles. The approach that has worked for me for over forty years adapts the analytic metric used by lawyers to analyze fact patterns, known by its acronym, the IRAC[63] formula, into a related method and applies its created cousin to my substantive area, damages analysis. The application of a companion of the IRAC formula also works for most types of forensic analysis, and I recommend it should be applied in every case. My method for forensic analysis is called FARC,[64] but before I explain it, I will discuss the lawyer's analytic metric, IRAC.

THE LAWYER'S METRIC: IRAC

To wade through the minefield of legal reasoning, lawyers and law students have historically developed the IRAC formula: Issue, Rule, Analysis (or Application), and Conclusion. The IRAC structure is the basic building block of legal analysis. The beauty of the analytic model is that it allows the complexities of the law to be reduced to a simple, analytic equation.

To apply the IRAC formula, one first identifies an issue of law based on the relationship of the identified facts to the relevant law. (If it's a contract question, look at contract law; if it's a crime, look at criminal law, etc.) When a legal issue is identified, the related rule is stated based on an existing statute or case precedent. Then, the facts are analyzed in relation to the rule (or *applied* to the rule) to derive the conclusion. If a rule requires that a certain circumstance be present in order for the rule to apply, then the absence of that circumstance helps one reach the conclusion that the rule does not apply.

As an example of the application of the IRAC formula, let's consider the simplest fact pattern imaginable (after it is initially

63. The acronym stands for Issue, Rule, Analysis (or Application), and Conclusion.
64. FARC stands for Facts, Assumptions, Rationale, and Conclusion.

cluttered with irrelevant paraphernalia). John Smith received a telephone call that his 12-year-old daughter, Sarah, seriously twisted her ankle in a Saturday soccer game and was taken to the local emergency room by her mother, Trish. Trish called John and said that he should come to the hospital immediately. John raced from his office—working on a crash project on a Saturday morning—and headed to Shady Glen hospital to attend to the situation. Several blocks from his office, John breezed through a stop sign without coming to a complete stop and was soon pulled over by motorcycle patrolman Jones. John politely argued with Officer Jones, describing the medical emergency nature of the situation, but Jones issued a "failure to stop" citation to John which carried a $250 fine. At John's traffic court hearing two months later, Judge Eldon J. Reasonable patiently listened to the testimony of Officer Jones and defendant John Smith. Should Judge Reasonable convict John Smith of the crime alleged against him?

Issue: Does John's "breezing through" the stop sign constitute a violation of the Vehicle Code?

Rule: California Vehicle Code Section 22450(a) states: The driver of any **vehicle** approaching a **stop** sign at the entrance to, or within, an intersection **shall stop** at a limit line, if marked, otherwise before entering the crosswalk on the near side of the intersection. [emphasis added]

Application/Analysis: Officer Jones's testimony states that John did not stop at the stop sign, but "breezed through," lowering his speed to "four or five miles per hour" before accelerating again. John testified that he was very concerned about his daughter's health and had to get to the hospital quickly, and that was the reason for possibly failing to come to a complete stop. The Vehicle Code states that the driver "shall stop" without any provision for anything less than stopping before the driver enters the intersection. (There could be a defeating condition of exception in the Vehicle Code allowing less than a complete stop for exigent circumstances, but there isn't one in Section 22450(a)).

Conclusion: John violated the Vehicle Code by failing to come to a complete stop and is guilty of the misdemeanor outlined in Section 22450(a).

Unfortunately, John loses his traffic ticket case. It is rare to be involved in the application of a rule as simple as "Failure to stop is a violation of the law."[65] In this conditional proposition, there is one condition (failure to stop) and one conclusion (violation of law). In reality, most rule-based reasoning involves a complicated law that has a conjunction of conditions connected by "AND" and the possibility that there are defeating conditions ("UNLESS") that will negate the conclusion. Furthermore, the underlying facts never have "values" as simple as TRUE or FALSE; they are always UNDECIDED at the outset of the matter. So the ultimate conclusion rests on the evolving discovery of the existence of the facts, the conjunction of the many conditions of the law,

65. More realistic examples of rules of law would be: California Civil Code §1608: If any part of a single consideration for one or more objects, or of several considerations for a single object, is unlawful, the entire contract is void. Or, California Penal Code §242: Battery is defined as "any willful and unlawful use of force or violence upon the person of another." Most legal propositions are more complex than the simple example I use to introduce the IRAC formula.

and the possible existence of defeating conditions that will negate the logic of the rule. Note that the IRAC metric can usually be applied to each condition and each defeating condition of the entire proposition.

Proponents of the IRAC formula suggest that it is almost always a valid way—although not necessarily the only way—to organize legal analysis. Opponents of the formula say that its simplistic nature masks the series of complex interrelated steps that lawyers need to use to analyze and write about legal problems in a sophisticated manner. Regardless of the criticism, the IRAC rule is an effective analytic tool for forcing complex legal facts and propositions into a framework of logical analysis. And, its pattern of step-by-step analysis is often used by lawyers to analyze every aspect (facts, issues, rules, conclusions) of a litigation matter, including the analyses of forensic experts.

In my early years of practice as a forensic consultant, I struggled with trying to "quantify" the analytic mental process I went through to take complex factual situations and apply them to financial models (my area of expertise) to reach conclusions that were supportable as legal opinions, meaning those conclusions that would satisfy a standard of reasonable certainty in a court of law. It was also difficult to teach my staff how to replicate my thinking process, one that I thought was effective for reaching expert witness opinions and conclusions. As I analyzed my dilemma, I returned to my legal training and began to tailor the IRAC methodology to my substantive area, which happened to be economics and valuation. I developed the FARC methodology: Facts, Assumptions, Rationale, and Conclusion. Like its cousin, IRAC, the FARC methodology is not the answer to all of the complexities of an expert witness assignment, but it is one more tool in the arsenal of the qualified professional who finds herself in the litigation arena.

The adaptation of the IRAC formula into the FARC methodology works for most areas of expert witness testimony, and it forces the expert to think like a lawyer, a skill that is extremely helpful when defending the opinion in litigation, particularly on cross-examination.

THE FORENSIC'S METRIC: FARC

A competent expert analysis is a blending of underlying facts, reasonable assumptions, substantive theory, and legal theory. The facts and assumptions of a particular case must be interwoven with substantive and legal rationale in order to derive a conclusion. The proper combination of all four components (facts, assumptions, substantive theory, and legal theory) will yield a supportable expert analysis, one that will be defensible in a court of law. In order to analyze and present a competent opinion, it is extremely helpful to have a consistent approach to the analysis that will withstand legal scrutiny and cross-examination. A step-by-step application of the FARC methodology provides this consistency, and the metric can be applied to every step of a substantive analysis in developing the expert's final opinion.

Facts are historical or present truths. A fact is something that has occurred or is known to be true. In a contested matter, an underlying fact can be agreed upon or disputed. In a forensic analysis, the consultant may be asked to assume the existence of a particular fact or may perform alternative analyses, based on fact A or fact B. As an example of alternative facts, there may be a dispute about the degree of injury suffered by a plaintiff, ranging from slight/none to significant/severe. A vocational rehabilitation expert may be asked to perform a "return to work" analysis based on these extremes, or some range of them. Examples of other facts would be things like historical earnings of a plaintiff, a construction defect ("the roof leaks"), or the necessity of certain medical expenses. A fact is usually the basis of each step of a forensic consultant's analysis. The FARC methodology requires the consultant to clearly identify the fact on which this step of the analysis is based, and it is the starting place for analyzing a particular step of forensic analysis. "Is the fact correct?" "Is the fact agreed upon or disputed?"

There are many situations in which one party to a dispute will request the forensic consultant to assume the truth of an underlying fact, and it is certainly reasonable for the consultant to do so, as long as the assumed fact is not contrary to the professional's judgment. And, the forensic consultant should be careful to stay within her field in evaluating the reasonableness of assumed facts, as subsequently discussed. Many cases will require alternative analyses based on different factual assumptions, deferred to the later judgment of the ultimate fact finder's conclusion.

Assumptions are suppositions, either the supposing of a hypothetical fact to be true or supposing a connection between a fact and a substantive theory. Assumptions are necessary for at least two reasons in expert analysis: sometimes facts are missing (or disputed) and must be assumed to exist, and assumptions are used to connect facts to substantive theory. An example of the first use of an assumption would be filling in a gap in the facts with a reasonable assumption. Say an economist doesn't know the amount of a person's employment benefits, so she assumes the benefits are a "normal" level of employment benefits for the job description of the plaintiff. That is an assumption used to fill a gap in the facts: you know the person had employment benefits, but you are assuming the amount of them. Also, assumptions are used to connect facts to the substantive theory; for example, adopting the assumption that a reasonable approach to determine the speed of a vehicle in an accident is to measure and analyze the skid marks left on the road. And, the connection assumption between the facts and the substantive analysis must make sense (i.e., be reasonable). In other words, the accident reconstruction expert isn't going to use astrology to determine the speed of the vehicle; he is going to measure and analyze skid marks to draw his conclusion, a scientifically recognized methodology. Recognizing that assumptions are required in every expert analysis, it is critically important that the assumptions used by the forensic expert are reasonable in light of the historical facts of the case and a realistic expectation of what would have happened to the plaintiff in the "but-for world."[66] As a general proposition, in the development of any expert analysis, the more uncertain the data supporting an assumption is, the more conservative (or careful) the assumptions should be.

Certain assumptions are within the realm of the forensic consultant's knowledge and experience and should be subject to

66. The "but-for world" is the term used to describe the hypothetical future that would have happened to a plaintiff if the event in question had not happened. For example, the plaintiff would have continued his employment, or the contract would have been fulfilled, or the patient wouldn't have died.

the consultant's opinion as to their reasonableness. (A real estate appraiser being asked to comment on the "highest and best use" of the appraised property, for instance.) Other assumptions are not within the scope of the consultant's judgment, and should not be within the area of the consultant's opinion. (Example: a banking expert being asked to comment on the reasonableness of a customer's business plan.) Great care must be exercised when the expert is asked to opine on the reasonableness of assumptions the expert is asked to make. You want the assumptions to appear (and be) reasonable, but if they are outside your area of expertise, the competent expert will simply say, "I was asked to assume X or Y," and not opine on their reasonableness, simply stating that they are out of the consultant's area.

Still other assumptions fall within the "gray area" of the forensic consultant's knowledge and experience. (Example: the importance of a particular chief executive officer to the operations of a business and the resultant "key person" discount to be applied in a valuation may be an area where the business appraiser CPA has familiarity in some cases, but not in others.) Care should be exercised when dealing with these "hybrid" assumptions. Agreeing to the reasonableness of an assumption opens an expert up to cross-examination on background, education, and experience in the area of the assumption and, if the expert is stretching her expertise, that cross-examination will be used to discredit the expert in other areas of her testimony.

In short, assumptions are fundamental to most forensic consulting analysis in litigation. The forensic consultant's selected assumptions must be rationally based and in conformance with the existing facts. If the assumptions are not reasonable, the entire expert analysis is likely to be rejected.

Rationale is the process of applying reliable substantive principles and methods to facts and assumptions to derive supportable conclusions. By definition, rationale is the fundamental reason, or rational basis, for connecting the facts and assumptions to the conclusions. Stated informally, rationale is the "smell test" of reason as it is applied to facts and assumptions to derive conclusions. The process of applying rationale to facts and assumptions is undertaken many times in a forensic analysis. In litigation, the importance of good rationale is heightened because the opposing side is challenging every step of the forensic analysis, particularly the rationale of every step. If every step of the forensic analysis includes good, defensible rationale, the ultimate conclusion should make sense.

It is critically important to understand and accept that rationale is rarely perfect. There is often some "disconnect" between the facts and assumptions and conclusions. Competent opposing counsel will always try to stress the imperfections or "disconnect" in the rationale.

Every conclusion or sub-conclusion in an expert's analysis should be supported by several theories of rationale, if possible. These "layers" of rationale support the conclusion and make it very defensible. For example, to determine the amount of "fair compensation" for the owner/operator of a particular business enterprise, a CPA business evaluator would ideally employ as many of the following lines of rationale as possible:

- Develop an understanding of the background, education, and experience of the particular owner/operator along with a detailed description of the current duties, management skills, and number of hours worked.

- Undertake statistical studies of reported compensation of similarly situated officers in similar types of businesses.

- Analyze the compensation of the next level of management in the company and add some reasonable premium to those amounts as an indication of the reasonable value of the subject owner/officer.

- Obtain data on salaries of chief executive officers in the geographic area in which the company is located.

- If the company is not 100% owned by the subject owner/operator, seek to obtain some historical evidence of a negotiated salary amount among owners.

- Obtain the opinion of the owner as to the reasonable value of his or her services.

At every point of logic in a forensic analysis, the expert should strive to have several reasons (layers of rationale) for the decision that is being made. You want to be able to suggest that you "zigged" (instead of "zagged") at this particular junction because of x, y, z AND a, b, and c, if possible. Your rationale can never simply be "just because," or if it is, you won't carry the day with your resulting opinion.

Conclusion. Relying on historical facts, reasonable assumptions, and sound rationale, draw a conclusion for the particular step of the analysis that is supportable and defensible in the face of the arguments against it. If each step of the forensic analysis is reduced to a FARC analysis, the steps will each be supportable and defensible. Also, applying the FARC methodology will enable the consultant to objectively evaluate the logic of the step as part of the overall analysis, supporting the ultimate conclusion and opinion.

THE ATTORNEY'S CHALLENGE

The argumentative attack on the FARC methodology can be made on every step of the FARC metric. For example:

- The facts are wrong;
- The assumptions are not reasonable—either the assumption of the facts, or the assumption of the connection between the facts and the logic of the rationale;
- The rationale applied to connect the facts and assumptions to the conclusion is not sound;
- The conclusion does not logically follow the rationale.

There are two ways to test rationale: negatively and affirmatively. In litigation, the opposition generally challenges rationale negatively. They ask, "What's wrong with it?" Or, "How could this be different?" "You could have done x, and you didn't, right?" "You don't know [some irrelevant detail], do you?" They repeat the question about an irrelevant detail about ten times, hoping that it will look like the expert doesn't know anything. "Isn't it possible that your analysis is wrong?" (Any question that starts with "Isn't it possible..." deserves a yes.) If there is complicated logic, the opposition will seek to obfuscate it to make it look wrong. Remember, the opposition isn't necessarily looking for the truth; they just don't like your answer, so any way they can negate it is a "win" for them.

Rationale can also be supported affirmatively. That is the logical process of affirmatively defending the rationale. For instance:

- *X* conforms to traditional analysis, **AND**

- *X* conforms to the way that an independent evaluator (scientist, technical expert, accountant, regulator) of the situation would look at the issue, **AND**

- *X* conforms to the expert's experience, **AND**

- *X* makes intuitive sense.

It is not possible to create a formula for perfect rationale for solving any one issue, but it is important for the forensic consultant to understand that broad-based rationale results in very defensible conclusions. It is usually very easy for a conclusion to be supplanted if it has only one line of rationale (i.e., one study, one method, or one "comparable" sale). As previously stated, always try to have several supportable lines of rationale for every decision node in your analysis. Stealing a metaphor from Michael Lewis's *Premonition*, "the solution would be a layering of multiple strategies, sort of the way you laid slices of Swiss cheese on a sandwich, so that the holes did not align." The more layers of rationale supporting a conclusion, the more defensible the conclusion is.

The application of the FARC framework to every part of a substantive expert analysis is very effective, but it quickly shows that there is no absolute way to perform all different types of forensic analyses. Almost none of the types of analyses that forensic consultants do are "black and white." It is impossible to provide a formula to the consultant that will work to decide every factual or analytic situation. But the FARC methodology provides a framework for analyzing almost any kind of problem, resulting in a defensible, competent opinion. Understand that the lawyers will try to use the reverse of IRAC to dismember your analysis. They will suggest that the conclusion you have reached does not rationally follow the application of the specific rule of law to the (disputed and/or unclear) facts of this case. The application of FARC methodology enables the expert to objectively defend each step of the analysis and puts the forensic consultant on more level ground with the opposing attorney. While there is no absolute formula that can be applied to all forensic work, the unique circumstances of each case will require the analyst to apply a flexible framework of analysis that will lead to the best conclusion, and Facts, Assumptions, Rationale, and Conclusions is the most effective tool I have found in my practice of many years.

Finally, expert witnesses should understand the difference between an "affirmative" and a "negative" argument. A good forensic analysis is an affirmative argument—it is a positive assertion that a particular conclusion (an expert opinion about something) is the correct answer, or the most reasonable answer, to a question. "The actions of the defendant physician did not fall below the standard of care in this community," or "The business is worth $500,000," or "Ms. Smith's loss of earnings is $1,200,000," or "The construction of the residence falls below the community standard of care for this type of building." The analysis should be supported by facts, reasonable assumptions and sound logic, and arrive at a reasonable conclusion. The affirmative argument, or position, must be carefully calculated, considering both the strengths and weaknesses of the underlying facts and assumptions, with the goal of reaching a reasonable conclusion. The goal of an "affirmative" conclusion should be to make the analysis as supportable as is reasonably possible.

A negative argument does not contain any positive assertions, but instead is a criticism leveled at an affirmative assertion or opinion. It suggests a number of complaints regarding the affirmative assertion or opinion. Some negative arguments are meritorious, but it should be understood that it is always easier to argue negatively than to argue affirmatively. Negative arguments can be leveled at almost any part of the forensic consultant's analysis: the facts, the assumptions, the causal connection between the facts and the conclusion, or the conclusion of the analysis itself. Examples of negative arguments are "The facts that were relied on are wrong," "There is an error in the calculation," "There is insufficient data on which to base the conclusion reached," and, "The investigation did not eliminate all possible reasons that could have caused the problem." A good forensic analysis will anticipate the negative arguments that will be suggested later and try to affirmatively defend against them in the main analysis. There is no question that this suggestion is easier said than done.

CONCLUSION

The inexperienced expert witness often fears a litigation challenge to the conclusion he or she has reached. If, however, the analysis has been developed with a thorough understanding of the underlying facts, reasonable assumptions, and sound rationale, the conclusion will be intellectually supportable and will withstand any reasonable challenge. The expert witness is not an advocate for any client, but rather the advocate of the competently derived scientific or technical opinion, bringing great value to the litigation arena. He or she is able to provide competent, unbiased opinions that assist parties and the courts to resolve disputes. In cases that proceed through the entire litigation process, the qualified, knowledgeable expert should feel comfortable defending a well-developed and well-documented expert opinion.

CHAPTER 10

DOCUMENTING THE EXPERT OPINION

At the outset, let me encourage you to appreciate the importance of this chapter for understanding the art of expert witness testimony. Documenting your expert file may seem like an administrative clerical task, but I assure you it is nearly as important as the intellectual development of your opinion discussed in Chapter 9. A discussion of adequate documentation begins with the reminder that there may be varying requirements for a particular level of documentation in different types of litigation services engagements, depending on the area of expertise that is being rendered. An expert physician may have professional record-keeping requirements that differ from those of a forensic accountant or a building contractor who is engaged to render a litigation opinion. The forensic expert must maintain the minimum professional requirements in her particular field because she will be cross-examined about not keeping up to the specific profession's standards, and defending against that attack is the first reason to maintain competent documentation.

Documentation is the written record of the research and analysis that was undertaken to reach the expert opinion arrived at in the case. In the environment of litigation, documentation can be a two-edged sword. On the one hand, thorough documentation is necessary to record the details of the analysis. On the other hand, detailed documentation can be used against the forensic expert in cases where the underlying substantive analysis is inaccurate, inadequate, or incompetent. Even if the underlying substantive analysis is competent, improper[67] documentation can be used to criticize or cross-examine the forensic expert.

A well-documented, cross-referenced file is an essential resource to the testifying expert witness. At the deposition, a complete file shows the thoroughness of your work and the defensibility of your final position. The process of documenting the file solidifies the expert's rationale and exposes potential weaknesses before the analysis is completed. At trial, detailed documentation is critical to enable the expert to access data quickly in response to cross-examination questions. It is imperative for the testifying expert to be able to use the well-documented file as a working resource to support the ultimate opinion. It will contain the expert's analysis, a summary of the rationale, all supporting documents, and references to all research material used. During cross-examination, a well-placed cross-reference will often save the day.

A complete and well-documented file is a fine work product, in and of itself. In many litigation matters, no written report will ever be required, so the expert's file will effectively constitute that report. The practitioner should be keenly aware that any document may be taken from the file and enlarged into a trial exhibit. The testifying expert must remember that the opposition will take pages (or comments) out of context, blow them up, and argue from them in front of the jury. Every comment, conclusion or analysis in the file should be prepared with this fact in mind. In

67. "Improper" documentation doesn't mean bad or poor documentation; it means documentation that isn't strategically written to consider cross-examination.

the final analysis, though, well-documented work papers are an asset to the expert in litigation support services.

When the FARC methodology is used at each sub-step of the substantive opinion analysis (Chapter 9), the written documentation of the file logically follows the rationale of the facts, assumptions, rationale and conclusions. Each step of the analysis has been determined as a result of the application of the FARC logic, so documenting the logic in the expert's file or in a report is simply restating the steps of the FARC. The forensic expert should not fear disclosing her well-thought-out opinions in an organized, supportable way. Nevertheless, there are techniques of file documentation that will enhance the presentation of the ultimate opinion.

Adequate file documentation should include:

1. A complete record of all the material activities undertaken by the forensic expert.
2. Copies of all correspondence sent to or received from others in connection with the assignment.
3. Copies of the expert's significant notes of research, meetings, or conversations that have occurred during the expert's analysis.
4. Copies of all documents in your possession that were provided to you during the forensic assignment.
5. Copies or excerpts of all relevant studies on which you have relied during the course of your analysis, where practical to include them.
6. Copies of all ***final*** calculations and analyses that you have undertaken during the assignment and any final written opinions you have reached.

Proper documentation should be complete, accurate, and thorough. It should clearly identify the steps that the forensic expert has undertaken and it should be able to be followed and understood by a knowledgeable observer. Competent documentation of an expert's analysis should probably ***not*** include the following things:

1. Preliminary drafts of analyses or opinions.
2. Detailed lists of preliminary plans for the analysis.
3. Irrelevant scribblings or margin notes.
4. Review notes of senior staff with comments to make the analysis more supportable.

Over the years, I have developed a number of specific documentation techniques for litigation consulting files, and these techniques will increase your level of performance as a competent expert witness. Reminding you that some of them seem trivial—they aren't—I will discuss each one in some detail.

1. File index—create a file index that indicates every document you have received by the client and also identifies each section of your work (i.e., correspondence, billing, opinions and conclusions, analysis, support for analysis, research, notes of communications, summaries of relevant documents, etc.). You must have a practice of keeping and indexing all documents received and all communications with attorneys (and anybody else).
2. Index every document in your file and paginate every page of your file. (This practice may seem overly compulsive, but it is essential for cross-referencing and document access on cross-examination.) Over the years of my prac-

tice, many outside onlookers have suggested I keep files electronically (and I do), and not in paper form, but every litigation practitioner I know preserves electronic files, but prints out almost every page and physically files them. In my experience, lawyers want to see paper. In my historical firm, prior to its acquisition by CBIZ, we maintained files the old-fashioned way—in paper, with electronic backup. Now, working on very large cases, it's not always practical to reduce large electronic files to paper.

3. Organization of files—Adopt a consistent method of file organization for all cases.
4. Consider having a file intake system—a "received" date stamp.
5. Maintain copies of every document received from and/or sent to anyone in a litigation matter. Also, don't keep files in manila folders or redwell files; they will quickly become unmanageable. Any sizeable case file should be three-hole punched and organized in sequential notebooks with file tabs that follow the index at the front of the file. (Subject to the practicality of not printing every document in very large files.)
6. Cross-referencing and highlighting (discussed subsequently).
7. Have a practice of saving over computer files that are being developed rather than saving each iteration of the file. The earlier, incomplete analyses will be used by the opposing party (attorney) as cross-examination fodder and be taken out of context.
8. Do not remove notes (or anything) from your file; just know how to properly create them.
9. If the client's lawyer does insist that you remove something from your file, advise him that you are going to disclose that you removed it. (Discussed in detail on page 187.)

10. Learn how to take notes; they should be limited to issue-related facts of the case, not lawyer's strategy comments or client comments that are unrelated to facts. Do not note any of those comments, and immediately admonish the lawyer or client that conversations with you are generally not privileged.
11. File notes are not the place for impressions, preliminary opinions, casual observations, judgments (positive or negative) about documents, facts, or other information that is part of your file.
12. Create a little tick mark indication on every page of a file that you have looked at; and don't kid yourself, you need to look at every page of a file. That tick mark gives you comfort later in preparation for deposition, preparation for trial, and/or when you're on the witness stand and a piece of paper is shoved in front of you.... If your review tick mark is on it, you know that you have seen it and considered it.
13. Your staff should be trained in the rules of documentation.
14. No casual margin comments.
15. Use Post-it notes for casual non-file comments that are preliminary. Remove them after the comment has been considered and incorporated into the analysis.
16. If you have a review system where senior staff review the work of junior staff and make review notes, make it a practice to exclude those review notes from your file. They aren't germane to your analysis; they are simply a review of junior staff preliminary analysis that contributes to making your work more complete. It is the corrected work that comprises your file, not the senior person's review notes to correct it.

17. Staff preliminary notes of meetings and telephone calls should not be maintained as part of the file, particularly if you were in the meeting/call and took your own notes. The notes are duplicative and simply used to support and verify the accuracy of your notes of the meetings. After your notes have been clarified (and edited for accuracy), the staff's notes should be discarded. Your expert file should be limited to your reviewed and approved analysis of everything that you have considered that supports (or contradicts) your opinions and conclusions.
18. Your opinions and conclusions should be succinctly stated in writing in a separate conclusions section of your file. Although some consultants think that summarizing your opinions in writing is a bad idea, my experience indicates that a supportable opinion or conclusion can be reduced to writing, and the act of writing it significantly aids the development and supportability of the opinion.
19. A well-documented file is proof of a good analysis, and it is typically intimidating to the opposing counsel.
20. This comment doesn't exactly fit here, but it is important. Many professionals have a footer at the bottom of their emails saying something like "This email contains privileged and confidential information…." In contrast to that footer, a forensic consultant's email should contain a footer that says: "The contents of this email are NOT PRIVILEGED and are subject to discovery in cases in which [your name] is designated as an expert witness." Don't mislead your clients into thinking that communications with you are privileged because most, if not all of them, are not.

File index and organization: Your work file is the written record of the communications, research, and analysis that was undertaken to reach the expert opinion arrived at in the case. Your engagement frequently occurs over many months and it isn't practical to memorize the work you have done, and it certainly isn't possible to know the totality of your work in a case if you have a substantial forensic consulting practice. It is only logical to have a system of file organization and begin the contents of a work file with an index that identifies the documents you have been provided and the categories of the analysis you have undertaken.

Practice Tip. Adopt a consistent method of file organization for all cases. There is no "right way" to organize your files, but I have evolved the following five categories that seem to work for all the types of litigation consulting matters I do, and I think these categories will work for most any substantive forensic practice.

Section A—Engagement letter, written correspondence, billing, and emails. (Your file should include all emails sent or received by you or your staff, so make sure they are carefully written and advise clients that emails are not privileged communications.)

Section B—Report, conclusion, and analysis section. My work is financial, so my conclusions in a case are usually some quantification of damages, business valuation, lost profits, etc. My B Section is usually a set of financial schedules, or it may be a valuation report or a federal expert report (Federal Rules of Civil Procedure (FRCP) 26 report).

Section C—Support for analysis. This section contains all of the backup material for my analysis. Examples for a business valuation would be financial statement analysis of a company; market research for comparable stock sales information; relevant industry research for this business; research on the economic outlook in general; research and analysis on the current fair market value of the fixtures and equipment of the business, etc. Examples for a personal earnings loss analysis would be summary of the plaintiff's historical earnings; summary of historical employment benefits; research on work life and life expectancies; research on appropriate interest and discount rates to apply to future earnings losses, etc. Each item of support in Section C is cross-referenced into the analysis and conclusions in Section B.

Section D—File notes and document reviews. My personal notes of client meetings and telephone calls. Also included in this section are any written reviews of documents by myself or staff. In my practice, senior staff members read and prepare reviews of depositions, and these are in the D Section. Relevant facts are cross-referenced into Section B or Section C.

Section E—Client-provided documents. In large cases, the E Section of my file can include thousands of pages of documents.

Pagination, cross-referencing and highlighting: Many novices will initially ignore this suggestion, but after a few cases and a few times on the witness stand, the experienced expert witness will agree that paginating every single page of a file and consistently employing a detailed cross-referencing practice is essential to competent forensic consulting practice. And, the rule doesn't change whether it's a two-binder case or a twenty-two-binder case.

Have I mentioned that lawyers tend to like things on paper? I guess the reason is so they can physically look at documents, and in my practice, at least, we still reduce (almost) every document to paper. The exception to that rule is an occasional lengthy Excel spreadsheet with scores of pages that generally doesn't need to be looked at on a line-by-line basis, but only in totals. We don't always print those out; otherwise, everything is reduced to paper. (Of course, the exception here is the case with tens of thousands of documents, which requires a different document management system altogether.)

Every page of a file must be numbered. I have found an alphanumeric system to be most effective. In each section of my files, I have a document behind every tab, and I employ the numbering system C1.1, C1.2, C1.3, … C2.1, C2.2, C2.3…. In the E section, for instance (client documents), I can keep adding newly produced documents as they are provided. E27.1, E27.2,… E28.1, E28.2, etc. The order of newly produced documents isn't important as long as they are identified in the overall index and a cross-referencing system is used to identify the source of every relevant fact that the expert relies on in her analysis.

Cross-referencing is a practice that we accountants learned in our first jobs as auditors after college. It is as simple as it seems: it is a mechanism for identifying the source of every relevant fact used in the analysis, and it also shows (on the source document) where the fact is factored into the final analysis. At the risk of delving too far into the weeds, the following graphics are examples of cross-referencing techniques used to "source" factual information.

Practice Tip. Cross-referencing technique. Exhibits 10.2 and 10.3 are examples of "going to" cross-references and Exhibit 10.1 shows an example of a "coming from" cross-reference.

On the source document—usually a client document in my E Section—I will notate a circled page number at the bottom or to the right of the important fact, indicating that the fact "goes to" the referenced page. (The usual "destination" of the cross-referenced fact is my Support for Analysis section [C Section].) Any time I look at a source document and see a forward cross-reference (a fact "going to" another part of the file), I can tell where the analysis of this particular fact is undertaken. And, the facts on which you are relying can come from any source in your file: emails, client documents, deposition reviews, financial statements, medical records, etc.

In the analysis section of my file—usually either the B section or the C section of the file—I will show the source page by a cross-reference number at the top of, or to the left of, the fact that has been pulled forward from the client (or other source) document. When I am looking at the analysis section, I can see where every factual source comes from immediately by looking at its cross-reference.

Why undertake this meticulous exercise of cross-referencing? There are at least two reasons. First, you need to be able to carefully review your file in the course of finalizing your opinions, preparing reports, and preparing to testify. A cross-referenced file can easily be reviewed and checked for accuracy and completeness. Second, opposing lawyers are in the business of arguing against you, asking you why did you do this? Or, where did you get that? The competent forensic expert needs to be able to quickly find the factual source of every aspect of her analysis… emphasis here on the word "quickly." You need to be able to throw it back in their faces when they challenge you on aspects of your work, and the only way that you can competently do that is by having a meticulously detailed file, complete with every aspect of your opinion and conclusion tied into the underlying facts. Cross-referencing is the way to do it.

Computer protocol. Everything is done by computer, and your computer files are completely subject to discovery in a litigation matter. They must be produced to the opposition in response to a subpoena.

In the normal course of business, most people draft their work in stages, typically saving early drafts of their evolving work product. The normal, non-litigation practice would be to save backup iterations of an evolving work product in version 1, version 2, version 3, etc. Or, saving versions by date prepared or some other indication of the evolving nature of the work product. In a normal business practice, it might often be helpful to retrieve an earlier iteration of one's work to possibly take the project in an alternative direction, or for some other reason.

Saving iterations of work product does not work for a litigation practice when there is generally no privilege to protect the earlier versions of the product. The forensic consultant should employ a standard practice of iterating over previous drafts of work product, whether it is report drafting, financial analysis, or other substantive analysis. These earlier iterations of work product do not memorialize the consultant's final thinking on the subject, and the evolutionary thinking process is a devastating area for cross-examination by an argumentative opposing side to an issue. Opposing lawyers will use anything they can find to undermine your opinion, and your earlier, evolving thinking about your analysis and opinion is fertile ground for very messy cross-examination. Bluntly stated, you simply don't want to go there. A final point on this subject: you need to have a firm-wide practice of iterating over earlier work; it's not a very good position to just adopt it for an occasional litigation project and not adopt the practice for all of your work.

But all you need is one good cross-examination of Version 1, Version 2, and Version 3—when your final analysis is Version 7—to learn this lesson.

File notes. The reality is that you (or your staff) have to review documents and summarize them, and you have to take notes of communications with clients (you can't remember detailed facts from meetings and phone calls). There is no point in hiding the fact of file notes, but they have to be documented appropriately. The reason for *appropriate* note-taking is the reality that the notes are generally not privileged and they will be used for cross-examination.

One primary rule of note-taking is do not remove them from your file; simply take them appropriately. I have been in depositions of opposing experts where they either say they don't take any notes of conversations or phone calls (pretty hard to believe if you have a substantial practice) or they discard notes after they "have considered them." Seriously? To me, these are both untenable positions and ones that are subject to serious cross-examination that will undermine the overall credibility of the expert. "So, Dr. Smith, you don't take notes of meetings and conversations with attorneys?" "Is that because you have a perfect memory?" "Or, is that because you don't want us to see notes of what you talked about?" "Do you ever take notes of ***any*** meetings you attend?" "Are you able to remember all these facts in the many meetings that you undoubtedly have?"

"And, what is the logical basis to destroy notes that you previously took?" Answer: there is none. The forensic expert simply needs to understand what is and isn't appropriate to write down from conversations with lawyers and clients. Notes of conversations and phone calls should be limited to facts and not include any preliminary opinions or attorney strategies. As soon as you pick up your pen, recognize that these notes may be "Exhibit 1" in the trial that may take place in nine or twelve months and you will be asked about every line of the notes. You don't want them to say: "Lawyer is looking for the opinion that the defect was caused by the roofing company," or "Attorney needs a low appraisal." First of all, lawyers shouldn't be making these comments to an expert, but they do it all the time. Second, even if they do, the competent expert should respond appropriately ("I'm not in the business of finding a predetermined conclusion"), and the comment should be ignored and not written down. Also, the lawyer should be admonished that conversations with experts are not privileged, and he shouldn't be talking about case strategy with you. As I have noted repeatedly, many lawyers are not mindful of the lack of privileges with experts in their communications with us, except for some communications in states following the Federal Rules of Civil Procedure.

Then there is the subject of review-type notes of documents that you or your staff read and summarize. As a practical matter, you need these review notes to quickly read before the deposition and/or the trial and you need staff to take the first cut at reading and reviewing many documents that exist in some cases. Similar to notes of conversations, these notes should be limited to factual summaries of documents; they should not include opinionated comments like: "This report is really difficult to understand," or "This thing doesn't make any sense." The comment "I don't get this" doesn't bode well for file documentation, unless the thing that nobody "gets" is a primary source of the opposing expert's work. And, if it is, your team better spend some serious time trying to figure out what the document means—the other side might be seeing something that you don't!

All file notes should be written with a tone of objectivity, showing that your approach to the substantive issue in the case is detached and unbiased. This can be a difficult challenge because, from the initial call with the lawyer, he or she is arguing their case with you and to you. The lawyer has an adversarial, biased view of each issue of the case and they often start out pitching that story to their experts. The competent expert works hard to maintain a mental state of objectivity, and her ongoing notations during the preparation of a file should memorialize that reality. Your file notes should go overboard in showing objectivity, even when you are beginning to develop opinions that may favor your side of the case.

Practice Tip. Examples of inappropriate and appropriate file comments:

Notes of a telephone call with the retaining attorney:

- Inappropriate comment: "He needs a report that says there's insufficient data to form an opinion."
- Appropriate comment: "Is there sufficient information to form an opinion?"

In response to a financial discrepancy in a client's records:

- Inappropriate comment: "They must have two sets of books," or "Looks like fraud to me."
- Appropriate comment: "Not yet reconciled; appears to disagree with source document."

In response to a negative comment in a personnel file:

- Inappropriate comment: "Guy looks like a slacker," or "He's at the low end of the spectrum."

Appropriate comment: "Supervisor's review appears to be in lower performance range," or "Note range of review score."

Observing a doctor's comment in a medical record:

Inappropriate comment: "Guy is in extreme pain," or "Guy could be faking it."

Appropriate comment: "Patient's symptoms appear to be subjective," or "Note doctor's uncertainty about diagnosis."

Other examples of "bad" documentation:

"this agreement is unintelligible"

"lawyer wants a high value"

"other side has lied about everything in this case"

"wants to stall the discovery because real estate values are increasing"

"their position is way stronger than ours"

Generally, note the difference in documentation of making a conclusive statement ("This agreement is unintelligible") versus a more moderate statement ("Agreement may be unclear regarding x, y, & z"). More moderate documentation is more difficult to cross-examine later, whereas the conclusive, absolute statement is easier to take out of context.

Review notes. If you have a practice of reviewing a junior associate's work in written form, those review notes should be considered to be communications that are intended to correct the file, and not part of the file themselves. (Remember, there is no privilege to prevent the production of these documents; your personal practice or firm should consider having a policy of discarding them after they are used.)

Practice Tip. Because there is no privilege to prevent the production of review notes, consider implementing a policy within your firm of discarding review notes after they have been used.

Preliminary drafts. Preliminary drafts of analyses, calculations, or opinions, both hard copy and computer backup files, do not represent your final opinion or conclusion. I have discussed the practice of iterating over computer draft analyses. If earlier drafts are reduced to writing for internal discussion purposes in your firm, you and your firm should have a policy of discarding these preliminary drafts. These drafts do not represent your opinion or conclusions. If you have sent drafts to the attorney client, it is probably not appropriate to discard those types of communications; if emailed to a client, they should be preserved. Consider using the screen share feature of video conferencing to jointly review preliminary work product with your retaining attorney rather than emailing a document to the lawyer.

> **Practice Tip.** Clearly indicate that any preliminary calculations or reports are, in fact, drafts. Two simple ways of communicating the nature of such documents are the use of a "draft stamp" or the addition of the phrase "tentative and preliminary" to a document's footer. Another effective restriction on a preliminary document is the notation "Prepared for mediation or settlement discussions." Such a legend, if true, may provide some legal privilege to the subsequent disclosure of the document.

Importantly, the one exception to the "lack of privilege" of an expert's work is Federal Rule of Civil Procedure 26(b)(4)(B), which provides that draft reports, attorney comments regarding those drafts, and attorney communications to witnesses who are expected to prepare written reports are privileged from discovery. (See discussion in Chapter 14.) Absent this federal law protection (which may be adopted by a particular state), an expert's drafts are discoverable, and most litigation cases are in state court, at least in my experience.

Irrelevant scribblings or margin comments. These notations should not exist in a forensic consultant's file.

> **Practice Tip.** Include in your staff training a course on file etiquette, including proper documentation of formulas, computations, and source documents. All staff should understand that opinionated comments, extraneous comments or broad conclusions should not be noted in the work papers. Final opinions and conclusions are only within the province of the testifying expert and should not be made by any staff members other than the ultimate expert. It is also important to note that the practice of factual documentation without extraneous commentary also applies to computer-generated and retained information.

Lists of procedures to be performed. Because the litigation environment is dynamic in nature, any written list of procedures would inevitably require constant updating to remain current. Also, while you may have initially contemplated performing a particular procedure, you may later determine that the procedure was not necessary for the final analysis.

> **Practice Tip.** Refrain from including lists of specific procedures to be performed in your engagement files, because these will be produced to the opposition. Although you may have a reasonable explanation for considering certain procedures that you originally thought were necessary but were not ultimately performed, such questioning may detract from your final opinion and leave an unfavorable impression with the judge or jury.

Documentation of opinions and conclusions. Do not fear the documentation of a complete FARC methodology in the work papers (see Chapter 9). When properly applied, the FARC methodology forms the basis for a logical, supportable argument.

Practice Tip. The FARC methodology is a logic-based approach to analyzing almost any substantive issue. Including the steps of the methodology in the work paper file is recommended because it shows the logic of the expert's analysis and conclusions.

Overall practice/procedure for retaining transcripts. Don't keep copies of depositions (or trial testimony) you have given in other cases. Destroy or discard them at the end of the case. Why? In later cases, lawyers will ask you if you have transcripts of your earlier depositions or trial testimony, and there is no privilege preventing the production of those documents. Don't retain them; if there is anything remotely contradictory or confusing in them (even if it's not on point), they will only be used against you.

FRCP 26 list of expert testimony. FRCP 26(a)(2)(B)(v) requires the following disclosure in an expert's written report: "a list of all other cases in which, during the previous 4 years, the witness testified as an expert at trial or by deposition." (See Chapter 15 for other requirements for written reports.) The previous quote is the exact requirement for disclosure. In response to this requirement, I have seen other experts disclose case name, case number, names of attorneys representing the parties, the party who retained the expert (plaintiff or defendant), and the court in which the case was venued. This disclosure will only be used against the expert, so why disclose anything more than what is minimally required? Let the opposition go digging to find the details of your disclosure; don't make their job any easier.

CONCLUSION

In addition to being soundly developed, the expert's analysis should be appropriately documented. Proper documentation is thorough and complete; it does not minimize weaknesses in the analysis, but rather it considers them and incorporates them into the overall conclusions. Proper documentation considers the fact that the expert's work will be argued against, and preliminary and/or opinionated file comments will be taken out of context by the opposing side of the case.

EXHIBIT 10.1

"FARC" SHEET
("FACTS, ASSUMPTIONS, RATIONALE, & CONCLUSIONS")
JONES V. ABC COMPANY INC.
EARNINGS ANALYSIS

FACTS:

1. Plaintiff Mary Jones claims to have been wrongfully terminated at ABC Company Inc. on December 31, 2019.
2. As a senior shipping and receiving supervisor, her compensation was $28.00 for straight time and she qualified for overtime for hours worked in excess of forty hours per week at time and one-half times her straight time rate.
3. Her earnings records for 2016 through 2019 show straight time, overtime, and hourly rates as follows:

Mary C. Jones
Hire date: 9/22/12

	Regular Hours	Rate	Extension	Overtime Hours	Rate	Extension		Total Compensation
2016	1900	$ 25.00	$ 47,500	138	$37.50	$ 5,175	*E 10.2*	$ 52,675
2017	1876	$ 26.25	$ 49,245	160	$39.38	$ 6,300	*E 10.2*	$ 55,545
2018	1800	$ 27.25	$ 49,050	88	$40.88	$ 3,597	*E 10.3*	$ 52,647
2019	1863	$ 28.00	$ 52,164	184	$42.00	$ 7,728	*E 10.3*	$ 59,892

Calculations:

Average hourly rate:	$ 26.63
Average Ann'l Hours:	1,860
Average O.T. Hours	142.5
C.A.G.R. hourly rate	3.85%

[file page number]
E 10.1

4. Ms. Jones also participated in the employer's FICA contribution, an employer-paid medical plan at $330.00 per month in 2019, and a pension contribution of 3.0% of her total compensation.

ASSUMPTIONS:

1. To estimate Ms. Jones's loss of earnings, use her 2019 hourly rate as indicative of her after-termination but-for earnings. = $28.00
2. Grow her annual earnings at the average increase she experienced each year over the last four years. = $28.00 + 3.85% = $29.08
3. Use average annual hours worked (1,860) and average annual overtime hours worked (142.5) as indicative of the hours she would have worked in the post-termination period.

RATIONALE:

1. In the absence of information to the contrary, there appears to be no reason to conclude that Ms. Jones would not have earned in 2020 her 2019 earnings with an average increase.
2. It is reasonable to assume that her regular compensation and her overtime compensation would be based on the average annual hours (regular and overtime) she has worked over the last three years.
3. It is reasonable to assume that her benefits would have continued if she remained employed. Estimated benefits are approximately 15% of earnings.

CONCLUSION:

1. For 2020, use \$29.08 (\$28.00 × 1.0385) per hour as her base compensation.
2. Use 1,860 regular hours per year and 142.5 overtime hours per year to calculate her compensation estimate.
3. Add equivalent benefits as she historically earned.
4. Apply a growth factor of 3.85% annually to her earnings to project into the future until she mitigates her losses with earnings equivalent to her previous job.
5. Calculation of earnings base for analysis:

2020 earnings:			
	# Hours	Rate	Extension
Reg. time	1,860.0	29.08	$ 54,089
O.T. time	142.5	43.62	6,216
	Estimated 2020 Earnings		$ 60,305

EXHIBIT 10.2

22222 | Void ☐ | a Employee's social security number: 123-45-6789 | For Official Use Only ▶ OMB No. 1545-0008

b Employer identification number (EIN): 33-0001925

c Employer's name, address, and ZIP code:
ABC Company, Inc.
240 State Street
Phoenix, AZ 85003

d Control number: 222-234567-3

e Employee's first name and initial: Mary C. | Last name: Jones | Suff.

12740 Temple Avenue
Phoenix, AZ 85004

f Employee's address and ZIP code

1 Wages, tips, other compensation	2 Federal income tax withheld
52,675	6,422
3 Social security wages	**4 Social security tax withheld**
52,675	3,266
5 Medicare wages and tips	**6 Medicare tax withheld**
52,675	0
7 Social security tips	**8 Allocated tips**
E10.1	
9	**10 Dependent care benefits**
11 Nonqualified plans	**12a See instructions for box 12**
13 Statutory employee ☐ Retirement plan ☐ Third-party sick pay ☐	**12b**
14 Other	**12c**
	12d

15 State	Employer's state ID number	16 State wages, tips, etc.	17 State income tax	18 Local wages, tips, etc.	19 Local income tax	20 Locality name
AZ	91-2376-4	52,675	848	52,675		

Form **W-2** Wage and Tax Statement **2016**

Department of the Treasury—Internal Revenue Service

Copy A For Social Security Administration — Send this entire page with Form W-3 to the Social Security Administration; photocopies are not acceptable.

For Privacy Act and Paperwork Reduction Act Notice, see the separate instructions.

Cat. No. 10134D

Do Not Cut, Fold, or Staple Forms on This Page

22222 | Void ☐ | a Employee's social security number: 123-46-6789 | For Official Use Only ▶ OMB No. 1545-0008

b Employer identification number (EIN): 33-0001925

c Employer's name, address, and ZIP code:
ABC Company, Inc.
240 State Street
Phoenix, AZ 85003

d Control number: 222-234567-3

e Employee's first name and initial: Mary C | Last name: Jones | Suff.

12740 Temple Avenue
Phoenix, AZ 85004

f Employee's address and ZIP code

1 Wages, tips, other compensation	2 Federal income tax withheld
55,545	6,515
3 Social security wages	**4 Social security tax withheld**
55,545	3,444
5 Medicare wages and tips	**6 Medicare tax withheld**
55,545	0
7 Social security tips	**8 Allocated tips**
E10.1	
9 Verification code	**10 Dependent care benefits**
11 Nonqualified plans	**12a See instructions for box 12**
13 Statutory employee ☐ Retirement plan ☐ Third-party sick pay ☐	**12b**
14 Other	**12c**
	12d

15 State	Employer's state ID number	16 State wages, tips, etc.	17 State income tax	18 Local wages, tips, etc.	19 Local income tax	20 Locality name
AZ	91-2376-4	55,545	784	55,545		

Form **W-2** Wage and Tax Statement **2017**

Department of the Treasury—Internal Revenue Service

Copy A For Social Security Administration — Send this entire page with Form W-3 to the Social Security Administration; photocopies are not acceptable.

For Privacy Act and Paperwork Reduction Act Notice, see the separate instructions.

Cat. No. 10134D

Do Not Cut, Fold, or Staple Forms on This Page

E10.2

EXHIBIT 10.3

22222	Void ☐	a Employee's social security number 123-45-6789	For Official Use Only ▸ OMB No. 1545-0008
b Employer identification number (EIN) 33-0001925		1 Wages, tips, other compensation 52,647	2 Federal income tax withheld 5,950
c Employer's name, address, and ZIP code ABC Company, Inc. 240 State Street Phoenix, AZ 85003		3 Social security wages 52,647	4 Social security tax withheld 3,264
		5 Medicare wages and tips 52,647	6 Medicare tax withheld 0
		7 Social security tips (E10.1)	8 Allocated tips
d Control number 222-234567-3		9 Verification code	10 Dependent care benefits
e Employee's first name and initial Mary C.	Last name Jones / Suff.	11 Nonqualified plans	12a See instructions for box 12
12740 Temple Avenue Phoenix, AZ 85004		13 Statutory employee ☐ Retirement plan ☐ Third-party sick pay ☐	12b
		14 Other	12c
f Employee's address and ZIP code			12d

15 State	Employer's state ID number	16 State wages, tips, etc.	17 State income tax	18 Local wages, tips, etc.	19 Local income tax	20 Locality name
AZ	91-2376-4	52,647	568	52,647		

Form **W-2 Wage and Tax Statement** 2018

Department of the Treasury—Internal Revenue Service

For Privacy Act and Paperwork Reduction Act Notice, see the separate instructions.

Copy A For Social Security Administration — Send this entire page with Form W-3 to the Social Security Administration; photocopies are not acceptable.

Cat. No. 10134D

Do Not Cut, Fold, or Staple Forms on This Page

22222	Void ☐	a Employee's social security number 123-45-6789	For Official Use Only ▸ OMB No. 1545-0008
b Employer identification number (EIN) 33-0001925		1 Wages, tips, other compensation 59,892	2 Federal income tax withheld 6,867
c Employer's name, address, and ZIP code ABC Company, Inc. 240 State Street Phoenix, AZ 85003		3 Social security wages 59,892	4 Social security tax withheld 3,713
		5 Medicare wages and tips 59,892	6 Medicare tax withheld 0
		7 Social security tips (E10.1)	8 Allocated tips
d Control number 222-234567-3		9	10 Dependent care benefits
e Employee's first name and initial Mary C.	Last name Jones / Suff.	11 Nonqualified plans	12a See instructions for box 12
12740 Temple Avenue Phoenix, AZ 85004		13 Statutory employee ☐ Retirement plan ☐ Third-party sick pay ☐	12b
		14 Other	12c
f Employee's address and ZIP code			12d

15 State	Employer's state ID number	16 State wages, tips, etc.	17 State income tax	18 Local wages, tips, etc.	19 Local income tax	20 Locality name
AZ	91-2376-4	59,892	864	59,892		

Form **W-2 Wage and Tax Statement** 2019

Department of the Treasury—Internal Revenue Service

For Privacy Act and Paperwork Reduction Act Notice, see the separate instructions.

Copy A For Social Security Administration — Send this entire page with Form W-3 to the Social Security Administration; photocopies are not acceptable.

Cat. No. 10134D

Do Not Cut, Fold, or Staple Forms on This Page

E10.3

CHAPTER 11

THE EXPERT DEPOSITION (AND OTHER DISCOVERY DEVICES)

INTRODUCTION

The primary focus of this chapter is the strategies and tactics used by an expert to give expert testimony in deposition. The most effective deposition techniques are counterintuitive, and they deflect the lawyer's strategies for getting the most information from the expert. Before we discuss depositions, we will review the other forms of discovery and the expert's role in them.

Discovery is governed by the rules of civil procedure, the body of law that sets out the rules and standards followed by courts when adjudicating civil lawsuits (as opposed to procedures in criminal law matters). It is a mixture of different pretrial procedures by which a party can obtain facts and information relevant to the litigation from other parties, witnesses, or others. The objective of discovery is to educate both sides about the facts and arguments of the other to streamline litigation and to facilitate settlement of the dispute.

Much of every attorney's litigation practice comprises discovery procedures because only a small percentage of cases actually go to trial. The majority of litigation conflict is through the techniques of discovery, where lawyers advocate to obtain documents and information, seek admissions, and learn the opposition's positions in the case. Despite its noble purpose, the process of discovery is sometimes abused as a sword in litigation, designed to harass and burden opponents with unreasonable demands. To minimize possible abuses, a supervising court will occasionally order the appointment of a discovery referee to oversee the requests and responses of feuding litigants. A competent expert will not participate in abusing the process, but unfortunately, the expert is not the person leading the litigation team.

DISCOVERY DEVICES

The following discovery devices, though not as significant to the expert as the deposition, may involve the expert as a participant or consultant to the lawyer.

Written interrogatories are a formal set of written questions put forward by one party and required to be answered under oath by an adversary. They are intended to clarify matters of fact and help to determine, in advance, what facts will be presented at the trial of the case. They are sometimes referred to as requests for information, and the forensic expert can have a role assisting her lawyer to craft meaningful and penetrating questions about facts relevant to the litigation.

Because attorneys may help their clients answer interrogatories, interrogatory responses tend to be more finely crafted than answers to deposition questions. The number of questions included in interrogatories is usually limited by court rule. For example, under the Federal Rules of Civil Procedure, each party may only ask each other party twenty-five questions via interrogatory unless the court gives permission to ask more. In the Federal Rules of Civil Procedure, Rule 33 governs interrogatories, and it is set forth at the end of this chapter.

Requests for admission. A request for admission is a discovery device that allows one party to request that another party admit or deny the truth of a statement, under oath. If admitted, the statement is considered to be true for all purposes of the current litigation. Parties may also use this discovery device to request that other parties verify that documents are genuine. Rules regarding requests for admission vary by jurisdiction. Requests for admission are generally used toward the end of the discovery process to settle uncontested issues and simplify the trial. Federal Rule of Civil Procedure 36 governs requests for admission, and is set forth at the end of this chapter.

Request for production of documents. A request for production is a legal request for documents, electronically stored information, or other tangible items. Any party to the litigation may request that another party provide any documents in its possession pertaining to the subject matter of the lawsuit. The responding party is required to furnish copies of any documents that are responsive to the request, except for those that are legally privileged. The responding party also can submit a response to the requestor explaining why the documents cannot be produced. For example, the responding party may indicate that documents are unavailable because they have been destroyed, that it would be unduly burdensome to produce the documents, or that the documents are not in possession of the responding party. However, the requestor may then file a Motion to Compel discovery to ask the court to order the responding party to produce documents. Federal Rule of Civil Procedure 34 governs requests for production, and is set forth at the end of this chapter.

Declarations. In the environment of litigation, it is not unusual for lawyers to draft declarations for their clients and other witnesses, including expert witnesses. A declaration is a written statement, under oath, given by a witness in the discovery phase of a lawsuit.

Early in my career I had a lawyer provide me with a declaration "of mine" to sign and be submitted to the court. I had previously met with this lawyer and told him of my preliminary financial analysis of his client's situation in a complicated divorce from the client's spouse of thirty years. California is a community property state, so long marriages frequently involve complex untangling of intermingled financial lives and valuation of jointly-owned assets. In this case, the lawyer had taken my preliminary analyses of the situation and written it into declaration form, showing it to me for the first time to sign under penalty of perjury to be submitted to the court. Of course, there is always a deadline. It seems that nothing ever gets done ahead of time in litigation—lawyers are always under the gun to get today's product out the door before the unyielding five o'clock deadline. There I was, reading "my" declaration for the first time and being pressured to sign it. As lawyers almost always do, they see the world from the perspective of their argument and they state everything with that bias. As an example, one lawyer describes a vehicle going "slightly over the posted speed limit" while the other one describes the same vehicle traveling "at a great rate of speed." The competent expert should describe facts and conclusions without argument; in this hypothetical, simply stating that "my analysis indicates the vehicle was traveling at 49 miles per hour in a 45-mile-per-hour zone."

The point of this long-winded story is that my client's lawyer had drafted a very argumentative statement of my preliminary opinion that would have been devastating to me if it showed up in court. Fortunately, I had the strength to resist the lawyer's determination for me to sign the declaration, requiring it to be significantly toned down before I would sign it. In fact, in that case, we did end up in court, and I distinctly remember the feeling when the judge was looking at me, reading my declaration, and accepting my statements as my sworn testimony. I was relieved that I didn't let my client's lawyer bully me into overstating my opinions.

THE EXPERT DEPOSITION

THE BASICS

A deposition upon oral examination is a pretrial discovery procedure used to obtain facts relevant to the litigation. The witness is asked questions under oath by an examining lawyer, usually in the informal setting of a conference room in the opposing attorney's office. The questions and answers are transcribed by a court reporter verbatim, and many times the deposition is videotaped by a certified videographer. Because of liberal discovery rules, almost any question can be asked during the deposition. Federal Rule of Civil Procedure 30 governs depositions by oral examination, and is set forth at the end of this chapter.

While the official purpose of a deposition is to obtain relevant facts, the practical purpose of an expert deposition is broader. Recognizing that litigation is an argument, the deposing lawyer's objective is to obtain any information, on the record, that can be used to advance the opposing side of the argument at issue. Such information could include information to discredit or disqualify the witness from testifying on an issue. It could also include statements of agreement to particular facts that benefit the opposing side, or concessions that the assumptions made by the expert are not perfectly supportable. Another purpose is impeachment of the witness: if testimony at trial is different from the deposition testimony, the witness can be impeached with the deposition transcript at trial. Finally, a deposition intends to solidify the totality of an expert's opinions during discovery so the opposing side knows every opinion the expert will testify to at trial. This last purpose is critical for the expert to understand because failure to include an important opinion in the deposition testimony will likely lead to exclusion of the opinion at trial.

Generally, a deposition is a losing proposition for an expert. The expert witness will testify under oath about every aspect of his involvement in the case, including research and analysis leading to the expert's opinion and conclusions. Because the deposing attorney is trying to obtain any information that can be used to discredit, impeach, or disagree with the expert's opinions, an expert's deposition is a minefield full of booby traps that must be avoided. A sophisticated knowledge of the strategies and tactics of the deposing attorney is essential to the deponent's ability to minimize the harm suffered by experts in deposition.

Depositions are often considered to be the most important (and routine) events during the course of litigation because most cases settle before trial based on the opposing lawyer's evaluation of testimony and the demeanor of witnesses. Depositions establish the majority of the evidentiary record in a lawsuit and they become the basis for settlement, trial preparation, or motions to exclude a witness's testimony. (See discussion of *Daubert v. Merrell Dow Pharmaceuticals* in Chapter 5.)

There are important strategies and tactics for depositions used by both deposing lawyers and the witnesses being deposed. One element of the art of expert witness testimony is to thoroughly understand the deposing lawyer's strategies in the expert witness deposition and provide your expert testimony in response to that strategy. In this chapter, I will address both the expert's and the lawyer's strategies.

THE EXPERT'S STRATEGIES AND TACTICS IN DEPOSITION

In organizing this chapter, I put the attorney's strategies and tactics after the expert's, but I suggest you jump forward and read that section of the chapter before you read the expert's strategies and tactics. (See page 194.) The expert's strategies and tactics are more meaningful in the context of understanding the attorney's role in the deposition.

From the expert's perspective, an initial fact to contemplate is that virtually nothing that happens during the deposition is important in the moment it happens. The significant part of the deposition is the creation of the deposition transcript (or video) that can be used later. To successfully give an expert deposition, the deponent must remember this important fact and resist the temptation to lecture the opposing lawyer or get angry or otherwise emotionally involved in the process. Such mistakes only serve the opposition by creating a careless record that will be highlighted at trial and used to impeach the witness's testimony.

Planning for the deposition. The expert must prepare for and give an effective deposition. The expert's analysis should be completed before the scheduled deposition; however, the expert should not prepare a report or reduce her conclusions to writing unless she is asked to do so by her party's lawyer, or it is required under Federal Rules, or required by applicable professional standards.[68] The expert should insist on a detailed briefing with her party's lawyer before the deposition to discuss her testimony. It is advisable to conduct a rehearsal with mock cross-examination to ferret out potential weaknesses in testimony. Remember, however, that none of these meetings should be assumed to be privileged.

In contemplating your expert deposition, you should think about the major points of logic in your analysis and practice articulating your rationale for these logical points. This "practice" should also be extended to weaknesses in the analysis; the expert needs to be able to put his best foot forward on both strengths and weaknesses.

An expert's strategy toward a deposition will be different if the case is expected to settle versus going to trial. If settlement is expected based on discussions with your lawyer, the expert's strategy will be to be more open and expansive in explaining her analysis and opinions. In a settlement strategy, the expert's objective will be to educate the opposition on the strengths of the anal-

68. The Uniform Standards of Professional Appraisal Practice (USPAP), for example, require the preparation of an appraisal report in connection with the rendering of an appraisal opinion.

ysis with less fear of exposing the expert's opinion to cross-examination at trial. If trial is anticipated, the expert's strategy in the deposition will be more closed, with concern for educating the opposition to the subtleties of the analysis and providing fodder for cross-examination at trial. A third strategy of completely educating the other side may be employed if it is anticipated that the opposition is trying to disqualify the expert based on a *Daubert*[69] challenge. In that case, the expert must make a complete record showing that the expert has considered and competently evaluated all relevant facts and applied a supportable, logical analysis to those facts to arrive at a defensible conclusion.

Realities of the expert deposition. The environment of the deposition appears to be informal, but the deposition itself is not. It is a formal discovery proceeding, the record of which has serious consequences to the expert and the overall case. It is critically important that the expert witness doesn't succumb to the casual environment of the deposition setting and let her guard down during the proceeding.

The opposing lawyer has several objectives in the expert deposition. She begins the deposition with limited knowledge of the details of the expert's analysis and opinion[70] and her first objective is to learn everything about the expert's involvement in the case. The opposing lawyer may be polite and friendly, but she is trying to harm you and your substantive position, to the detriment of your client. The ultimate objective of the opposing side of the case is to argue against your position, not to be convinced of the correct-

69. *Daubert v. Merrell Dow Pharmaceuticals* is discussed in Chapter 5.
70. There may have been a pre-deposition expert report or production of the expert's file, somewhat mitigating this statement.

ness of your view of the case. The experienced expert witness will keep this in mind during the course of the deposition and limit her answers to the questions asked and not volunteer any additional explanation beyond a narrow interpretation of the question.

The natural tendency of a knowledgeable person explaining something is to try to clearly and completely explain the subject to the listener. This is *not* the expert's job in a deposition, nor is it a wise tactic. The expert's role is to answer the question asked—only the present question—and answer it truthfully. The expert's job is not to educate the uninformed questioner about the subtleties of the analysis that has been undertaken, unless the questioner is smart enough to back the deponent into a corner by asking for precise details of the analysis. And, not all lawyers are adept enough to accomplish that task.

Recognize that the opposing lawyer's representations are not entirely truthful, and they should be taken with a grain of salt. For instance, the representation "I'm only trying to find out your opinion and the bases of the opinion" is not completely true. The opposing lawyer is trying to obtain any piece of information that she can use to discredit or disqualify the witness.

The opposing lawyer would like to get the witness to make a statement (or give an answer) that harms the witness's position and helps the deposing lawyer's position. From the opposing lawyer's perspective, the most effective response from an expert witness is a concise, simple answer (ideally an unqualified "yes" or "no") to a question that presents a fact or assumption in favor of the deposing lawyer's argument. A clear, simple deposition answer to a precise question is the most effective response that can be used against the expert at trial. (It is obviously a failure if the expert witness gives the lawyer that answer, but if the perfect question is asked, the truthful answer must be given, even if it is harmful to the expert's opinion.)

Specific strategies and tactics for the expert. Don't allow yourself to be bullied. In a situation where the opposing lawyer is getting emotional or pushy, try to relax and calm yourself, falling back on the Ten Commandments for Effective Expert Depositions (presented subsequently). Remember that the only result of the deposition is a written transcript; the transcript does not show the emotion of the moment.

Recognize that you have rights as a witness. A lawyer should not be asking questions that are not relevant to your background, education, experience, analysis and opinions in the present case. The lawyer may ask about personal things with the intention of intimidating you. One problem is that the lawyer at your side is your client's lawyer, not your lawyer. Your client's lawyer is representing the client, not you at the deposition. Don't feel like you are represented, because you are not. In effect, you are representing yourself.

If you get into a difficult situation that you don't know how to resolve, be sure to make a record that properly states your position. An occasional situation will occur when your client's lawyer will instruct you not to answer a question. (In fact, there are very few times when this instruction is appropriate, but that doesn't stop some lawyers from so instructing you. The only time that an instruction not to answer to an expert witness is appropriate is if some privilege is being violated, and that is rarely the case with an expert. As has been discussed, there are virtually no privileges that cover an expert, except for the exchange of draft reports and related communications under Federal Rules. See Chapter 14.) But if the situation occurs, you will most likely decide to follow the client's lawyer's instruction. The opposing attorney may grill you about whether the lawyer "represents you" (he doesn't) or whether you are going to follow his "incorrect instruction." When this situation occurs (or any similar one where you are unsure what to do), simply state on the record that you are unsure what you should do, state what you are deciding to do, that you are acting in good faith and, of course, if a judge instructed you to answer the question (or comply with the request), you would certainly do it. You have a right to make a record that protects you and your professionalism. Don't be afraid to use your rights.

Don't let the opposing lawyer interrupt your answer. Sometimes the deposing attorney doesn't like your answer and, in that situation, you are not telling her what she wants to hear. The lawyer may interrupt you with another question or try to cut you off. If that occurs, politely state on the record that you are not finished with your answer and you would appreciate not being interrupted. Of course, you can only do this if you are answering the question asked and not rambling on and on.

Personal questions are not appropriate, but the attorneys have a lot of latitude in inquiring of the expert witness. A proper question only has to be designed to lead to relevant evidence, however. Remember, your client's lawyer doesn't really care if you are being exploited; he is only interested in protecting the client. Examples of irrelevant questions are:

a. Did you consume any alcohol in the last twenty-four hours? (That general question is not appropriate. It is appropriate to ask if you have consumed any alcohol or taken any drugs that would have any effect on your ability to testify today. So, if I am asked if I have had a drink or taken any drugs, my answer would not just be a "yes" or "no"; it would be: "I have not taken any drugs/drinks that would have any effect on my ability to testify today.")

b. Where were you born? (No big deal, but it is just an example of a lawyer starting to ride roughshod over a witness.) It is not relevant. The question, "When were you born?" would at least elicit your age, which is arguably relevant in determining your experience. But "where" you were born is irrelevant.
c. Another question that is often asked is "What do you think about the opposing expert witness?" Or, "Do you know of Dr. Smith's reputation in the community?" These are tempting questions to answer, but they should not be answered. Why? Because they are "no-win" questions. First of all, you are not an expert in "reputations" or "what you think of someone," so the questions are outside of your area of expertise. Also, they are "no-win" questions because, if you say Dr. Smith is a great guy, you will hear that answer in front of the jury in trial. If you say Dr. Smith is a hack, that comment will never be heard again. So, when I am asked that question, I very carefully state that I know Dr. Smith, but it is not my place or my area of expertise to comment on his reputation. I continue to state that my refusal to directly answer that question should not be negatively interpreted for Dr. Smith; I just don't have an opinion on that question. If I am pushed by the lawyer, I will use the following example: "Mr. Jones, I have an opinion about your tie, but it's not appropriate for me to state that opinion in this deposition and have it considered to be expert opinion because I am not an expert in ties any more than I am an expert in other experts' reputations or whether they are good guys or good gals."

d. A good response to a question that you believe is completely irrelevant is: "If you can tell me what relevant evidence that question might lead to, I will gladly answer it." Questions like, "Where were you born?", "Where did you serve in the military?", or "Were you in the military?" do not seek to find relevant evidence and are therefore not appropriate.
e. My purpose in discussing these personal-type questions is providing the expert with an awareness of the degrees of control in the expert deposition. Some lawyers will begin to push the envelope to gain control of the proceeding. I suggest that the competent expert witness politely push back on these overreaches.

There are other questions that need careful responses because they border on "trick" questions. Here are some examples:

a. If an expert report was prepared, the following comment doesn't apply because the expert opinion was formed when the report was signed.

   Sometimes an examining lawyer will ask, "When did you form your opinion?" I suggest caution in answering this question. To an expert witness, the word "opinion" is a very precise term. It is a formal conclusion arrived at after careful consideration of all relevant facts and the adoption of reasonable assumptions. An opinion is not something that the expert arrives at two or three days before the deposition while having a beer on his back porch. The question "When did you arrive at your opinion" is a trap for the unwary. If you say you arrived at it three days ago as you were completing your analysis, then, "What did you do for the last three days?" "Did you consider anything else?" "Did you consider x, y, and z…?" These problems have brought me logically to the conclusion that I don't form my opinion until I put it on the record in a deposition. That is the formalizing of a well-thought-out expert conclusion.

To dodge and rephrase this question is not an improper, evasive technique, although at least one lawyer has suggested that it is. The reason that I formalize this precise definition of "opinion" is that if I learn some significant fact or realize some other revelation at 8:00 a.m. on the morning of my deposition, I certainly would change the preliminary opinion that I had reached the night before. So if I am asked the "when did you form your opinion" question, I politely respond that the term "opinion" is a big deal in my work and I will formulate my opinion in a few minutes when you ask me for it.

b. One of the best strategies for a deposing lawyer is to push the expert witness "off his page" in the deposition by asking questions that are outside of the witness's opinion or area of expertise. Sometimes these questions are tempting to answer because they seem so simple, or supportive of the expert's client's position in the litigation. Expert beware: there is little upside to answering this type of question and a lot of downside. First of all, if a subject is outside of the expert's area, he will likely not be allowed to respond to the question at trial, so there was no value in answering the question in a way that was supportive of the expert's client's position. Answering a question outside of the expert's qualified area will expose him to cross-examination on background, education, and experience in the subject area, causing the expert to be diluted in his qualifications in all of his areas of expertise and being exposed to the challenge of why he is attempting to give an opinion in an area in which he is unqualified. A competent expert will work hard to "stay on the page" of his qualifications and areas of expertise.

An example of the "stay-on-the-page" strategy in my area is instructional here. A damages expert frequently relies on a vocational rehabilitation consultant to opine on employment alternatives for an injured plaintiff. The opposing lawyer may ask, "Do you agree with the vocational expert's opinion that Mr. Smith can likely perform the duties of job x or job y?" The logical, informal answer might be, "Sure, that seems reasonable to me," but beware that the opinion is outside of the damages expert's area of expertise. He or she will now be exposed to the cross-examination discussed previously. The correct answer is, "I have no opinion on X because it is outside my area of expertise."

c. "Have you discussed any weaknesses in your analysis or opinion with Mr. Jones, your client's lawyer?" Of course, there are some weaknesses in every argument or opinion, so it is foolish to not have thought about the question and have some answer at the ready. Obviously, testifying about weaknesses isn't going to be your strongest testimony, but a competent expert better have something to say in response to this question.
d. "What underlying facts, if different, would cause you to change your opinion?" Similar to the previous comment about weaknesses, there are certainly some hypothetical facts that would cause an expert to change her opinion. You should be able to list a few hypothetical facts, hopefully ridiculous ones, that would change your opinion.

e. "Have you removed anything from your file?" The answer to this question should be a clear "no." This is a reality that a competent expert should be aware of from the outset of a litigation matter, and proper documentation procedures should ensure that all documents are retained and there are no improper notes or margin comments in a file. When your lawyer tells you in a phone call that "the other side are a bunch of jerks," that's just not something that is relevant factual information that you write down in your telephone notes. Also, your firm should have established procedures regarding associates' notes, specifically that they are not included in the expert's work file; but this also means that they can't be kept in a separate file held by the associate. Such a file would certainly be subject to discovery, so the procedure should include discarding of associates' notes after they are summarized (to whatever extent they are) and included in the work file.

f. "Have you been asked to remove anything from your file?" This is a question that every good lawyer should ask in an expert deposition. Here's my recommendation to the expert. If your client's lawyer asks to review your file prior to deposition, that's fine, but tell him not to ask you to remove anything from the file because (1) you are not inclined to remove documents, and (2) you will be asked <u>if you were asked</u> to remove anything, and you will answer truthfully. Furthermore, chances are the removal of the document (or merely asking) will call more attention to the document and make it a bigger issue than leaving it in the file. If the issue is brought before a court, the document will probably have to be disclosed and the entire attempt to hide it will be foiled. Try to dissuade your client's lawyer from asking or insisting that any documents be removed from your file.

g. "Have you produced all notes or memoranda of any communications that you contemporaneously took? (If not, why not? Where are they? Did you destroy them? If so, why?)" Some experts have the practice of [supposedly] either not taking notes or summarizing them into the file or their report and then destroying them. I find either of these practices to be foolish. First, who among us has such a photographic memory that he can function at a high professional level without taking notes of meetings or telephone calls? And, even if someone does, the practice of "not having any notes" smacks of deception. If an expert destroys his notes after rereading them or summarizing them, why is there a need to destroy them, unless the expert is preventing the opposition from seeing them? I suggest that the more appropriate practice is to be aware that all of your notes will later be produced and, recognizing that fact, be careful how you take them. Don't write down irrelevant information ("the other side are liars") or information that shouldn't be discussed with an unprivileged expert witness. If a lawyer starts talking about litigation strategies and/or weaknesses in the case, remind him or her that this conversation is probably not privileged and we should probably change the subject.

h. If an attorney is good enough to ask a very precise question (most of them aren't) to which you don't like the answer, try to provide an answer with some qualifications in it. That way, it is harder to use the question/answer in trial.

Ten commandments for effective expert depositions. Years ago (in 1985), I coauthored an article[71] in which the following "Ten Commandments for Effective Expert Depositions" were published. Over the last thirty-five years, not much has changed in expert deposition strategy; here they are as originally written:

1. ***Tell the truth, but answer only the question asked.*** Do not volunteer information and avoid long, narrative answers. The more topics that you bring up in your answer, the more questions the examining lawyer will ask. The deposition is an opportunity for the opponent to obtain information; it is not the trial.
2. ***Think about the question before answering it.*** This will give you the time to formulate an appropriate response. It will also give your party's lawyer time to analyze the question and interpose any objections. Remember that the examining lawyer will attempt to develop an informal, but rapid conversation to elicit from you as much information as possible. Watch out for an examiner who attempts to catch you off guard with a casual friendly manner or flattering questions.
3. ***Do not answer a question unless you understand it.*** If a question is unclear, ask the examining lawyer to repeat or rephrase the question or have the court reporter read the question back.
4. ***Do not guess or speculate.*** If you do not know the answer to the question, say so. If you are not sure, qualify your answer by saying "approximately" or a similar qualification. Beware of hypothetical questions. Before answering a hypo-

71. *"The CPA as an Expert Witness,"* Business Valuation News, 1985, co-authored by myself and attorney Michael W. Prairie.

thetical, make sure that all essential facts or assumptions are included. Remember that at trial, a portion of the deposition may be taken out of context and used to impeach you.

5. ***Do not bring notes, diagrams, books or other written material to the deposition unless they are required by a subpoena or unless you have been instructed by your party's lawyer to bring them.*** If asked to testify regarding documents or other exhibits, take the time to review them carefully before answering questions about them. (This commandment is a little out of date. The current best practice is for the expert to bring the complete case file to the deposition.)
6. ***Listen carefully to objections made by your party's lawyer.*** The objection may be intended to alert you to a trick question or some other problem with the question. If your party's lawyer instructs you not to answer a question, follow his instructions, even if the examining lawyer threatens you with court sanctions. (See recommendation for making a record earlier in the text.)
7. ***Do not argue or become angry or hostile with the examining lawyer.*** Such a reaction will communicate to the examining lawyer a lack of confidence that will be exploited at trial. It may also alert the examining lawyer to weaknesses in your theories or conclusions. As a general proposition, work hard to maintain a calm, collected attitude during the deposition.
8. ***Even if the question calls for a yes or no answer, ask to explain your answer briefly if a qualification or explanation is necessary.*** However, do not be concerned if your answer does not supply all information which would be required for a complete understanding of the topic.

Your party's lawyer will decide whether to obtain a more complete explanation during the deposition or at trial.

9. ***Watch out for questions which involve absolute terms, such as "Have you identified all of the documents which you have reviewed?" or "Are there any other facts that you have relied upon?"*** If possible, provide a qualified answer in the event that you inadvertently failed to identify a pertinent document or fact.
10. ***Do not memorize your answers in advance of the deposition.*** Provide a direct and factual response to the questions.

As in life, it is easier to read and understand the Ten Commandments than it is to live by them, but at a minimum, you should review them before every deposition you are called to attend. I think that knowing the Ten Commandments is "Expert Witness 101," and knowing how to apply them judiciously is "Expert Witness 401." In short, you don't have to rigidly apply every one of them all the time in deposition. Use your judgment.

Other comments on the expert's deposition considerations. One technique deposing lawyers will use is to be very informal at the outset of the deposition, creating a comfortable environment, kind, helpful. "We're just here to understand what you have done in this matter." In your mind, you should be hearing: "I just want to get you to say anything that I can use to embarrass you, tie you up, destroy you on the witness stand, impeach you…." That's the purpose of the deposition from the opposing lawyer's perspective.

You are only in an expert deposition because the other side disagrees with you. It is possible—but extremely unlikely—that you will convince the other side of the merits of your position. That's not going to happen, no matter how "right" you are. That's not how litigation works. Unfortunately, both sides tend to dig in to their respective positions and not look at the other side openly. You should assume that the other side is passive-aggressively trying to destroy you and your opinion. Any thought to the contrary is simply fantasy. You should act accordingly to use your knowledge and skills to advance your opinion in the litigation.

If your client wants to attend your expert deposition, you should call him or her aside and have a private conversation, with or without the attorney. It is important for the client to understand the counterintuitive tactics of the expert deposition. The client will expect the expert to "knock the ball out of the park" with deposition testimony. I tell clients that most expert depositions are defensive propositions for the expert and the best thing I can do is get finished without giving out too much information, because the information will be used against me at a later time. The client needs to understand that the deposition isn't the place to make the intense subtle arguments that will be made at trial; the best thing that can happen is that I can get out of the deposition without having to completely bare my soul. It is strategically helpful to have your client understand this before they attend your expert deposition. If you don't have this conversation with the client, he will be jumping out of his chair, wanting you to throw all these punches, and he needs to understand that the deposition is more of a defensive exercise where you are trying to extricate yourself without being too badly bloodied.

A good lawyer will explore the fine points and subtleties of your arguments. The average lawyer will often allow you to state a more general point without refining it and, if you can get away with answering a question generally (and truthfully), that is your best strategy. I want to get out of the deposition by having put enough substantive points on the record that I can raise them at trial, but if possible, I want to get out of there without having to enumerate all the subtle fine points of the argument.

If an expert finishes a deposition and feels that he has really crushed it—explained himself, proved his point, educated the other side, convinced the other side of the merits of his opinion, etc.—the expert has probably completely "lost" the deposition. If, on the other hand, you walk out of the deposition feeling that they "didn't understand anything I said," you probably did a good job.

The role of experts in depositions. The expert should assist the lawyer for his party in preparing for the deposition of the opponent's expert by providing the lawyer with background information about the education, experience, and reputation of the opponent's expert. The expert should advise the lawyer where to probe for weaknesses in the methodology and analysis used by the opponent's expert in reaching her opinion. For example, the opponent's expert may have skipped some steps in the analysis or failed to review important records that would affect her conclusions. The expert should suggest deposition questions to her party's lawyer and, if possible, attend the deposition of the opponent's expert. The expert must be mindful, however, that any written communications between the expert and the retaining lawyer are generally discoverable, unless they fall within FRCP 26.

THE ATTORNEY'S STRATEGIES IN EXPERT DEPOSITIONS

This section is written as advice to lawyers for taking effective expert depositions and is included to educate expert witnesses on lawyers' tactics. I previously suggested that this section should be read before The Expert's Strategies and Tactics in Deposition to set the stage for the expert's understanding of the process.

The role of the lawyer in depositions. Lawyers use depositions to find facts, evaluate witnesses, learn the expert's analysis and opinion, evaluate the case for settlement, and impeach witnesses at trial. A good deposition gets to the core of the issues that the expert has analyzed by forcing the expert to reduce a complex analysis to basic steps and understandable terms. Good deposing attorneys are not intimidated because they lack substantive knowledge of the expert's field. The lawyer doesn't need to know as much as the expert; he or she only seeks to learn the totality of the expert's opinions and the bases for them.

Practically, it is important for the lawyer to memorialize the expert's complete analysis so there is no surprise at trial. The Rules of Civil Procedure require expert witnesses to state all opinions on the record in deposition, and no additional opinions can be developed after the deposition.[72] Consequently, a competent deposing attorney will "box in" the expert to be sure that all opinions have been presented and no stone has been left unturned.

72. The exception to this rule is rebuttal opinions. The expert witness cannot rebut another expert whose deposition has not yet happened.

Examples of "Boxing-In" questions: "Have you told me all of your opinions?" "Is there any assumption or basis of [this specific] opinion that you haven't told me about yet?"

A deposition is a two-way street for a lawyer. An experienced expert witness will not volunteer any information that is not specifically asked for, so the deposing lawyer will have to prod to force the expert to disclose the totality of the expert's analysis. Strategically, the lawyer should be careful not to disclose his or her trial tactics in the process of the expert deposition. It is tempting for the lawyer to argue with the witness about points that the lawyer feels strongly about (or points where the expert is weak), but in the process of argument, the lawyer is showing his hand. If the lawyer shows his hand by arguing the weaknesses of the expert's position at deposition, the lawyer doesn't win at the deposition; he should save the good stuff for trial.

The lawyer can affirmatively win at deposition, but the expert can only minimize his loss. The lawyer wins by obtaining all the subtleties of the expert's opinion without disclosing any of the lawyer's trial strategies. Also, the lawyer wins by getting crisp one-word answers to questions that include facts and assumptions that go against the expert's position. However, to be most effective, the damaging questions and answers must be narrow and precise. Complex questions with narrative answers are not generally effective for impeachment testimony at trial. The expert only wins (minimizes his loss) if he or she discloses very little information while the lawyer shows all of his arguments against the expert's position.

The lawyer's preparation should include:

1. A discussion with his or her own expert about the nature of the analysis, anticipated opinions of the opposing expert, and the reputation of the opposing expert.
2. Inquiry of the lawyer's colleagues about previous opposition or retention of the opposing expert.
3. Performing some research in the expert's substantive area so the lawyer has some familiarity with the subject matter before the deposition.
4. Review of other deposition transcripts of the opposing expert.
5. If the procedural rules in the jurisdiction don't already provide for production of the expert's file, an agreement with opposing counsel to obtain the expert's file prior to the deposition.
6. Consideration of a video deposition, a more expensive but very effective tool for obtaining more candid testimony on important issues.

An effective deposition is usually executed pursuant to a plan in which the attorney has formulated objectives for the deposition. The deposition plan should identify the lawyer's purpose of this deposition: Learn opinions? Test opinions? Evaluate strengths? Pin down a particular point? Gauge effectiveness of expert? Discredit expert? Recognize, however, that an argumentative penetration of the witness's weak points serves to educate the witness and prepare him or her for cross-examination at trial.

The notice of deposition should include a subpoena that requires the expert's production of the *entire* file, including all notes, memoranda, billing records, computer files and research material. It is helpful if the lawyer can obtain the file several days before the deposition.

THE ATTORNEY'S TACTICS IN EXPERT DEPOSITIONS

Obtain precise answers. The most beneficial expert deposition testimony elicits clear, concise answers to narrow questions that result in the expert's agreement with important facts and assumptions that support the opposition's argument. Consequently, it is necessary to form precise, unambiguous questions that don't logically permit an expert to hem and haw over the prefaces, qualifications, or adjectives used in the questions. Also, do not allow an expert to unnecessarily qualify answers to precise questions. If the expert insists on giving qualified answers, restate the question to remove the ambiguity from it so the expert is forced to precisely answer the question. Here is a sequential example:

> **Question:** Mr. Smith, after you met with the controller and discussed the available records, did you review the general ledger of the business to determine if certain expenses of the business were personal in nature?
> **Answer:** The controller advised me that there were a number of accounting records that would possibly identify personal expenses charged to the business, and I was able to review invoices and credit card statements that I summarized to come up with what I believe are personal expenses charged to the business.

The lawyer has asked a complicated question that gives the witness the opportunity to give a vague, imprecise answer. A compound, general question may be effective in getting the witness to talk, so the question may have some value, but using that deposition testimony at trial will not be very effective. Let's work toward a better technique to corner the expert (in several steps):

> **Question:** Mr. Smith, did you review the general ledger of the business to determine if certain expenses of the business were personal in nature?
> **Answer:** I reviewed numerous financial records provided to me by the controller and, based on credit card statements and invoices, I created a summary of personal expenses charged to the business that I have in Exhibit D. *[Closer, but the witness just distracted the lawyer by taking him to Exhibit D.]*

The answer sounds pretty good, but the lawyer still has not elicited the precise answer that will be able to help him in trial. Try this:

> **Question:** Mr. Smith, did you review the general ledger of the business?
> **Answer:** I reviewed all of the financial records of the business provided by the controller. *[This answer could be objected to as nonresponsive, and it probably should be. It is amazing how often an expert can get away with this type of answer with no follow-up by the lawyer.]*
> **Question:** Mr. Smith, let me ask you again. Did you review the general ledger of the business?
> **Answer:** No, but I didn't think it was important to see it. *[The lawyer could make a motion to strike everything after "No" because it is nonresponsive to the question.]*
> **Answer #2:** I didn't think it was important to do that, so I didn't. *[Witness is smoother in dodging the question by putting the qualification before the "Yes" or "No."]*
> **Question:** I am not asking you whether you thought it was important. Did you review the general ledger of the business?
> **Answer:** No.
> **Question:** So, to be clear, just please tell me: Did you review the

general ledger of the business? *[The attorney needs this concise question to get a precise question and an unambiguous answer. The attorney can use this question and answer in trial and no one will be confused. The witness did not review the general ledger.]*
Answer: No.

This sequential exchange is an example of a witness trying to dodge a question, first by talking about the controller and then by distracting the lawyer with some related information ("Here's Exhibit D"). Then, the witness tries to muddy the record by throwing in "I reviewed all documents provided by the controller." The witness's third try is to sneak in "I didn't think it was important," either before or after the "No." In this exchange, the early vague testimony is the fault of the lawyer because of the complicated question. The precise question is "Did you review the general ledger?" Questions that are limited to one phrase or one thought are much more effective questions that will elicit deposition testimony that can be effectively used at trial to either buttress the opposition's argument or impeach the witness. The masterful expert witness will understand the skillful attorney's objectives and employ strategies to try to frustrate the attorney's goal. And, the witness will often be successful with the typical, "average" lawyer.

Sequencing. Carefully planned sequencing of the areas of inquiry is critical for conducting an effective expert deposition, and sequencing doesn't necessarily mean following a logical chronological order of inquiry. At the outset, in the deposition of an experienced expert witness, there is a very narrow window of opportunity for the deposing attorney to gain advantage. Very near the beginning of the deposition, the expert should be quickly asked about the assignment and the expert's opinions, leaving less important areas of inquiry for later. There is little benefit in spending the first minutes of the deposition with perfunctory admonitions that the expert has heard dozens of times before or easy questions about education and experience. The experienced witness has heard these questions many times and they allow the expert to get comfortable in the deposition rather than immediately be put on the hot seat to answer challenging questions.

From the expert's perspective, if a deposition begins with minimal admonitions and questions that immediately get to the heart of the expert's analysis, the expert should be on guard that this is a capable lawyer and the deposition will be a challenging one.

Another aspect of sequencing is the strategic use of ***not*** following a tightly organized order of inquiry into each area of the expert's analysis. There may be a benefit to either ignoring an intellectual point of inquiry or leaving it "hanging" until later, and out of context, in the deposition. At trial, there is no requirement to use deposition questions and answers in the order they were asked, so an incriminating answer given out of context is just as valuable as one given in context.

Admonitions. The extent of the use of admonitions in an expert witness deposition requires judgment on the part of the deposing attorney. With inexperienced witnesses, the attorney may need to make a record about the witness's understanding of the deposition procedure, the force of the oath, and the fact that the witness understands the questions that he will answer. In the deposition of an experienced expert witness, however, lengthy admonitions are usually an unnecessary waste of time.

If the expert has significant deposition experience, the lawyer should simply establish that fact and that the expert is thoroughly familiar with the deposition procedure (one or two questions!). The lawyer can then directly proceed into the substance of the expert's analysis. In my years of testifying, I have never had an admonition read back to me in trial, leading me to conclude that they are an unnecessary waste of time (and deposition strategy).

> **To the Expert:** Enjoy the vacation of this type of examination. Use this time to collect your thoughts and relax, size up the lawyer, think about the weaknesses in your analysis so you can finesse your answers, and get ready for possible meaningful examination that might be coming later. Probably not, though, because this attorney is wasting valuable deposition time on unimportant stuff.

Background, education, and experience. Several considerations are important in this area. The inquiry should only be made if there is a concern that the expert may not be qualified to give the opinion he or she is rendering. If this inquiry is even necessary, it should *not* be made at the beginning of the deposition. The expert's background is the witness's most comfortable area and he/she should not be given the opportunity to get comfortable at the beginning of the deposition. If you, the opposing counsel, anticipate that the deposition will be used at trial in lieu of testimony, why should you qualify the opposing expert witness?

> **To the Expert:** If a deposing attorney begins with a significant inquiry into your background, education, and experience, the expert should sit back and enjoy the easy cross-examination.

For the experienced expert, there is little exposure to this type of questioning. The longer the attorney stays in this area, the less time he is spending in more important, possibly dangerous areas. Enjoy the ride.

Attitude and demeanor. The deposing attorney may vary his/her attitude and demeanor depending on many different factors. A less experienced witness may be somewhat intimidated by an aggressive approach. A cool, calm, and collected approach is probably more effective with an experienced expert witness. The chance is that the "nice guy" will get more information than the obnoxious antagonist.

To the Expert: I suggest that the witness's emotional temperature should be inversely proportional to the deposing lawyer's attitude and demeanor. Although I always recommend staying calm, when the deposing attorney increases the heat in the deposition, I particularly calm down. It is my experience that the emotionally charged lawyer is trying to use that emotion as an intimidating factor, and the experienced expert should recognize that fact and respond with the converse emotion—calm.

Administrative. Near the outset of the deposition, but not at the very beginning, the lawyer should cover the following areas:

1. Review the deposition subpoena with the witness and ask the witness to confirm that he/she brought everything that was requested to the deposition.
2. Ask the witness to describe everything in the file. (This is a valuable question because it forces the expert to work through the file and allows the examining attorney to sit back and observe the process, with an occasional

question like, "What was the importance of that document in your analysis?" And, the attorney may be pleasantly surprised to learn that the overworked expert has not reviewed some important documents in the file, or doesn't understand their significance.)

3. Ask the expert what documents were requested for the case. (What documents were provided? What requested documents were omitted? Does the expert's engagement letter say that these documents are ***required*** to do the analysis? If they weren't all provided, how can the analysis be complete? But save this argumentative question for trial.)
4. Inquire about billing to date. How much time has the expert spent on this case? How much time has been spent by the expert's employees? (It is sometimes a little embarrassing for the expert to realize the relationship of the witness's time to staff time in the engagement. Who is the expert? The person here testifying or the person or people back at the office who did most of the groundwork? Again, a question for trial.)

Mechanics of taking the deposition. Take prepared notes to the deposition, which include a broad outline, a checklist, and a ***few*** specific questions in key areas. Don't be obsessive about preplanned questions or note-taking in the deposition; much more is learned by listening intently and going with the flow of the answers. Don't feel that you have to immediately follow up on any loose ends; make a note (discreetly—the experienced expert is watching you) to come back to open items later rather than follow up right away.

Substance of expert's analysis. The deposing attorney should identify each step of logic taken by the expert in developing his/her conclusion. Example: "Give me a broad overview of the steps you have taken in your analysis." (Chronologically, in order of importance, or any way the expert will provide the steps.)

Methodical approach. Once the expert's analysis is reduced to five or six major steps of logic, each step should be examined methodically. With respect to each major step, the following inquiry should be made:

1. Why is this particular step necessary at all?
   a. Could this step have been eliminated?
   b. Has the expert performed this type of analysis in the past without including this step?
2. What was the specific outcome of this particular step?
   a. On what facts is the outcome based?
   b. On what observations is the outcome based?
   c. On what assumptions is the outcome based?
   d. On what judgments is the outcome based?
3. Generally, what other outcomes are possible for this step in an analysis?
   a. What facts would cause a different (lower, higher, stronger, weaker, etc.) outcome at this step of the analysis?
   b. If expert opines to some ***inadequacy*** about the underlying situation, what in his/her opinion would constitute ***adequacy***? (Or vice versa.)
   c. If expert opines to some ***failure,*** what in his/her opinion would constitute ***success***? (Or vice versa.)
4. When inquiring about the expert's opinion about a quanti-

fiable issue, what is the range of reasonable outcomes, if a range can be quantified?

a. For example, if lost profits are stated to be $50,000, what is the reasonable *range* of lost profits? $40,000 to $60,000?? Zero to $10,000,000??
b. For example, if fact X was concluded by the expert to be unacceptable conduct or below the standard of care, what would have to be different about fact X to be acceptable or within the standard of care?

5. "Have you told me every fact and assumption on which you have relied to come to this conclusion?"

Make the expert argue with himself/herself. With respect to a particular outcome for one of the expert's logical analytic steps, ask what facts of this case support a higher outcome or a lower outcome? A similar outcome? A different outcome? Try to force the expert to argue the strengths and weaknesses of his/her conclusion.

Follow through on equivocal answers.

1. Answer: "*X* is ***generally*** true." **Next question:** "When would it not be true?"... "Not ***generally*** true?"
2. Answer: "True, based on what I know now." **Next question:** "What else would you need to know to make it unequivocal?"

Communications with others. It is well known that experts' communications with counsel and others are not privileged (except in limited circumstances under FRCP 26).

1. Ask the expert to name every person with whom he or she has communicated in connection with the particular case.

The reason for and nature of each of these communications should be explored in the deposition.

2. The expert should be asked about every meeting he has had with his client's attorney. The date, time, place, reason for the meeting and parties in attendance should be inquired about. The lawyer should fully inquire about the purpose of each meeting and the results of that meeting. Also, were any documents or reports given to the lawyer at the meeting? Were any notes taken? If so, are copies of these reports and/or notes present in your file? If not, why not?
3. All discussions by opposing counsel with opposing expert witnesses in deposition are discoverable. After every break, inquire about the details of any discussions that the expert witness had with his/her client's attorney. (Remember, you're only going to get one chance during the day to ask this question meaningfully, so wait until it counts.)
4. Review all notes of meetings that are present in the expert's file. If notes are not included in the file, ask if notes were taken. Were they destroyed/discarded? Does the expert normally attend meetings without taking notes?

Two-way street. A deposition is a two-way street, requiring the lawyer to disclose his/her questioning strategies to the expert witness. Be sensitive to this fact and try to be discreet about inquiring into areas in which you believe the expert is somewhat weak and that you intend to explore more heavily at trial. Don't argue with the witness and don't heavily pursue areas in which you feel the expert is weak. Consider saving your inquiry for trial.

This point is important and it is often ignored by attorneys who just can't resist arguing with the opposing expert. Let the expert "blow a theory past you," particularly if you think it is weak and you will cross-examine him on the point at trial. On the night before trial, when I am rereading my expert deposition for the last time, I often smile and realize that the cross-examining lawyer is sitting at his or her house doing the same thing. If I was grilled in the deposition on some weakness in my analysis, I will be particularly careful about practicing my testimony on the point. If the lawyer didn't grill me on some weakness, I just might think I fooled him with it and I am not inclined to work so hard to practice my testimony on that point.

Some Practice Pointers:

1. Treat objections as though they are just a formality of the deposition. After the objection, refocus attention on the witness and seek the answer to the question that was just asked.
2. Try to avoid arguments with opposing counsel. They educate the witness about critical issues. Arguments also tend to increase the tension in the room and make an experienced witness less inclined to offer valuable information. A less experienced witness may respond differently, however.
3. If the opposing lawyer is making speaking objections, ask him or her to limit the objections to proper legal objections stating only the basis of the objections. Speaking objections tend to educate the opposing expert witness about subtleties of facts and arguments of the case.
4. As you conclude your inquiry into each substantive area or "step" of the expert's analysis, ask the expert if there is anything about step x "that you haven't told me?" An experienced expert will respond, "Not that I can presently think of." At this point, the lawyer should seek a com-

mitment that if the expert does think of anything about step x between now and the signing of the deposition, the expert will write in the fact that he/she has thought of.

5. Another question in response to the expert's equivocal answer to the previous question is to ask the witness if she is aware of the significance of the deposition for learning the expert's *entire* analysis. "This is your opportunity to state all of your opinions so please state on the record that this is your complete analysis."
6. Inquire if the expert has any other work planned in this matter. Specifically, are there any steps that he/she intends to complete? Has his lawyer asked him ***not*** to perform any steps?
7. Inquire about the expert's availability for trial on the scheduled trial date.
8. When you are defending the deposition of your client's expert witness and the deposing attorney has brought the opposing expert witness as a consultant, ask that consulting expert witness to preserve a copy of his/her notes for production at the time of that witness's deposition. (They are notes; they were taken in the course of the expert's work; there seems to be no good reason why they should not be preserved and produced. You might even try to get them marked as an exhibit to the present deposition.)

Some additional questions the lawyer may wish to consider:

1. Have all your professional opinions or conclusions reached in this case been explored in this deposition?
2. Is there anything you would like to add so as not to be misunderstood?

3. How sure are you about your opinions?
4. If you had an unlimited budget in this case, what additional steps would you perform?
5. Have you been involved in drafting any legislation in your field?
6. How many other cases have you performed for the lawyer who has retained you in this matter?
7. How many other cases have you handled for this lawyer's law firm?
8. Have you socialized with this lawyer?
9. Have you removed anything from your file?
10. Were you asked to remove anything from your file?
11. Have any written materials been destroyed or discarded?
12. Have you retained previous drafts of your analysis? If so, provide them. If not, why not?
13. Have you provided any written materials to your client's lawyer that are not photocopied in your file?
14. Do you have a computer file or storage device that has a copy of any documents that are not presently in your file?
15. Have you discussed any weaknesses in your analysis with your client's lawyer?
16. You have made calculations based on the opinions of other experts [retained by your clients] in this matter. Have you made any calculations based on the other side's experts? If not, why not?

Other questions that the expert may answer. (These questions are really irrelevant and should be answered with "I don't know" or "I don't have an opinion," but many experts will answer them.)

1. Are you familiar with the opposing expert?
   a. Is he/she credible?
   b. Tell me about his/her reputation
2. Do you think the opinion of Dr. Expert, another expert on the deponent's same side of the case, is reasonable?
   a. Why?
   b. Why not?

CONCLUSION

The deposition is arguably the most significant event in litigation because most cases settle before trial based on the lawyers' assessment of the evidence and the witnesses' performances in depositions. For an expert witness, the deposition is a losing proposition. The examining attorney begins the deposition with minimal knowledge of the expert's analysis and opinion, and the deposition proceeds to obtain every detail of the expert's work. While the stated purpose of the deposition is to obtain information about the expert's substantive analysis, the hidden purpose is to get any information that can disqualify the expert or refute her analysis. The expert's knowledge of the attorney's strategies and tactics will arm him or her for this skirmish and enable the forensic consultant to minimize the potential harm of this discovery event. The chapter includes the "Ten Commandments for Effective Expert Depositions," which provide guiding principles for the forensic consultant's comportment in the heat of battle.

CHAPTER 11 APPENDIX
FEDERAL RULES OF CIVIL PROCEDURE
(RULES IN EFFECT AS OF JULY 2022)

RULE 30—DEPOSITIONS BY ORAL EXAMINATION

(a) **When a Deposition May Be Taken.**

(1) *Without Leave.* A party may, by oral questions, depose any person, including a party, without leave of court except as provided in Rule 30(a)(2). The deponent's attendance may be compelled by subpoena under Rule 45.

(2) *With Leave.* A party must obtain leave of court, and the court must grant leave to the extent consistent with Rule 26(b)(1) and (2):

(A) if the parties have not stipulated to the deposition and:

(i) the deposition would result in more than 10 depositions being taken under this rule or Rule 31 by the plaintiffs, or by the defendants, or by the third-party defendants;

(ii) the deponent has already been deposed in the case; or

(iii) the party seeks to take the deposition before the time specified in Rule 26(d), unless the party certifies in the notice, with supporting facts, that the deponent is expected to leave the United States and be unavailable for examination in this country after that time; or

(B) if the deponent is confined in prison.

(b) **Notice of the Deposition; Other Formal Requirements.**

(1) *Notice in General.* A party who wants to depose a person by oral questions must give reasonable written notice to

every other party. The notice must state the time and place of the deposition and, if known, the deponent's name and address. If the name is unknown, the notice must provide a general description sufficient to identify the person or the particular class or group to which the person belongs.

(2) *Producing Documents.* If a subpoena duces tecum is to be served on the deponent, the materials designated for production, as set out in the subpoena, must be listed in the notice or in an attachment. The notice to a party deponent may be accompanied by a request under Rule 34 to produce documents and tangible things at the deposition.

(3) *Method of Recording.*

(A) Method Stated in the Notice. The party who notices the deposition must state in the notice the method for recording the testimony. Unless the court orders otherwise, testimony may be recorded by audio, audiovisual, or stenographic means. The noticing party bears the recording costs. Any party may arrange to transcribe a deposition.

(B) Additional Method. With prior notice to the deponent and other parties, any party may designate another method for recording the testimony in addition to that specified in the original notice. That party bears the expense of the additional record or transcript unless the court orders otherwise.

(4) *By Remote Means.* The parties may stipulate—or the court may on motion order—that a deposition be taken by telephone or other remote means. For the purpose of this rule and Rules 28(a), 37(a)(2), and 37(b)(1), the deposition takes place where the deponent answers the questions.

(5) *Officer's Duties.*

(A) Before the Deposition. Unless the parties stipulate otherwise, a deposition must be conducted before an officer appointed or designated under Rule 28. The officer must begin the deposition with an on-the-record statement that includes:
(i) the officer's name and business address;
(ii) the date, time, and place of the deposition;
(iii) the deponent's name;
(iv) the officer's administration of the oath or affirmation to the deponent; and
(v) the identity of all persons present.
(B) Conducting the Deposition; Avoiding Distortion. If the deposition is recorded nonstenographically, the officer must repeat the items in Rule 30(b)(5)(A)(i)–(iii) at the beginning of each unit of the recording medium. The deponent's and attorneys' appearance or demeanor must not be distorted through recording techniques.
(C) After the Deposition. At the end of a deposition, the officer must state on the record that the deposition is complete and must set out any stipulations made by the attorneys about custody of the transcript or recording and of the exhibits, or about any other pertinent matters.
(6) *Notice or Subpoena Directed to an Organization.* In its notice or subpoena, a party may name as the deponent a public or private corporation, a partnership, an association, a governmental agency, or other entity and must describe with reasonable particularity the matters for examination. The named organization must designate one or more officers, directors, or managing agents, or designate other persons who consent to testify on its behalf; and it may set out the matters on which each person designated will testify. Before or promptly after the notice or subpoena is served, the serving party and

the organization must confer in good faith about the matters for examination. A subpoena must advise a nonparty organization of its duty to confer with the serving party and to designate each person who will testify. The persons designated must testify about information known or reasonably available to the organization. This paragraph (6) does not preclude a deposition by any other procedure allowed by these rules.

(c) **Examination and Cross-Examination; Record of the Examination; Objections; Written Questions.**

(1) *Examination and Cross-Examination.* The examination and cross-examination of a deponent proceed as they would at trial under the Federal Rules of Evidence, except Rules 103 and 615. After putting the deponent under oath or affirmation, the officer must record the testimony by the method designated under Rule 30(b)(3)(A). The testimony must be recorded by the officer personally or by a person acting in the presence and under the direction of the officer.

(2) *Objections.* An objection at the time of the examination—whether to evidence, to a party's conduct, to the officer's qualifications, to the manner of taking the deposition, or to any other aspect of the deposition—must be noted on the record, but the examination still proceeds; the testimony is taken subject to any objection. An objection must be stated concisely in a non-argumentative and nonsuggestive manner. A person may instruct a deponent not to answer only when necessary to preserve a privilege, to enforce a limitation ordered by the court, or to present a motion under Rule 30(d)(3).

(3) *Participating Through Written Questions*. Instead of participating in the oral examination, a party may serve written

questions in a sealed envelope on the party noticing the deposition, who must deliver them to the officer. The officer must ask the deponent those questions and record the answers verbatim.

(d) **Duration; Sanction; Motion to Terminate or Limit.**

(1) *Duration.* Unless otherwise stipulated or ordered by the court, a deposition is limited to 1 day of 7 hours. The court must allow additional time consistent with Rule 26(b)(1) and (2) if needed to fairly examine the deponent or if the deponent, another person, or any other circumstance impedes or delays the examination.

(2) *Sanction.* The court may impose an appropriate sanction—including the reasonable expenses and attorney's fees incurred by any party—on a person who impedes, delays, or frustrates the fair examination of the deponent.

(3) *Motion to Terminate or Limit.*

(A) Grounds. At any time during a deposition, the deponent or a party may move to terminate or limit it on the ground that it is being conducted in bad faith or in a manner that unreasonably annoys, embarrasses, or oppresses the deponent or party. The motion may be filed in the court where the action is pending or the deposition is being taken. If the objecting deponent or party so demands, the deposition must be suspended for the time necessary to obtain an order.

(B) Order. The court may order that the deposition be terminated or may limit its scope and manner as provided in Rule 26(c). If terminated, the deposition may be resumed only by order of the court where the action is pending.

(C) Award of Expenses. Rule 37(a)(5) applies to the award of expenses.

(e) **Review by the Witness; Changes.**

(1) *Review; Statement of Changes.* On request by the deponent or a party before the deposition is completed, the deponent must be allowed 30 days after being notified by the officer that the transcript or recording is available in which:

(A) to review the transcript or recording; and

(B) if there are changes in form or substance, to sign a statement listing the changes and the reasons for making them.

(2) *Changes Indicated in the Officer's Certificate.* The officer must note in the certificate prescribed by Rule 30(f)(1) whether a review was requested and, if so, must attach any changes the deponent makes during the 30-day period.

(f) **Certification and Delivery; Exhibits; Copies of the Transcript or Recording; Filing.**

(1) *Certification and Delivery.* The officer must certify in writing that the witness was duly sworn and that the deposition accurately records the witness's testimony. The certificate must accompany the record of the deposition. Unless the court orders otherwise, the officer must seal the deposition in an envelope or package bearing the title of the action and marked "Deposition of [witness's name]" and must promptly send it to the attorney who arranged for the transcript or recording. The attorney must store it under conditions that will protect it against loss, destruction, tampering, or deterioration.

(2) *Documents and Tangible Things.*

(A) Originals and Copies. Documents and tangible things produced for inspection during a deposition must, on a party's request, be marked for identification and attached to the deposition. Any party may inspect and copy them. But if the person who produced them wants to keep the originals, the person may:

(i) offer copies to be marked, attached to the deposition, and then used as originals—after giving all parties a fair opportunity to verify the copies by comparing them with the originals; or

(ii) give all parties a fair opportunity to inspect and copy the originals after they are marked—in which event the originals may be used as if attached to the deposition.

(B) Order Regarding the Originals. Any party may move for an order that the originals be attached to the deposition pending final disposition of the case.

(3) *Copies of the Transcript or Recording.* Unless otherwise stipulated or ordered by the court, the officer must retain the stenographic notes of a deposition taken stenographically or a copy of the recording of a deposition taken by another method. When paid reasonable charges, the officer must furnish a copy of the transcript or recording to any party or the deponent.

(4) *Notice of Filing.* A party who files the deposition must promptly notify all other parties of the filing.

(g) **Failure to Attend a Deposition or Serve a Subpoena; Expenses.** A party who, expecting a deposition to be taken, attends in person or by an attorney may recover reasonable expenses for attending, including attorney's fees, if the noticing party failed to:

(1) attend and proceed with the deposition; or

(2) serve a subpoena on a nonparty deponent, who consequently did not attend.

RULE 33—INTERROGATORIES TO PARTIES

(a) **In General.**

(1) *Number.* Unless otherwise stipulated or ordered by the court, a party may serve on any other party no more than 25 written interrogatories, including all discrete subparts. Leave to serve additional interrogatories may be granted to the extent consistent with Rule 26(b)(1) and (2).

(2) *Scope.* An interrogatory may relate to any matter that may be inquired into under Rule 26(b). An interrogatory is not objectionable merely because it asks for an opinion or contention that relates to fact or the application of law to fact, but the court may order that the interrogatory need not be answered until designated discovery is complete, or until a pretrial conference or some other time.

(b) **Answers and Objections.**

(1) *Responding Party.* The interrogatories must be answered:

(A) by the party to whom they are directed; or

(B) if that party is a public or private corporation, a partnership, an association, or a governmental agency, by any officer or agent, who must furnish the information available to the party.

(2) *Time to Respond.* The responding party must serve its answers and any objections within 30 days after being served with the interrogatories. A shorter or longer time may be stipulated to under Rule 29 or be ordered by the court.

(3) *Answering Each Interrogatory.* Each interrogatory must, to the extent it is not objected to, be answered separately and fully in writing under oath.

(4) *Objections.* The grounds for objecting to an interrogatory must be stated with specificity. Any ground not stated in a timely objection is waived unless the court, for good cause, excuses the failure.
(5) *Signature.* The person who makes the answers must sign them, and the attorney who objects must sign any objections.

(c) **Use.** An answer to an interrogatory may be used to the extent allowed by the Federal Rules of Evidence.

(d) **Option to Produce Business Records.** If the answer to an interrogatory may be determined by examining, auditing, compiling, abstracting, or summarizing a party's business records (including electronically stored information), and if the burden of deriving or ascertaining the answer will be substantially the same for either party, the responding party may answer by:
(1) specifying the records that must be reviewed, in sufficient detail to enable the interrogating party to locate and identify them as readily as the responding party could; and
(2) giving the interrogating party a reasonable opportunity to examine and audit the records and to make copies, compilations, abstracts, or summaries.

RULE 34—PRODUCING DOCUMENTS, ELECTRONICALLY STORED INFORMATION, AND TANGIBLE THINGS, OR ENTERING ONTO LAND, FOR INSPECTION AND OTHER PURPOSES

(a) **In General.** A party may serve on any other party a request within the scope of Rule 26(b):

(1) to produce and permit the requesting party or its representative to inspect, copy, test, or sample the following items in the responding party's possession, custody, or control:

(A) any designated documents or electronically stored information—including writings, drawings, graphs, charts, photographs, sound recordings, images, and other data or data compilations—stored in any medium from which information can be obtained either directly or, if necessary, after translation by the responding party into a reasonably usable form; or

(B) any designated tangible things; or

(2) to permit entry onto designated land or other property possessed or controlled by the responding party, so that the requesting party may inspect, measure, survey, photograph, test, or sample the property or any designated object or operation on it.

(b) **Procedure.**

(1) *Contents of the Request.* The request:

(A) must describe with reasonable particularity each item or category of items to be inspected;

(B) must specify a reasonable time, place, and manner for the inspection and for performing the related acts; and

(C) may specify the form or forms in which electronically stored information is to be produced.

(2) *Responses and Objections.*

(A) Time to Respond. The party to whom the request is directed must respond in writing within 30 days after being served or—if the request was delivered under Rule 26(d)(2)—within 30 days after the parties' first Rule 26(f) conference. A shorter or longer time may be stipulated to under Rule 29 or be ordered by the court.

(B) Responding to Each Item. For each item or category, the response must either state that inspection and related activities will be permitted as requested or state with specificity the grounds for objecting to the request, including the reasons. The responding party may state that it will produce copies of documents or of electronically stored information instead of permitting inspection. The production must then be completed no later than the time for inspection specified in the request or another reasonable time specified in the response.

(C) Objections. An objection must state whether any responsive materials are being withheld on the basis of that objection. An objection to part of a request must specify the part and permit inspection of the rest.

(D) Responding to a Request for Production of Electronically Stored Information. The response may state an objection to a requested form for producing electronically stored information. If the responding party objects to a requested form—or if no form was specified in the request—the party must state the form or forms it intends to use.

(E) Producing the Documents or Electronically Stored Information. Unless otherwise stipulated or ordered by the court, these procedures apply to producing documents or electronically stored information:

(i) A party must produce documents as they are kept in the usual course of business or must organize and label them to correspond to the categories in the request;

(ii) If a request does not specify a form for producing electronically stored information, a party must produce it in a form or forms in which it is ordinarily maintained or in a reasonably usable form or forms; and

(iii) A party need not produce the same electronically stored information in more than one form.

(c) **Nonparties.** As provided in Rule 45, a nonparty may be compelled to produce documents and tangible things or to permit an inspection.

RULE 36—REQUESTS FOR ADMISSION

(a) **Scope and Procedure.**

(1) *Scope.* A party may serve on any other party a written request to admit, for purposes of the pending action only, the truth of any matters within the scope of Rule 26(b)(1) relating to:

(A) facts, the application of law to fact, or opinions about either; and

(B) the genuineness of any described documents.

(2) *Form; Copy of a Document.* Each matter must be separately stated. A request to admit the genuineness of a document must be accompanied by a copy of the document unless it is, or has been, otherwise furnished or made available for inspection and copying.

(3) *Time to Respond; Effect of Not Responding.* A matter is admitted unless, within 30 days after being served, the party to whom the request is directed serves on the requesting party a written answer or objection addressed to the matter and signed by the party or its attorney. A shorter or longer time for responding may be stipulated to under Rule 29 or be ordered by the court.

(4) *Answer.* If a matter is not admitted, the answer must specifi-

cally deny it or state in detail why the answering party cannot truthfully admit or deny it. A denial must fairly respond to the substance of the matter; and when good faith requires that a party qualify an answer or deny only a part of a matter, the answer must specify the part admitted and qualify or deny the rest. The answering party may assert lack of knowledge or information as a reason for failing to admit or deny only if the party states that it has made reasonable inquiry and that the information it knows or can readily obtain is insufficient to enable it to admit or deny.

(5) *Objections.* The grounds for objecting to a request must be stated. A party must not object solely on the ground that the request presents a genuine issue for trial.

(6) *Motion Regarding the Sufficiency of an Answer or Objection.* The requesting party may move to determine the sufficiency of an answer or objection. Unless the court finds an objection justified, it must order that an answer be served. On finding that an answer does not comply with this rule, the court may order either that the matter is admitted or that an amended answer be served. The court may defer its final decision until a pretrial conference or a specified time before trial. Rule 37(a)(5) applies to an award of expenses.

(b) **Effect of an Admission; Withdrawing or Amending It.** A matter admitted under this rule is conclusively established unless the court, on motion, permits the admission to be withdrawn or amended. Subject to Rule 16(e), the court may permit withdrawal or amendment if it would promote the presentation of the merits of the action and if the court is not persuaded that it would prejudice the requesting party in maintaining or defending the action on the merits. An admission under this rule is not an admission for any other purpose and cannot be used against the party in any other proceeding.

CHAPTER 12

EXPERT WITNESS TESTIMONY: EFFECTIVE DIRECT EXAMINATION

Courtroom scene from the trial of defendants Bill Gambini and Stan Rothenstein in the 1992 film, *My Cousin Vinny*:[73]

Witness: I'm a special automotive instructor of forensic studies for the Federal Bureau of Investigation.

Attorney: Uh-huh. How long you been in that position?

Witness: Eighteen years.

Attorney: [showing photo exhibits] Now, Mr. Wilbur, these are photos of tires belonging to the, uh, defendant's car, and these are photos of the tire marks left by the assailants' car as it fled the convenience store. Now, are you familiar with these?

Witness: Yes, I am.

Attorney: Could you elaborate please, sir?

73. Expert witness testimony scene between district attorney Jim Trotter (actor Lane Smith) and expert George Wilbur (actor James Rebhorn) from *My Cousin Vinny*, 1992, 20th Century Fox, directed by Jonathan Lynn.

Witness: We compared the tire marks outside the convenience store with the rear tires of the defendant's car. *[with emphasis:]* They're the same model, and size, of tire. Michelin model XGV, size 75R, 14 inch wheel.

Attorney: *[emphatically reiterating:]* They're the same size, and model tire. Anything else, sir?

Witness: Yes indeed. The car, leaving the convenience store, spun its rear tires dramatically and left a residue of rubber on the asphalt. Now, I took a sample of that rubber and analyzed it. I also took a sample of the rubber from the rear tires of the defendant's Buick and analyzed that too.

Attorney: What kind of equipment did you use to find this out?

Witness: I used a Hewlett-Packard 5710A dual-column gas chromatograph with flame analyzation detectors.

Attorney: Uh-huh. Is that thing turbo-charged? *[laughter]*

Witness: Only on the floor models.

Attorney: Now, Mr. Wilbur, what was the, ah, result of your analysis?

Witness: The chemical composition between the two samples was found to be … identical.

Attorney: I – dentical! No further questions, Your Honor.

The transcript of this courtroom exchange doesn't quite give it the life that the movie does; nevertheless, it is a wonderful dramatization of expert witness testimony. The expert appears to have a strong position based on his analysis and the lawyer orchestrates the testimony perfectly, complete with a bit of humor to entertain the jury. From the expert's perspective, this is how every direct examination should go, but unfortunately, it doesn't happen that way very often.

THE BIG PICTURE

Effective direct examination testimony doesn't begin at trial, it begins at the outset of the case. From the initial contact with the potential client—usually the client's attorney—everything that happens in the case should be designed for presentation at trial, or protected from being a problem at trial. The challenge of effective direct examination is to get a compelling story presented to the trier of fact while keeping their interest and ensuring their comprehension of the relevant material. Direct testimony is the climax of the expert's entire effort in the litigation proceeding. It seems like it should be a straightforward exercise, but its many facets make its success a tall order.

Direct exam involves the skill of reducing complex information to straightforward, understandable terms while not being condescending to the listener; maintaining a logical method of presentation; using the skills of persuasion while not appearing to be overly persuasive; understanding the needs of the listeners; teaching effectively; and, working jointly with the examining lawyer to share the burden of the presentation. Effective direct examination requires careful preparation—jointly with the examining lawyer—and a nuanced understanding of sophisticated trial techniques.

First and foremost, the expert is a teacher. Experienced teachers know their success is about much more than the delivery of content. Teachers succeed by understanding the needs of their listeners and delivering presentations that fulfill those needs with relevant content. Successful teachers take a pulse of the class often in order to gauge how interested their students are in the subject matter and whether something needs to be done to increase their participation, interest, or both. Unfortunately, an expert witness can't ask jurors how they feel about the lesson that is being presented, but she needs to be mindful of the level of interest in the minds of the listeners, and strive to reach them. Similar to a teacher, the witness has analyzed a complicated problem, brought her expertise to bear on the problem, solved it, and now wants to communicate the results of her analysis and opinion to some nontechnical listeners.

The expert's first task on direct examination is to tactfully build credibility through foundational testimony that shows you are a qualified person who is trustworthy, who has done a thorough, competent analysis, who brings some scientific objectivity to the problem at hand, and who is worthy of being believed. You're not a pompous know-it-all; you're just a hardworking professional who was retained to look at a problem, analyze it, and derive a fair, balanced, supportable conclusion. You realize that there may be an opposing expert who sees the problem and solution differently, but you have no personal problem with that individual; you just believe he is not looking at the facts or the problem correctly. You also have no bias for or against your client or the opposing client; you are providing technical services to help the court and the jury understand a problem that is beyond their common, everyday knowledge.

PREPARATION

The expert has prepared a thorough analysis, considered the strengths and weaknesses of the substantive arguments, and derived opinions and conclusions that conform to the expert's substantive specialty. During the course of the forensic workup, the expert has received input from both the lawyer and client and, hopefully, the expert has properly tempered any biased, argumentative positions that have been presented to her by the client or the lawyer during the analysis phase. In this regard, I frequently have commented that some of the most strenuous arguments I have had are with my own clients, and I am proud to stand strong against my clients' occasional attempts to get me to say something that I don't think is defensible. The moral of the story is: Don't let your clients bully you—and they will try to from time to time. Stand your ground.

One of the most difficult arguments I encounter from my own clients as a forensic expert goes something like this. The trial system is adversarial, and everyone knows there's a tendency to compromise positions put in front of the judge or jury. The client says: If you, the expert, just put forth a "middle of the road" (defensible!) opinion, we run the risk of your middle position just being averaged with the other guy's extreme position. Therefore, we need you to be as extreme as you can be in arriving at your opinion. (Remember, my opinions are damage numbers, so it's easy for me to quantify "extreme" as either too high an amount or too low an amount, but every area of technical expertise has a range of reasonableness to its conclusions.)

I respond to this argument with several points. First, the most defensible position to advance at trial is a balanced position that takes into account both the strengths and weaknesses, and doesn't just focus on the strengths of the argument. The listeners will see through an extreme argument and are more inclined to accept a balanced analysis, leading to a reasonable conclusion. Second, I am the one testifying under penalty of perjury, and I have an obligation to present an objective opinion to the court. The crass wisecrack is "pigs get fat and hogs get slaughtered." Don't let a lawyer or client push you into overstating (or understating) your most balanced position. It will come back to haunt you. And, being discredited on one aspect of your analysis will tend to carry over to discredit your entire opinion.

Once the expert's opinion is derived, the expert-lawyer team must decide how to present the analysis on direct examination. Both the expert and the lawyer succeed in trial based on their credibility in front of the court and the jury. Belief in the expert's case comes from a thorough, competent analysis of the facts and substantive theories resulting in an objective, defensible opinion. So, the real preparation for direct examination runs throughout the expert's involvement in developing the opinion. In a perfect world—which rarely happens—the expert is on the "right side of the case" with a very sympathetic client, great facts, a tremendous lawyer, a bulletproof opinion, and a judge who leans toward your client's side of the case. But, welcome to the real world of litigation: two parties are disputing the facts, the law, and every technical point relating to their larger disagreement.

At trial, the interaction between the expert and the lawyer is a carefully coordinated dance that must be structured from their agreement on how to present the material to the trier of fact. Collaborative preparation between them can help each to understand the perspective of the other, leading to an excellent outline of the expert's direct examination. And, every expert witness direct examination should be the result of a carefully constructed outline.

The expert's direct examination should proceed from a script, but the testimony must not appear scripted. Nothing that is said on direct examination should be articulated for the first time. Both the expert and the lawyer should have practiced every question and answer so there is a logical flow to the testimony. Some authorities say it is never a good idea to ask the expert to write the direct examination questions, but I respectfully disagree. The concern might be that the questions will be too technical, possibly too "in the weeds" and not big-picture enough. That is certainly a possibility, and a joint review of the planned direct examination should allay this concern. Then again, depending on the sophistication of the lawyer, I will suggest that the expert is often better qualified to structure the direct examination. Over the years, I have been involved in many trials where the lawyers just aren't that good at structuring a direct examination story generally, and they aren't sufficiently skilled at telling a technical story in my area. In those cases, I believe I am the better scribe of the direct examination, but I always politely defer to my client's lawyer, the quarterback of the trial. (Sometimes you have a Super Bowl player and other times you are playing at the local high school level.) I always offer my proposed script to the lawyer only as a proposal, deferring to him or her for the final call, but about 85% of the time the lawyer takes my advice.

For the witness, one preparation technique is to reduce technical concepts to simple examples, then practice saying phrases that illustrate the example. As an example, I was recently explaining a basic lost profits formula to a jury. The formula is: lost revenue minus variable costs saved equals lost net profit. That rule sounds great to a CPA, but it doesn't make any sense to a layperson. The listener might not understand the concept of revenue or the concept of variable costs, and why they have to be subtracted to arrive at net lost profit, so the entire concept has to be explained. So, I constructed the following script with my examining lawyer to try to illustrate the point:

… after the context of my analysis was explained…

Question: So, you compared the company's projected revenue after the water damage to the actual revenue received after the damage to estimate the total amount of lost revenue in 2019, correct?

Answer: That's right…. By subtracting the <u>actual</u> revenue they received from the <u>projected</u> revenue (they expected to get), I arrive at the estimate of lost revenue.

Question: And, what exactly is "revenue"?

Answer: Revenue is the total sales of the company… the total amount that customers pay to the business for products sold.

Question: So, you first figured out how much revenue they lost, right?

Answer: Yes. [returning to the point for the second time.]

Question: And how much revenue did you estimate they lost?

Answer: By comparing ABC's actual revenue received after the flooding to the projected revenue for the same period, I estimate they lost $206,000 in sales, or revenue. *[Third time!]*

Question: But after you calculate lost revenue, I see that you continue with some additional subtractions from the lost revenue before you calculate total net lost profits. Why is that?

Answer: Well, it's important to understand that a loss of revenue doesn't equal a loss of net profit. There is another step in the analysis. I have to subtract the costs they saved by not receiving the expected revenue.

Question: Hold on a minute, Mr. Brinig. Can you explain that concept to me?

Answer: Sure. This is the concept of variable costs. These are the costs that change as revenue changes. If revenue goes down, variable costs go down, and vice versa. For example, if Home Depot doesn't sell a

$1,000 tractor, the measure of their loss isn't $1,000. It's true that they have lost revenue of $1,000, but they still have the tractor that cost them $600 that they didn't sell. So their net loss from that failed sale is only $400. The formula to calculate the net lost profit is lost sales revenue ($1,000 in my Home Depot example) minus the variable costs saved (the cost of the tractor - $600), and that results in net lost profit ($400).

Question: So, here, after you estimated lost revenue, you subtracted an estimate of the "variable costs saved" to arrive at net lost profit, correct?

Answer: [repeating the complicated concept—again!] That's right. I have to reduce the lost revenue for the costs that the business saved by not receiving the revenue—the sales—and that's what this step in the analysis does. And, in this case, I estimated the variable costs to be 35% of the lost revenue, and I based the 35% on the company's actual experience over the last five years.

Question: So, can you please tell the jury about your exact calculations here?

Answer: Here, I estimated the revenue they lost to be $206,000, based on comparing the projected revenue to the actual revenue they received in the year after the water damage... then I subtracted 35%—the variable costs they saved, or didn't have to spend—from the lost revenue... arriving at $133,900 of loss.

Question: So, what is the result of your calculation?

Answer: As this exhibit shows, I conclude that the lost profits to the company for 2019 were $133,900.

Before trial, I practiced this example with my lawyer (and myself) several times. I made sure that I had easy, understandable numbers for the Home Depot example and I used consistent terms throughout the example. Even though it was obvious to me, I made sure that my lawyer asked me for my conclusion at the end of the section.

Expert testimony is about teaching, and the words that are used are important. They create images, and you want the images to be consistent with your opinion and your client's side of the case. Think about ways to create an interesting image of a complicated test or analysis that an expert might have undertaken. Maybe a description of the origin of the type of test being performed is an interesting historical fact to include in the introduction to the explanation. Or, for example, an analysis of a construction defect might include some photographs of poorly designed versus well-designed structural features (windows, doors, etc.) as a context for the specific analysis undertaken by the expert. In the preparation phase, give careful thought to the context of your expert testimony presentation and work to make it relevant to both the overall facts of this case and the common experience of jurors.

I am reminded of some other expert testimony in *My Cousin Vinny* by the Academy Award–winning actress, Marisa Tomei. She is the unwilling automotive expert for the defendants, explaining the concept of positraction to the jury, saying that "everybody knows when your car is stuck in the mud in Alabama, one wheel spins and the other does nothin', that's positraction." As her explanation ends, the camera pans to an older woman on the jury who is nodding affirmatively and quietly muttering, "Uh-huh." This is a perfect example of creating an image to illustrate a technical point.

Another important consideration during pretrial preparation is the use of visual aids to support expert testimony. Scientific and technical evidence is complicated, and simply presenting it to a jury orally can be limiting. Many listeners learn and understand concepts visually rather than aurally, and well-done trial graphics are often an essential component of competent expert testimony. The variable here is the definition of "well-done" graphics. Many times the graphics will be too complicated to simplify testimony. Charts are visual depictions, not listings of numbers or formulas. For instance, a timeline must sequentially explain a chronology and not be overwhelmed with dates, times, and activities. For a complicated sequential depiction, consider using overlays or animation to continue to build a simple story into a more complex one; don't start with the complete story and try to explain it. The graphic should speak for itself with very little explanation. Finally, be mindful of the perception of overkill by using professionally prepared graphics, as opposed to nicely prepared handwritten charts. There's no perfectly correct answer to the graphics problem; these are all just important considerations to discuss with the lawyer and client during the trial preparation phase.

Finally, recognize the psychology of decision-making in the minds of most people. People don't generally make decisions probabilistically or analytically, although technical experts tend to think in those terms. People make decisions narratively, from the perspective of stories. Jurors want their decisions to fit in with their perception of fairness, not necessarily technical correctness.[74] Hopefully, your opinion is technically correct, but think about its presentation in the context of the theme and fairness of the overall position of the case as seen by your client's side of it. Expert testimony must resonate with a group of ordinary citizens who are not technicians and who are trying to be fair. Don't forget the technique of leading the fact finder to the precipice of a conclusion, but letting the juror come to the conclusion himself or herself. This allows the juror to be invested in the decision-making process and not just be told what the answer is. There are no perfect approaches to presenting expert testimony, but the skilled expert is wise to be open to varied techniques of presentation.

74. And, beyond my understanding of decision-making, many psychologists suggest that people make decisions viscerally, not necessarily logically. People "feel" what is the right decision to the problem and then they interpret facts to support their subconscious conclusion.

IMMEDIATE TRIAL PREPARATION

In addition to your overall preparation—knowing your facts, knowing your arguments, and planning your presentation—the practice of putting yourself in the right mindset before you testify is very beneficial. It's the difference between thinking positively about something and thinking negatively about it, and the mental framework shouldn't be ignored. Immediately before you testify, there is great benefit to calming yourself and thinking positively about yourself, your client, and your position. After all, you wouldn't be at this point in the process if you didn't believe in what you are about to testify to, so get on board with the program mentally. You should also think positively about the judge, the jury, and the courtroom personnel. I like to even give the other side of the case the benefit of the doubt, believing that they firmly believe in the truth of their positions in the case and not drawing negative inferences about them because of our disagreements. This is part of the art of expert witness testimony.

The expert must establish credibility without pontificating or being condescending. I suggest the expert should initially think of herself as the junior person coming into the courtroom. Understand that at trial, the lawyers have already been in the courtroom for many hours establishing goodwill connections with the jury, the judge, and the staff. The expert is walking into a group of people who have already developed some relationships, although very controlled by court protocol, and the expert is the "new kid on the block." And, she won't be there for very long in relation to the others. So the expert must be mindful of the sociological dynamics of the participants and act accordingly at the beginning of her interaction with the people in the courtroom. A deferential attitude is probably in order at the outset, but sometimes there may be reasons to be more assertive. Self-confidence is essential, but it must be subtly masked from the observers. At the very least, the art of expert witness testimony requires consideration of this courtroom dynamic.

Be aware that expert witnesses are not particularly favored by judges and court staff. The sad reality is that experts are often perceived as "bought and paid for" mouthpieces for their side of the case. From an outsider's vantage point, the perspective is easy to understand. Experts are very highly paid witnesses, and there seem to be enough of them in the marketplace to disagree on every technical issue presented to them as a group. Lawyers often have the observation that they can find an expert to say whatever is needed to support their position in a particular case. There is some unfortunate truth to this observation, although some of the "purchased" opinions are pretty flaky. In the planning stages of direct examination, it is important for the expert to understand the perception of expert witnesses by the courts and the public.

As part of your immediate trial preparation, think about the perception that is created if the expert witness enters the courthouse with the retaining lawyers or fraternizes with them at the breaks or at lunch. I suggest that the expert should appear detached from these professionals, conveying the image of an objective professional who is simply entering the scene to provide information to the judge and jury. And, be mindful of the negative perception resulting from goodbyes, handshakes, and any remote appearance of celebration. The expert should both arrive and leave the courtroom humbly, showing respect for the entire judicial process.

ACTUAL DIRECT EXAMINATION
(some of this is still preparation, though)

Foundational testimony. As previously stated, it is important for the expert to come into the courtroom with a degree of humility and establish her credibility from the ground up. There is a careful balance when an expert comes in to establish her credentials, because she has to present enough background, education, and experience to qualify as an expert witness on the one hand, but on the other hand, the witness is coming into a group of people who don't know her and she has to immediately start bragging about how qualified she is to render opinion testimony in this case. This situation calls for some thoughtful personality considerations: you don't want to appear to be the know-it-all; you need to establish your background, education, and experience somewhat humbly, and you should consider working jointly with your lawyer to have him or her drag it out of you a little bit. You probably really know your stuff and your case, but the listener doesn't have that level of confidence in you; you have to earn it. And, you can lose whatever momentum you might build by coming into the courtroom and being cocky or appearing to be overly knowledgeable.

The legal purpose of foundational testimony is to qualify the witness as an expert witness, although the practical purpose of the testimony is to establish the expert's credibility and professional expertise. The qualification of an expert is a legal question to be decided by the judge, not the trier of fact (usually a jury). Generally, the expert will testify about her education, professional credentials, employment experience, academic affiliations, publications, and previous qualifications as an expert witness. As a practical matter, the expert should prepare the foundational testimony with the lawyer to strive to make the qualifications relevant to the issue at hand and as interesting as possible. Any weaknesses in the expert's qualifications should also be dealt with affirmatively in foundational testimony to deflect the effect of a challenge that may be forthcoming. For instance, if the expert hasn't handled the exact issue in the present case in a previous matter, a series of questions relating to the similarity of other cases handled by the expert should be addressed.

Example: A business appraiser is testifying on the value of an optometry practice, the first time she has ever valued this type of professional practice.

Question: Ms. Swanson, you're testifying today on your analysis to determine the fair market value of Dr. Smith's optometry practice, correct?
Answer: Yes.
Question: You have valued many types of professional practices in the past ten years, haven't you?
Answer: Yes, I have performed fair market valuations for probably twenty or twenty-five professional practices in recent years: medical practices, dental practices, podiatry practices, veterinary, financial consulting.... Quite a few different professionals.
Question: And, what are the similarities in different types of professional practices that affect their fair market value?
Answer: Well, professional practices are all service businesses, where the main driver of the revenue is the professional services of the owner/professional; they are all licensed and operate under state licensing regulations; they all have a client base that values the services of the owning professional; they can only be sold to

a limited number of similarly licensed buyers; there is reported market data for transactions of different types of practices.... Many similarities of different types of professional practices for valuation purposes.

Question: Now, Dr. Smith's practice.... is the first optometry practice you've been asked to value in a court proceeding, correct?

Answer: That's right. This is the first optometry valuation I have testified to. *[Don't hide from that weakness in your qualifications. Always deflect weaknesses affirmatively.]*

Question: Are you comfortable with your analysis and conclusions of the value of Dr. Smith's practice, given your experience valuing many types of professional practices and the valuation similarities between all these types of practices? *[Note the positive way of phrasing the question as opposed to stating the qualification as "even though you haven't valued an optometry practice before?"]*

Answer: Absolutely... I approach the valuation of all professional practices in the same general way.... I was able to analyze the profitability of Dr. Smith's practice the same way I would analyze any professional practice, and I investigated the market transaction data for optometry practices the same way I would look at any market data for other types of professional practices.

Question: In your opinion, you should approach the valuation of an optometry practice the same way you would generally approach the valuation of these other types of practices?

Answer: That's correct. These valuations are all of professional practices, and the fact that Dr. Smith's is an optometry practice doesn't take it out of the category of "professional practices." I don't want to infer that they are all exactly the same, but they are all professional practices with the same professional service-type characteristics.

Question: Let's turn to your analysis of Dr. Smith's practice....

There are many styles of foundational testimony, and no one approach is right for every expert and every case. I think a degree of modesty is appropriate, maybe having the lawyer draw out the expert so she doesn't appear pompous or over-confident. On the other hand, the jury needs to know that this expert is a highly qualified person who has undertaken a serious study of the facts and developed conclusions that are credible, supportable, and correct. The lawyer and expert may consider a little "day in the life" testimony to make the expert's work more interesting to the lay listener. The subtle skill here is the balance between too much, too little, and not coming on so strong that the listener is alienated.

I suggest that the first question of an expert witness on direct examination should be, "Good morning, Dr. Jacobs. What are you here to testify about today?" The answer should be one, two, or three highlights of the anticipated testimony so the jury understands the context of this witness's testimony. This introductory statement of the issues should be done without conclusions to avoid an objection of lack of foundation (it hasn't been laid yet) and to interest the minds of the jurors in the questions at hand. Without this introduction, the jury will struggle to understand exactly why they are hearing about the education and background of this physician, engineer, or economist. Set the stage for your testimony by telling your lawyer (and the listeners) the reason for your being there. Then, foundational testimony should move into your background, education, and experience, the three areas that are the legal basis for qualifying a witness to render expert opinion testimony. (See Exhibit 12.1 for example of proposed script.)

At the end of foundational testimony, many lawyers like to specifically request the judge to declare the expert qualified to render expert testimony. If the foundational testimony has proceeded without argument, it is probably beneficial to have the judge certify the expert as qualified, creating a positive impression in the minds of jurors. Some trial lawyers disagree on this strategy, but I am hard-pressed to understand what is wrong with it, unless you all believe that there may be some hesitation on the court's accepting the expert as qualified.

It is also possible that the opposing side may take the expert on *voir dire*, which is effectively a cross-examination of the expert's qualifications to render the opinion that is forthcoming. If there is any uncertainty about the expert's qualifications in the present case, the lawyer and the expert should have considered that possibility in their preparation and prepared the expert to defend why she is qualified to render the opinions she will be presenting to the jury. Importantly, the defense of qualifications should be done affirmatively in the foundational testimony with the intention of deflecting the anticipated attack on *voir dire*. In my experience, unless the expert is really reaching out of her area of expertise (which she shouldn't be doing), judges will usually allow the expert testimony to be admitted into evidence, with the admonition that any weaknesses in the expert's qualifications should go to the weight given to the evidence presented.

Another reason supporting a court's admission of expert testimony is that the exclusion of the testimony is an appealable decision by a trial court. Trial judges are a little bureaucratic in their decision-making processes, not wanting to make waves in the litigation continuum, and not wanting to be reversed on appeal. The exclusion of expert testimony is certainly a matter of judicial discretion, but the wrongful exclusion of the testimony is reversible error. Judges may differ in their views about experts, but they aren't inclined to exclude a litigant's expert at the time of trial after the party has spent thousands of dollars on expert witness fees preparing for trial. Don't get me wrong: exclusion can and does happen from time to time, but there is a tendency to allow expert testimony if there is any plausible connection between the expert's qualifications and the issue on which the expert is testifying.

Much of the discussion of direct exam preparation and the best structure of expert testimony should be directed to the lawyer who is planning the trial, but I am dealing with the art of expert testimony, so I am speaking to expert witnesses. In a perfect world, we all hope that our retaining lawyers are Clarence Darrows who can brilliantly lead us through direct examination, but I have worked in the real world for forty years and my reality is that planning my direct examination is at least a 50/50 proposition between my lawyer and me, and often it's 20/80. So I am telling you, the expert, how to plan for direct testimony, and I hope your lawyer is capable of handling his half of the process, but we're never sure of that until the day of trial. Even if your lawyer ends up being the perfect director, you should still plan your own direct testimony and advise your lawyer of your proposal for how to best present your evidence and opinion. The average lawyer desperately needs your help, and a very good lawyer will at least want to consider your views on how to present your direct testimony. Do this in the form of your proposed script of your testimony, complete with questions for the attorney to ask. (See Exhibit 12.1, "Foundation for Direct Examination," at the end of this chapter.)

Consider the technique of front-loading the expert opinion. Once the expert's credentials and qualifications are established, it may be advisable to begin the structure of testimony with the conclusion. The temptation is often to proceed in chronological order, but a linear organization makes more sense with a fact witness than an expert witness. It makes perfect sense to have a fact witness tell his story sequentially, because that's the way life happened. But an expert's analysis is often tedious, and digging into the chronology of the steps isn't always the best way to start. Give consideration, at least, to an order of presentation that is designed to interest the audience, and it may not be the chronology of the way that you investigated and analyzed the facts of the case. The conclusionary testimony can always be backfilled to support the detailed analysis, so consider getting more quickly to the final answer.

Some less-experienced trial lawyers tend to ask closed, cross-examination type questions of an expert on direct examination, and the result of this is usually disappointing. Closed questions are questions that call for a "yes" or "no" answer; they don't seek a narrative or explanatory response. With closed questions, the lawyer is effectively testifying and simply asking the expert to confirm or deny everything the lawyer is saying. The expert does not get the opportunity to explain the steps of the analysis and the logic of why she did what she did. The expert should be sensitive to this potential problem in the preparation phase and encourage the less-experienced lawyer to ask open-ended questions. The lawyer should be the conductor of the orchestra, not the soloist. The expert is the soloist.

Whom to talk to. Normally, a teacher speaks to students, the listeners of the information conveyed. Without being patronizing, the expert should do the same, and try to do it conversationally. When the lawyer is asking a question on direct exam, it is logical to look at him or her, and then comfortably turn to the jury to provide the explanation that the question seeks. In a bench trial, look at the judge with the answer to the question. Don't follow this suggestion rigidly, but simply do it conversationally, the same way you would talk to a group of people at a gathering. Sometimes it may be appropriate to continue looking at the questioner for a short answer and be careful not to be pandering to members of the jury. And, if the expert can structure the opportunity to stand, perhaps annotating a chart or even preparing a simple chart, it is often a beneficial presentation mode instead of sitting throughout the entire performance.

Substance of testimony. The expert is basically a teacher of a complicated technical subject. The challenge is to make a difficult lecture interesting and easy to understand, trying to meet the needs of the layperson listener. Recognize that you can only make five or six major points in the course of an hour of direct examination and be careful not to get caught in tedious details that will be lost on the audience. An interesting story must have clear breaks within it so the listener knows when one point has been concluded and the next step of the outline is beginning. It's ultimately the lawyer's job to structure these breaks, but the expert should identify them in the preparation phase.

Scope of the expert's assignment. After foundational testimony and the qualifications of the expert are established, the expert and the attorney should set forth the origination of the expert's involvement in the case. It seems logical that the substance of expert testimony should begin with an introduction to the expert's involvement in the matter, and this can be done formally or informally, depending on the lawyer's feeling of the pulse of the courtroom. Depending on the respective styles of the lawyer and the expert, the formal inquiry could be: "Dr. Jacobs, when did my office first contact you in this matter?" And, "What was it that you were asked to perform in this case?" Or, if the judgment of the lawyer dictates a less formal introduction, the expert could be asked: "Dr. Jacobs, you and I have known each other for quite some time, haven't we?" "And, I have retained you several times over the past few years to review my clients' records in cases I have been involved in, isn't that right?" (Maybe I am repeating myself here, but don't hide the fact that you have worked for this lawyer's clients in other matters; deal with this alleged "weakness" affirmatively.) Then, "Turning to this case, what exactly did I ask you to do?" Or, "What exactly did you do?"

Methodology. Keep in mind that there is no single way to structure expert testimony, and it is difficult to generalize about different types of substantive testimony. After foundational testimony and the scope of assignment, an overview of the available approaches to solving the technical problem at issue should probably be presented to the judge or jury. The presentation should assess the strengths and weaknesses of the available methods and their applicability to the facts of the case, leading to the conclusion that the methods chosen in this particular situation are the best ones to address the question at hand. Clear reasoning should be stated for the rejection of methods that were not ultimately used in reaching the conclusions. Personally, I think an intermittent outline structure is helpful to the listener, and it's also a helpful technique for leading the questioner. For example:

> **Answer:** When I am asked to estimate the fair market value of a business, I always begin by considering the three accepted approaches to valuation: the cost approach, the income approach, and the market-data approach.
>
> **Question:** Please tell the jury how you applied the first of these approaches to Acme Manufacturing Company....

Or, an example of an outline approach for a vocational rehabilitation expert:

> **Answer:** When I evaluate an individual for possible mitigating earnings, I want to consider three things: the medical condition of the individual, the level of physical restrictions that the medical condition causes, and the availability of qualifying jobs in the individual's proximate employment area.
>
> **Question:** Please tell the jury how you approached determining the medical condition of Mr. Jones in this matter.... [i.e., the first thing...]

When dealing with a complicated analysis, I personally think it is helpful to frequently break it down to "the following three steps," or "there are four factors to consider when analyzing problem X." The lawyer can then ask the witness for an explanation of step #1, then step #2, etc., and it helps organize the presentation in the minds of the listeners. Again, there's no absolute right way to present complicated information, but you certainly don't want to get bogged down in minutiae. That will definitely lose the listener.

Dealing with the judge. Occasionally, and usually only in a bench trial, the judge will interrupt expert witness testimony with questions for the witness. This situation requires the expert to walk a very fine line that can be dangerous if stepped across. In the easiest situation, if the judge's questions are in conformance with the expert's testimony, the expert can simply buttress or clarify her opinion by explaining the situation to the judge. These questions from the bench are helpful to focus the expert on areas of possible confusion or misunderstanding on the part of the court, and the expert can clarify these points. There are at least two other types of questions from the bench, however. One is the question where the judge obviously disagrees with the expert's analysis or conclusion, but the question can be either introspective or argumentative. While there is no absolute right way to deal with the response, the obvious approach is caution. The expert wants to be helpful to the court, try to advance his or her position, and not antagonize the judge in any way.

If the question indicates disagreement with the expert's position, but it is introspective, the expert can proceed with something like: "Well, I think a different underlying assumption may be appropriate, Your Honor, and if I adopt that, then [the answer comes out the way I analyzed it]…." Or, "The basis of my analysis is the assumption that __________, which disagrees with the way I believe you are approaching the question." Of course, if the judge's underlying assumption leads to a different conclusion than that reached by the expert, the expert should concede, "If the court's underlying assumption is correct, then the answer would logically be __________. Respectfully, Your Honor, the [plaintiffs/defendants] believe the correct underlying assumption is X."

Under no circumstances should the expert ever argue with the judge. The expert's opinion is based on the application of science or technical analysis, and it follows a path of reason. If different inputs are made to the analysis, the outcome would certainly be different. The expert should concede (if it's obvious) that, given the judge's different assumptions, the analysis would proceed to a different conclusion. The place to disagree with the judge is to acknowledge that underlying inputs may be different and the result of changing those inputs will alter the conclusion.

As a worthwhile training technique, consider listening to some recorded arguments of Supreme Court hearings where a justice is obviously disagreeing with an argument of counsel and observe the way that very skilled lawyers respectfully respond to the justice's questions and/or disagreements. Again, there is no perfectly correct answer to this situation, but thoughtful, anticipatory consideration of dealing with judges is a wise use of an expert's preparation time.

Use of trial graphics. Expert testimony is often very complex, and explaining it to laypeople is a challenging task. It is usually helpful to employ some visual aids to demonstrate the steps of the expert's analysis and a summary of her conclusions. When considering these trial aids, the expert should put herself in the mind of the observer and contemplate what visuals will best simplify and convey the work of the expert to a layperson. And, trial graphics can help to "order" the steps of an expert's complicated process.

I am a certified public accountant (and non-practicing lawyer), not a graphic artist. So I don't know how to make beautiful graphics, but I know how to teach basic finance and accounting to laypeople who don't have strong analytic backgrounds. I know that more than four or five numbers on a trial graphic are too many, and I know that a simple timeline to demonstrate the chronology of a case (or the chronology of technical analysis) can be extremely helpful. I also suggest that a sequential buildup of a visual graphic can be very helpful and that putting too much detail on a chart will quickly lose the viewer. If a chart is to include a lot of detail, it should be composed of overlays or animation so it can be presented one step at a time. The viewer can be brought along through the development process.

In my opinion, there is little benefit to presenting scientific or sophisticated financial formulas visually. Here is an example of the formulas for acceleration and force. Do they mean anything to you? (They don't to me, I will confess.)

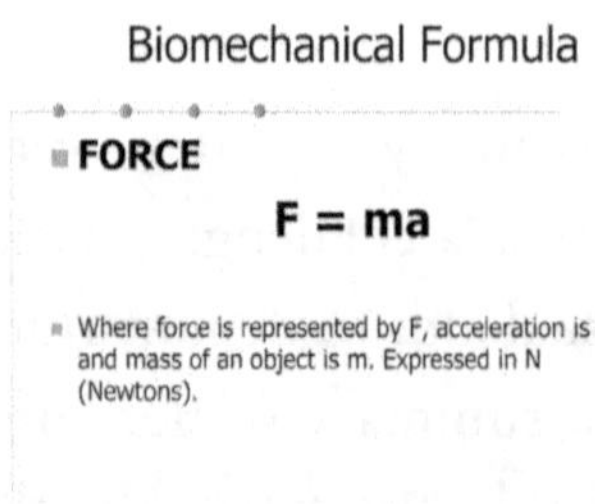

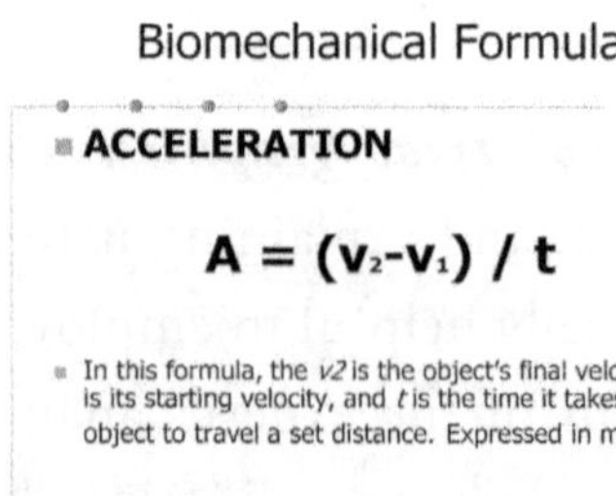

As an alternative to scientific or technical formulas, I might suggest something that resonates with almost any viewer: a simple picture.

Here's what happens when the force of a collision is relatively small:

Here is a medium level of force:

"And here is the level of force that occurred in the rear-end crash into my client's car in this matter, ladies and gentlemen:"

The majority of people are visual learners, so simply talking through your forensic analysis will not convey the information in a way that's best for the majority of the population to understand it. Careful consideration should be given to the use of simple graphics to illustrate and organize your testimony. The key here is ***simple***. Here are two examples of simple graphs that readily show something graphically that a series of numbers would not demonstrate:

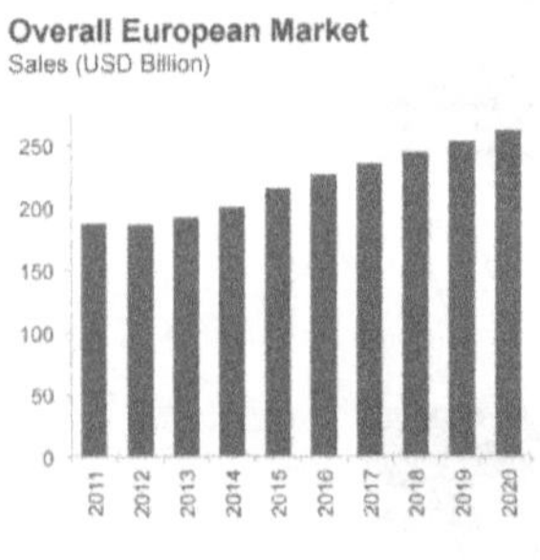

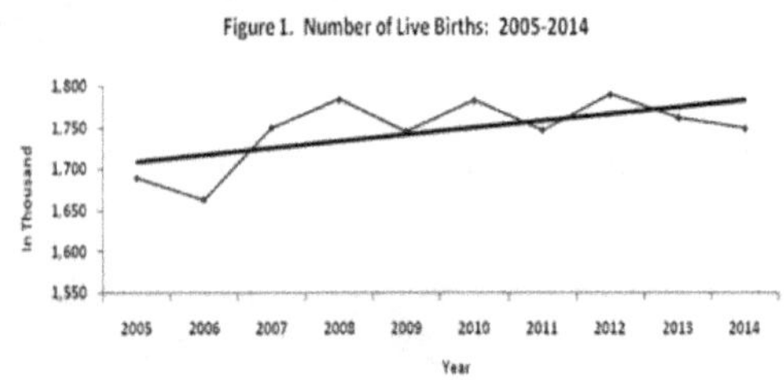

Contrast the previous two graphs to the following graphs, which are certainly colorful,[75] but pretty meaningless (to me, anyway). Neither of these graphs conveys a clear, simple point:

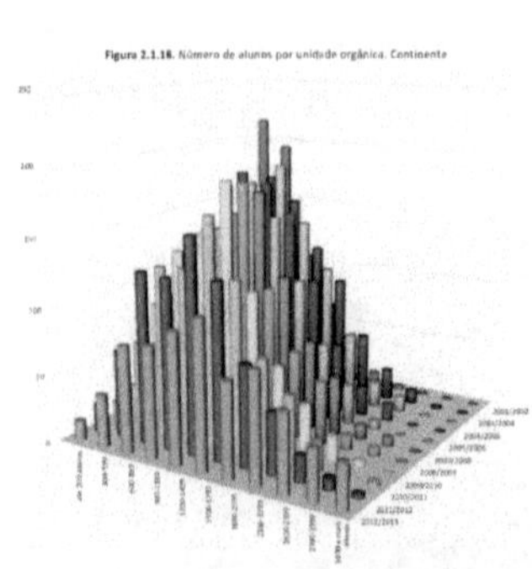

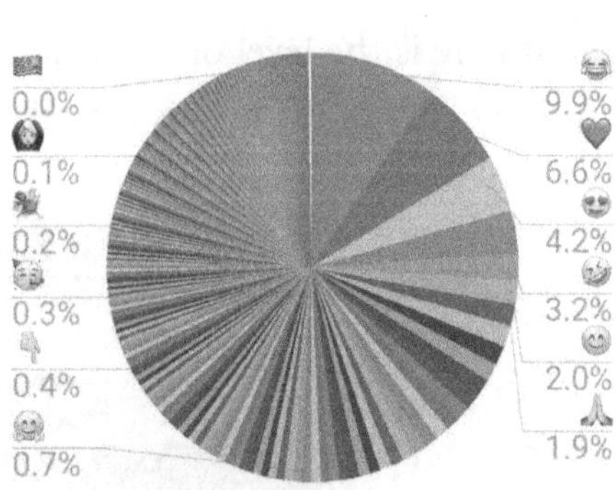

75. Sorry, folks. In the drafts of the book, these graphs are in color, but the printing costs increased $21 per book to keep them that way. Use your imagination!

Dealing with weaknesses in the analysis. It is critically important to present the weaknesses of a substantive analysis during direct examination and, don't kid yourself, every analysis has some weaknesses. Presumably, the expert has considered and incorporated the weaknesses into the opinion, and presenting them on direct examination enables the expert to contextualize them, downplaying their importance or their negative effect on the final conclusions. Strategically, it is always advisable to affirmatively disclose the weaknesses in an offensive posture, rather than to defend against a challenge during cross-examination.

Using humor in the courtroom. Be very careful with humor for several reasons. First, the entire proceeding isn't particularly lighthearted, so humor isn't a terribly natural fit. Second, jurors aren't particularly excited about being on jury duty, so they don't have a lot of tolerance for the "jolly old" expert witness or lawyer. Third, in this politically charged environment, people react so differently to various stimuli that it's hard to know what might work. Finally, highly skilled technical experts generally aren't the greatest comedians, so proceed at your own risk.

Here is an example where I used humor and got lucky with the situation. I had completed my one-hour economic damages testimony in front of a jury in a straightforward breach of contract case. Cross-examination was fairly perfunctory and not at all hostile. The judge was a very cheery woman and the attitude of everyone in the courtroom felt pretty light. I finished my testimony at 11:30 a.m., and just as I finished, the judge hesitatingly looked up at the lawyers, sort of inquiring what should "they all" do, if anything, before the noontime break. The court could proceed to do some mundane administrative stuff; they could read some deposition testimony aloud, or they could break early for lunch. In the momentary silence after her inquiry, I piped up and said, "I could go another half an hour, if you need it, Your Honor." Everyone in the courtroom cracked up and the judge smilingly said, "You know, I think we'll just take an early lunch today. See everyone at 1:30." Sometimes humor can work, but use it very carefully.

People's perceptions and sensitivities. Here's an example of people's varying reactions to words and comments. I testified in a trial several years ago where one of the accounting experts (not me, thankfully) described himself in what I thought was a cute, appropriate way, saying in response to a cross-examination question, "I'm just the bean counter, I don't know about the quality of management," or some issue distantly related to his accounting testimony. After the trial when the lawyers interviewed the jurors to learn their impressions about the case, one of the members of the jury was offended by the "bean counter" comment, thinking it had something to do with a Hispanic slur. I get it. The term "bean counter" has been used forever to cynically describe an accountant. I certainly don't think of it as any type of racial slur, but this member of the jury did.

UNIQUE PRESENTATION SKILLS

A good expert witness should be the person whom others would like to have a drink with after work or a casual chat at one of her kid's soccer parties. I don't know how to tell people to be likable, but expert witnesses should be mindful to try to be that person, without being phony about it in any way.

I recently had a judge friend of mine tell a story about two business executives who were testifying in his courtroom. These C-suite witnesses were self-made men and they were testifying on the opposing side of a case against a young former employee who was alleging wrongful termination. Apparently, the facts of the case could have gone either way—they were complicated—and it wasn't a clear case of retaliation against this employee. The point the judge was making was that these two executives were subtly pompous and condescending, and their attitude really turned off some members of the jury. In the end, the jury found in favor of the terminated employee, and my judge friend believed that it was primarily because of the negative vibe of the testimony of the executives. A witness—particularly a high-level witness, or an expert—has to be sensitive to the perceptions of jurors and very careful not to alienate these people.

I have the good fortune of knowing a lawyer named Paul Marchegiani, a lecturer at the University of Chicago School of Law who teaches a class he has designed called "Presence: Performance Skills for Lawyers." Professor Marchegiani has a background in music and acting, and he has developed strategies from that perspective designed for trial lawyers to help them succeed in court. Some of the approaches may not always be practical given the size and sophistication of the particular case, but all of the tips are valuable for experts to consider in preparation for expert testimony in the courtroom.

Immediate Trial Preparation.

1. Familiarize yourself with the space (i.e., the courtroom and courthouse) if at all possible. Much of what makes us feel "at home" in a given space is familiarity. Understanding the

sights, sounds, smells, and feeling of the room we are about to enter alleviates some of the mystery and stress, and allows us to partially eliminate—or at least not worry about—one variable in our expert testimony. Notice the quality of the light, the ambient noises, the smell of the room... this is what the judge and jury are living in for much of their day. Experience it alongside them. If you can't get into the exact courtroom space beforehand (ideally the day before testifying), choose the courtroom next door. Notice how witnesses sound on the microphone (if there is one). Can you hear them? Are they close to the jury? Far away? Where do the lawyers stand... at a podium, or are they able to roam freely?

2. Box Breathing.[76] This is a form of yogic deep breathing, a simple but powerful method of focusing on your breath that can help you get, and stay, calm. The common name, "box breathing," refers to the fact that a box has four sides, a concept represented by breathing while you slowly count to four a total of four times—four counts of breathing in, four counts of holding your breath, four counts of exhaling and four more counts of holding after you exhale. The technique recommends repetition of the entire process four times.

Any meditative calming practice before the expert testifies is helpful. In times of stress, your sympathetic nervous system is on high alert. Box breathing can help you move out of that state by tapping into the bodily system responsible for rest and digestion—the parasympathetic nervous system. The parasympathetic nervous system is the opposite of the sympathetic nervous system, otherwise known as "fight or flight."

76. "How Box Breathing Can Help You Destress, Cleveland Clinic, August 17, 2021, https://health.clevelandclinic.org/box-breathing-benefits/

"When a person is anxious," says Melissa Young, MD, of the Cleveland Clinic, "they breathe shallowly and quickly, which actually creates more anxiety within the body. We can use breathwork to move out of the fight-or-flight state and into that parasympathetic nervous system."

3. Regarding scripted testimony, there are several techniques that lawyers and witnesses can use to prevent the exchange from coming across as overly rehearsed, and to help them nimbly handle objections and interruptions as they occur. The goal here is to get both the lawyer and the witness "out of their heads" about the testimony. People sense when there's a disconnect between the words we say and what our bodies are saying. Ideally the two should be aligned, and the trick to this is to stand up (or use whatever parts of our bodies are available to us if we cannot stand) and *activate our whole self* as we practice. Some of these novel exercises might seem a little unorthodox in the legal realm, but they really do work as preparation techniques, and seasoned actors and other performers often use them to get out of their heads for performance. After a testimony script is (nearly) memorized, try these techniques:
   a. Stand about ten feet away from the lawyer and gently/slowly toss a light ball back and forth as you practice the testimony, keeping eye contact with each other as you toss and catch the ball. Keep the ball in motion regardless of who is speaking. After you go through the testimony, ask yourself whether there were areas that you stumbled over in terms of the substance of the testimony. Maybe the witness doesn't know those as well as he needs to, or maybe they're framed awkwardly and

need to be rewritten. Then, have another person or two join and continue tossing the ball among the three to four of you while going through the testimony again. This exercise serves several purposes: (1) the testimony will have more natural flow; (2) the two people will be more connected as lawyer and expert, and better able to pace the testimony and work together; and (3) by adding other people to the ball-tossing exercise, you subconsciously broaden your focus to include the silent jury and judge. For extra points, if one of the extra people is a member of the legal team, they can insert objections as you continue to toss the ball around, and the lawyer has to respond while keeping the ball moving.

b. Another way to get the testimony into the witness's "body" is to practice it while walking around the room, *not* looking at the other person, but exploring objects in the space that catch your eye. Maybe it's a flickering light, or a chip in the wall paint, or an unusual gadget in the middle of the conference table. Study the objects as you recite your script, and move on to something else that catches your eye when you lose interest in the prior object. Again, we're looking to (1) make sure we really have the testimony down pat, and (2) to get out of our heads about it and broaden our ability to take in the whole space when we are seated at the witness stand. It will seem so easy by comparison if you've had the chance to get the testimony in your body... it softens the witness's focus and slows the speaker down. This physical and mental state exudes presence and calm, and that's more effective expert witness testimony.

4. Status. We think a lot about the status of different people when we enter a courtroom, and these statuses can change at various times in the proceedings. At the top of the chain in all matters is the judge (though even the judge will occasionally give away some status to members of the jury when thanking them for their service, etc.). Lawyers should put themselves below the judge, but not too far below, or they risk coming across as unqualified. An expert witness should think of their status as more or less on par with the lawyer, but ultimately *just* below, especially when it comes to procedural and legal matters. There are ways to judiciously give away or take status when necessary. Using honorifics like "your honor" or "sir/ma'am" gives away status, as well as "please" and "thank you." These tools are always at your disposal if your status relationships begin to feel off-kilter. Posture, speech volume and clarity, and confident eye contact can help you make yourself larger and assume status if you feel yourself shrinking.
5. Physical Presence. How we enter a space provides our first impression to the jury. We should come across as relaxed and open, but also discreetly confident and positive. An acting methodology called the Alexander Technique[77] provides insight into a great way to get our bodies in alignment and free from tension so we can walk and speak with freedom and confidence. The Alexander Technique is a method of relaxation and releasing tension

77. "The Alexander Technique," Society of Teachers of the Alexander Technique (STAT), https://alexandertechnique.co.uk/alexander-technique/history. See also https://alexandertechnique.com/

in muscles that constrain our ability to use the whole body as the instrument of performance and communication. The method is used by performers of all kinds to develop and improve the use of their voices and create a whole presence to express themselves. The steps of the methodology are valuable to expert witnesses to enhance their communication ability.

6. Vocal Presence. Some quick rules of thumb from Professor Marchegiani's opera training:
    a. Vocal authority comes in part from freedom and resonance. We want to allow the voice to flow out of us and naturally bounce off all the resonators inside us. That adds vocal dynamism to make sure we can be heard.
        i. Freedom. Rather than forcing sound out, we want to allow ourselves to take deep and easy full breaths, where the diaphragm naturally lowers, the rib cage expands slightly all around (including into your mid-back), and the sound comes out unrestricted by your shoulders, throat muscles, and tongue.
        ii. Resonance. Sound requires space to amplify and resonate. We have several places in our bodies that amplify sound naturally and add interesting color and overtones.
            1. Space. First, we need space above the vocal cords to amplify the sound wave coming off the vibration of the vocal cords in the first instance. This space is created by gently raising our soft palate (where the uvula dangles from) and gently lowering the larynx. The trick here is not to use our muscles to force it. Think about the beginning

of a yawn and you'll get the sense of expansion there. Or speaking like Julia Child is another technique that is helpful.

2. Air. A steady flow of breath keeps the vocal cords purring. The more one speaks with this *legato*, the more pleasing and gentle the sound. Then we must thoughtfully incorporate pauses and dynamics in our speech to keep it expressive and "in the moment." That creates a pleasing musicality and authority to our speech that will keep the listeners engaged.
3. Resonance. Sounds created by our vocal cords and amplified in the voice box then have to travel out of our bodies. They bounce around different cavities and bones as they do this. Hum gently up and down, and you'll see that higher notes resonate at the tip of the nose and maybe even up between the eyes. Lower notes will cause your sternum to vibrate. Explore those sounds, and use gentle humming to wake up all those resonators, big and small. If you're stuffed up, this is especially important (again, gently). Humming or singing in the shower is a great way to do this, since the steam can help loosen any phlegm.
4. Vocal health. We get into trouble when we try to muscle the voice, or we don't speak with enough full, easy breath support. Easy and gentle is the key. Rely on your resonators, not your muscles, to create big and dynamic sounds.

FINAL RANDOM TIPS FOR TESTIFYING

I offer these points to put on your checklist of considerations for testifying. Taking my list in total, you may find one or two of them helpful to elevate your game. I am committed to sharing everything I know to help raise your forensic consulting practice to an art form.

Protocol around the courthouse:

1. It is inappropriate to have any communication with a juror in a case in which you are involved. This prohibition extends even to casual, non-substantive conversations. The best advice is to completely avoid the potential situation by not lingering in the areas where jurors are likely to gather. Jurors have been advised of this protocol, so they tend to be mindful of the prohibition of communication with parties, lawyers, or witnesses, and they will know you're not being rude by not being casually polite to them.
2. Think of everyone you might encounter within ten blocks of the courthouse as a member of the jury, and conduct yourself accordingly.
3. In and near the courtroom, I suggest you maintain a very detached association with the lawyers and the clients who have hired you. You don't want to look like an integral part of the litigation team; you want to look like an independent professional who was called in to solve a problem.
4. Although it has to be done sometimes, try not to huddle with the litigation team anywhere near the courtroom on the breaks.
5. Needless to say, don't walk in and out of the courthouse with your team.

In the courtroom:

1. Enter the courtroom somewhat timidly. Be very polite, but not effusive, to the courtroom staff.
2. When you arrive on the witness stand, you will be asked to state your name and spell your last name. At that moment, look respectfully at the court reporter who is probably sitting almost in front of you, and politely spell your name to him or her.
3. Most courtrooms have a law enforcement person (bailiff or sheriff) who is responsible for security, order, and some other administrative tasks in the room. In my experience, those individuals tend to be authority-type personalities, and I go out of my way to treat them with deference and strictly obey their directives.
4. In addition to employing some relaxation techniques discussed previously, put yourself in a positive mental frame of mind in anticipation of your testimony. It's analogous to an athlete believing she can break the existing record or win the game. Spend a few conscious moments thinking positively about yourself and your position in the case.
5. Don't allow yourself to think negatively about the jury, the jury system, or an individual juror. Reaffirm to yourself that the American judicial system is the best dispute-resolution method in the world and that you are contributing to the justice system.

Clothing suggestions:

1. For men, wear a white shirt rather than light blue or other color when you testify; it won't show you are sweating.
2. I heard one lawyer tell a group of expert witnesses not to wear monogrammed shirts to testify in jury trials; he didn't think they looked appropriate.

3. I can't intelligently comment on the details of the proper dress code for female expert witnesses, but I would simply tell women experts to be mindful of the appropriate attire for the situation.
4. I don't want to look like a lawyer in a gray pin-striped suit (and I kind of look like a lawyer), so I choose to wear a conservative sport coat and slacks instead of a suit. I simply want to avoid—as much as I can—looking like "just another lawyer" and appearing to be part of the "team."

Physical conduct:

1. Don't appear too comfortable or too familiar in the courtroom or courthouse setting. It's true that I have been there hundreds of times and I know a lot of lawyers, but I go out of my way to look like the opposite of "big man on campus," fraternizing with different lawyers (and even judges) whom I have gotten to know over the years.
2. The same thing is true in the deposition setting. I go out of my way not to be "buddy-buddy" with my retaining lawyer, even though the two of us might have gotten personally familiar with each other over the course of the case. There is no reason to give out that information to the opposing counsel.

SOME PITFALLS TO BE AWARE OF

I will share a few embarrassing stories from my career as reminders to expert witnesses of what not to do in the courtroom.

First is a story about the importance of detailed preparation with your lawyers. About fifteen years ago, I was testifying in a case of fire loss to a business in Las Vegas, Nevada. The primary financial issue in the case was the amount of lost profits to the plaintiff's business resulting from four fires at the defendant's adjacent premises. The plaintiff claimed the defendant was negligent in operating its recycling business by allowing more than one fire to ignite on the premises, causing damage to plaintiff. As the financial expert in the case, I had reviewed and analyzed historical financial statements to understand the profitability of the plaintiff's company to use as a basis for a lost profits calculation. In one of the historical years, there was a relatively small amount of miscellaneous income from a property insurance reimbursement from damage to a vehicle a few years earlier, completely unrelated to the present fire issue. I excluded the amount from my calculation of "historical average profitability" because it was not an operating item of the company's revenue, it was extraordinary, and not recurring. It was also an immaterial amount of about twelve thousand dollars having insignificant effect on the historical average earnings.

Outside of my knowledge of the proceedings, insurance coverage had been a huge issue in the trial. Apparently, the plaintiff had already received an insurance reimbursement from some equipment insurance, and the present fight related to the real estate property insurance. (It is well understood that the fact of a defendant's insurance coverage is not to be mentioned in the course of a trial. The litigation is between plaintiff and defendant, not between plaintiff and defendant's billion-dollar insurance company.) During a fairly routine cross-examination of me, the opposing attorney asked me why I had subtracted this $12,000 item from profits in that historical year in my analysis. I responded, "It was a non-operating insurance reimbursement from a truck that was damaged in an accident." Another defendant attorney immediately objected to my answer, and the objection was sustained, and the judge struck my answer from the record. (No further discussion of the subject occurred at this point.) Okay, that was the end of it, I thought… my testimony on lost profits proceeded uneventfully.

Immediately at the end of my testimony, while I was still on the witness stand, the opposing lawyer stood up and said, "Motion to strike this witness's entire testimony." The judge said, "Granted!" The judge then politely looked at me and said, "Thank you for your testimony, Mr. Brinig," and then looked at the jury and said, "Please disregard the entire testimony of this witness because the court has granted the motion to strike the testimony." I felt the color drain out of my face as I slinked out of the courtroom, completely embarrassed by what had just happened.

I don't know who to blame for that fiasco, me or my lawyers, but it highlights the importance of pretrial preparation. Yes, it was an out-of-town case and I just showed up at the courthouse at the appointed time without much trial preparation with my lawyers—a breach of one of my inviolate rules. On the other hand, the issue of insurance was such a big deal in this case that my lawyers should have admonished me—more than usual—to steer clear of anything related to insurance in my testimony. The moral of the story is prepare, prepare, prepare. Make sure you know where the mines are buried in the minefield, and don't step on them. In this case, I sure stepped on one.

My second story relates to the witness's interactions with the judge, and unfortunately, this one also happened to me. Frequently, an impossible question will be asked on cross-examination, one that's ridiculously complicated and/or unintelligible. When it happens, it's a question that I know I'm not going to answer. So I'll give it an "I don't know" or an "I don't understand the question" response. In a case about nine years ago, after such a question had been asked of me, an objection was raised by my client's lawyer and there was a long pause while the judge began rereading the question on his monitor and contemplating his ruling on the objection. In the uncomfortable silence, I foolishly butted in, looked at the judge and said, "I think I can help you out, Your Honor." (I was going to tell him that I couldn't answer the question, regardless of what he did with the objection.) The judge obviously didn't appreciate my assistance because he harshly responded with: "I don't need your help, thank you," and he proceeded to rule on the objection (I don't even remember which way).

The reality is that being a trial judge is sometimes a boring job, sitting there watching litigators argue, listening to testimony, and ruling on objections. The judge is dying for something to do, and he doesn't need a smart-aleck witness telling him how to do his job. This lesson falls in the "stay in your lane" category of advice: you do your job of witnessing and let the judge do his or her job of judging.

One of my distinguished colleagues, Paul Regan, tells a vaguely similar story where he once answered a question on cross-examination in a federal court trial, saying something like, "I have only calculated the damages, Mr. Attorney; whether the defendant's actions *caused* these damages is up to the jury to decide." In that case, Regan notes that a cantankerous old federal judge instantly pounded his gavel and jumped all over him, saying, "What am I, chopped liver? I'm the one who tells the jury what they're going to decide, Mister. Not you!"

I will close my embarrassing stories with one in which a judge admonished me for saying something improper on the witness stand. Sometimes a witness is precluded from talking about certain aspects of a case that are considered "off limits." There may be a motion *in limine* that precludes lawyers and/or the witness from raising certain facts and issues or another reason that something cannot be discussed (violation of privilege, correction of testimony after a deposition that is excluded, etc.). Just because a witness isn't allowed to talk about a particular issue doesn't necessarily mean that the cross-examining lawyer is precluded from barking around the edges of that issue, in a way that is embarrassing for the witness.

I experienced a situation in a jury trial where I was precluded from testifying about an adjustment that needed to be made to my calculation because the adjustment was based on some inadmissible evidence. Consequently, I was advised by my lawyers that I was not allowed to testify to the adjustment. In the course of the jury trial, the cross-examining lawyer raised the issue with me, suggesting that I had not properly fixed something that should be fixed in my analysis. (He was right!) I responded, "Well, I could have made the adjustment for x and y, but I didn't, and I'm not allowed to talk about that." My testimony proceeded uneventfully, until the morning break when the jury was excused.

After the jury left the courtroom, the judge looked sternly down from the bench and scolded me that "You will not make any statement like that again in this courtroom, Mr. Brinig." OUCH!!!! I guess I shouldn't have said that. The message here is that if the witness is not allowed to talk about something, not only should he not ***talk*** about it, but he also shouldn't even say he's ***not allowed*** to talk about it.

AND THERE ARE GOOD DAYS TOO

I wish the following story had happened to me, but it happened to my longtime business partner, Bob Taylor. Bob is an MBA/CPA and one of the smartest business valuation and economic damages experts I know. He is a very experienced expert witness who has testified in hundreds of depositions and trials over the past thirty years.

Bob was involved in a very contentious litigation matter that was venued in the State of Idaho, and he was required to testify in a jury trial in Boise. His issue was lost business profits of a client who was a distributor of office supply products to customers that were "protected accounts." The supplier of the office products began selling to, and encroaching on, the customers of Bob's client. On cross-examination, the opposing lawyer—who was not a particularly nice guy—grilled Bob on his calculation of the projected profits from the sale of the products, arguing that Bob's analysis was without merit because Bob had not made any subtraction for rent, utilities, receptionist wages, and other fixed costs (that shouldn't be subtracted anyway). In a particularly contentious exchange, the cross-examining lawyer challenged Bob with: "Just admit that your analysis is completely wrong and the alleged loss would be a lot lower if you properly subtracted the additional costs." Bob's response was: "Not at all. You are simply ignoring my explanation and attempting to confuse everyone." At that moment, in the middle of the second row of the twelve-member jury, a large man stood up, looked directly at Bob, and exclaimed to the entire courtroom, complete with a clenched fist: "You Go, Guy!"

At the time of the verdict, Bob's client was exceptionally pleased with the jury's decision. Back in our office, Bob's team had two dozen "You Go, Guy" T-shirts printed in various sizes, and, on casual Fridays, a number of these shirts can be seen around our offices in San Diego. As I said at the outset of this story, I only wish it had happened to me, but it couldn't have happened to a nicer, more competent guy than my partner, Bob Taylor. Some days everything goes your way.

CONCLUSION

I have suggested that the expert's conclusion and opinion be stated generally near the beginning of her testimony, but that is no reason not to tactfully restate the conclusion at the end of direct examination. Since the underlying rationale for the conclusion has been testified to, this final presentation of the expert's conclusion should be more detailed and contextual in light of the investigation the expert has undertaken. This is the expert's opportunity to state the logic of the final opinion, that "my review of the underlying factors of x, y, and z, and my application of the scientific principles of a, b, & c, leads me to conclude that the preparation of the concrete slab underlying the building was below the standard of care for this type of work regularly done in this community." In some cases, it may be appropriate for the examining lawyer to ask some buttressing questions that weave in important legal principles that will be given as jury instructions as part of the law of the case. For instance, questions like: "Mr. Green, are you comfortable telling the jury that you have reached this conclusion to a reasonable degree of certainty?" Or, I have heard the question to include "to a reasonable degree of medical certainty" in appropriate cases. The precise language of these questions is in the province of the examining lawyer, but the expert provides her suggestions in the proposed script of testimony.

The remaining concern I offer is regarding the lawyer who tries to nail the coffin shut with too many questions that elicit obvious, patronizing answers. Some lawyers have a tendency to "beat the dead horse" with questions that make the listeners roll their eyes. I don't know how the expert is in a position to control this unfortunate practice other than preparing direct examination testimony with the lawyer and getting a feel for the anticipated testimony and the lawyer's style. I do believe this practice detracts from effective direct examination testimony, and preparation by the lawyer and expert can mitigate the problem.

EXHIBIT 12.1: FOUNDATION FOR DIRECT EXAMINATION

WHITE VS. GREENE

BRIAN BRINIG

[Comment: I apologize for the granularity of this example, but I think it is important to show what I provide to lawyers for the script of my Foundation for Direct Examination. This is an example of the exact document I provide to my attorney as we prepare for my scheduled testimony in trial. This case involves a loss of earnings claim resulting from an automobile accident where the plaintiff suffered fairly serious back and bodily injuries, although he was able to return to his employment as a computer security consultant to a private university about five months after the vehicle accident. I was the economic expert retained by the defendant. IMPORTANT: I NEVER PREPARE THIS DOCUMENT BEFORE MY DEPOSITION AND I DO NOT TAKE A COPY OF IT WITH ME TO THE WITNESS STAND. I MAKE HANDWRITTEN NOTES OF MY ANSWERS AND I REFER TO THEM ON THE WITNESS STAND.]

To Attorney: This is only a proposed outline. We can review tonight or when we meet before trial.

1. Mr. Brinig, what are you here to testify about today?

    a. *The economic losses to Mr. Raymond White resulting from the injuries sustained in the motor vehicle accident on July 24, 2018.*

   b. *I was also asked to look at the economic analysis prepared by the plaintiff's expert, Christopher Reynolds, regarding Mr. White's loss calculations.*

2. What is your occupation?

   a. *CPA, and I specialize in forensic accounting—meaning calculating economic losses, economic damages, and business valuation analysis.*

3. How long have you been doing this type of work?

   a. *I have been doing this work for about forty years.*

4. Do you have any specific credentials that qualify you to testify about the economic losses to an individual?

   a. *CPA since 1977*
   b. *Senior member of ASA*
   c. *Past President of Financial Analysts Society of San Diego*
   d. *Member of various professional organizations relating to my work*
   e. *Officer of organizations relating to my professional work*

[Comment: I try to structure a short answer and then a longer answer so there is some variation to the pace of the examination. I also may vary the script between narrative answers and "outline points" answers.]

5. What is your education?
   a. *Georgetown Business School*
   b. *USD School of Law, I have a law degree, but I have never practiced law.*

6. Could you briefly summarize your employment experience?

[Comment: I obviously narrate the following answer. Here is just an outline.]

a. *Price Waterhouse… Arthur Young*
b. *1983 … Formed my forensic accounting firm that ran for 38 years and was sold about two years ago to a national financial services firm—CBIZ—where I presently serve as a Managing Director*
c. *AND, I am an Adjunct Professor at the University of San Diego School of Law where I have taught Finance & Accounting for Lawyers for about 25 years.*

[Comment: I want the lawyer to decide whether we should go into questions 7 to 9, based on her feeling about the needs of the jury.]

7. MAYBE SKIP QUESTIONS 7 – 9… YOUR CALL…. I know you have published a number of papers….. Would you tell the jury….. What books relating to your field have you written?

a. *The textbook,* ***Finance & Accounting for Lawyers****. I am the sole author…*
b. *I co-authored a technical publication called* ***The CPA's Guide to Litigation Support Services****….*
c. *I also co-authored another technical book called* ***Developing and Managing a Litigation Services Practice****…*

8. Any other publications over the years?

    a. *I have written twenty or thirty articles for journals and continuing education courses ... they are listed on my résumé.*

9. Please tell us about your teaching experience.

    a. *USD Law School—20+ years... I designed my course, Finance & Accounting for Lawyers... I also wrote the textbook for the class about ten years ago, and it's used in some other law schools as well.*
    b. *I do a fair amount of teaching of damages-type courses for different professional associations—AICPA, CalCPA, ASA, others... [Comment: I obviously narrate this answer.]*

10. Turning to this matter, were you retained by my offices to perform an analysis of the plaintiff's economic losses in this case?

    a. *Yes*

11. What specifically was your assignment?

    a. *To look at the historical earnings of Mr. White and his earnings after the auto accident, review the vocational rehabilitation report of Dr. Raymond Roberts, and estimate the economic losses experienced by Mr. White resulting from the accident.*

b. *I was also asked to look at the economic analysis prepared by Christopher Reynolds, the plaintiff's economist, regarding Mr. White's loss calculations.*

12. What documents did you review in preparation of your economic analysis?

   a. *I had Mr. White's W-2 forms from his employment from 2017 to 2020;*
   b. *The account of his use of sick and vacation time since the date of the injury;*
   c. *Social Security statement for Mr. White;*
   d. *A copy of his résumé;*
   e. *Dr. Raymond Roberts's vocational rehabilitation report;*
   f. *I had a number of depositions:*
      1. *Mr. White's deposition;*
      2. *Christopher Reynolds's deposition (and his entire file);*
      3. *Enrique Villareal—the plaintiff's vocational rehabilitation consultant;*
      4. *Raymond Roberts's deposition (defendant's vocational rehabilitation consultant);*
      5. *Dr. Angelo Minadeo's deposition (plaintiff's physician);*
   g. *Various other legal documents—responses to interrogatories, requests for admission, trial briefs…*
   h. *In summary, those are the documents I reviewed in preparation for today.*

13. You prepared financial schedules that summarize your analysis, correct?

   a. *Yes*

14. I am going to put up your conclusions schedule and ask you to explain it to us. [Lawyer puts up the exhibit.]

SUMMARY OF ECONOMIC LOSS

		Scenario 1 No Loss of WLE	Scenario 2 10% WLE Reduction
Past Period			
Loss of Earnings and Benefits	[C2.2]	$ 10,580	$ 10,580
Total Past Period		10,580	10,580
Future Period			
Loss of Earnings and Benefits	[B1.2]		213,923
Ergonomic Evaluation and Equipment	[B1.3]	7,554	7,554
Total Future Period		7,554	221,477
Total Economic Loss		**$ 18,134**	**$ 232,057**

15. You have two scenarios of losses here.... Would you explain the difference in the scenarios?

a. *The different scenarios are based on two alternative opinions given by Dr. Roberts, the vocational rehabilitation expert...*
b. *He gave the opinion that Mr. White would likely have either no loss of his work-life expectancy or a 10% loss of work-life expectancy.*
c. *Consequently, my two scenarios follow those two assumptions. Scenario 1 assumes no work-life loss and Scenario 2 assumes a 10% loss of the future amount of time Mr. White would likely work.*

16. It looks like both scenarios have the same Loss of Earnings and benefits in the past. Could you explain that??

    a. *Based on the summary of sick pay and vacation pay taken, Mr. White lost 200 hours of that time.*
    b. *I calculated his hourly rate at $41.80, based on his annual earnings divided by 2080 hours, and multiplied $41.80 times 200 hours.*
    c. *I also added FICA at 6.2% to that lost time, equaling $10,580 total past loss of earnings and benefits.*
    d. *And, the past losses are exactly the same in both scenarios.*

17. In both scenarios #1 and #2, I see you have the same number for "Ergonomic Evaluation and Equipment." Could you explain that amount?

    a. *Yes, those numbers are also the same in both scenarios …*
    b. *Dr. Reynolds has given the opinion that Mr. White may benefit from an ergonomic evaluation and $1,000–$1,500 in ergonomic equipment every three to five years over his remaining work-life.*
    c. *That opinion results in quantification of $7,554 in present-value dollars… the same in both scenarios.*

18. It appears that the one number that is different in the two scenarios is your future Loss of Earnings and Benefits. Would you explain that?

    a. *In order to calculate the future loss of earnings and benefits to Mr. White, I first estimated the present value of his life-*

time earnings, using a current estimate of his earnings as $118,449—same as Mr. Reynolds and Dr. Villareal.

b. *I added an estimate of benefits at 21.2%, based on the Bureau of Labor Statistics "Labor Costs for Employee Compensation" (FICA, Med Insurance, and Retirement)*
c. *I then projected the current earnings and benefits to Mr. White's statistical work-life expectancy (age 65.2)*
d. *I used an estimated growth rate on his future earnings of 2.3% (long-term future inflation estimates)*
e. *And I then discounted the future earnings projections to present value…*

19. Let me stop you there for a minute. That calculation gets you to his total lifetime earnings, not his economic loss, right?

    a. *That's right… that's the present value of his <u>total lifetime earnings</u>…*
    b. *I have to apply Dr. Roberts's estimate of the amount of his loss, which is 10% of those total earnings….*
    c. *That calculation results in the opinion of total loss of $213,923. That's my opinion of future lost earnings and benefits under the scenario that assumes he will have a 10% loss of work-life expectancy.*

20. So, please tell the jury your summary of your calculations of the losses for the two scenarios, Mr. Brinig.

    a. *Under Scenario #1, which assumes no loss of work-life, the total economic loss is $18,134, and….*

b. Under Scenario #2, which assumes a 10% loss of his work-life, my calculation of total economic loss is $232,057.

c. Those are my two alternative opinions of Mr. White's total economic loss as a result of the automobile accident that occurred on July 24, 2018.

21. Any other opinions you have reached in this matter, Mr. Brinig?

    a. No, sir. That's it.

22. Thank you for your testimony this morning.

[Comment: As you see, I am unsure if we should critique the other economist, so I completely defer the question to the attorney.]

23. [Do we want to critique Chris Reynolds (plaintiff's economist)? It's only the following things:

    1. He overstates his benefits by about 5% because he uses his specific retirement benefit from the Private University instead of a generalized retirement study—I say this is difficult to make a big point on… he is using ACTUAL instead of "theoretical"… the argument against him might backfire;

    2. He makes one of his calculations to age 67—Social Security retirement age… it's about 1.5 years longer than his statistical work-life estimate;

    3. He has half a year longer work-life expectancy than I use—not a big deal and difficult argument to say he's WRONG about it, although I think WLE should be calculated from date of injury, not the present.

CHAPTER 13

EXPERT WITNESS TESTIMONY: SURVIVING CROSS-EXAMINATION

THE BIG PICTURE

From the attorney's perspective, civil cases are generally won on direct exam, as opposed to cross-examination. If the expert witness and lawyer have done a good job with the analysis and a good presentation on direct examination, cross-examination will probably be fairly ineffective, but knowing the techniques for handling cross is always helpful. In short, the expert witness does not need to fear cross-examination if he or she has done a competent analysis and is aware of the opposing lawyer's tactics for cross. In the ideal case, the expert has a great substantive position with very few weaknesses, but unfortunately that isn't always the status of things. Sometimes the experienced expert witness must rely on technique to help finesse cross-examination.

The best preparation for cross-examination is performing a competent analysis and presenting it well on direct exam. Cross-examination intends to penetrate the weaknesses of an expert's analysis, but a thorough investigation by the expert will have considered any weaknesses and incorporated them into the workup of the case. A principal strategy of direct examination is to acknowledge and deflect weaknesses in the affirmative, rather than waiting to hear about them for the first time on cross-examination. Consequently, any flaws in the expert's analysis should have been presented to the trier of fact in the most positive light possible during direct examination, hopefully minimizing the effect of them on the expert's conclusion, as well as on cross-examination. When weaknesses are raised on cross, they can be responded to with, "Yes, I am aware of that fact and I have considered it in my analysis, as I stated on direct examination," or, "Yes, I am aware of that fact, but as I indicated, I didn't consider it critically important in light of x, y, and z."[78]

An expert witness's demeanor is always important, but particularly so on cross-examination. The witness is being challenged, and all eyes are on her in this critical moment. This is not the time to become defensive, hostile, or argumentative, no matter what challenges are made to the expert's credibility or analysis. The expert should always maintain a detached, non-adversarial manner on cross-examination. And the witness should be particularly sensitive to the natural tendency to change her personal attitude toward the cross-examining lawyer versus her treatment of the examining lawyer on direct. Different attitudes toward these two lawyers will telegraph an apparent bias to the listener in favor of one and opposed to the other. Treat these questioners similarly.

At first blush, it may appear that the areas of potential cross-examination of an expert are endless. In fact, cross-examination generally falls into one of the following five substantive areas:

78. I realize it isn't always this simple, but I am trying to share the best techniques possible to deal with cross-examination.

a. Lack of qualifications.
b. Superficial or incomplete analysis.
c. The analysis was based on erroneous facts.
d. The conclusions are incorrect (bad analysis and/or rationale).
e. The conclusions are inconsistent with other analyses or testimony previously given.

When potential cross-examination is boxed into these categories, it becomes much less intimidating and the witness's planned defense becomes more manageable. Each one of these areas can be defended against.

I will also discuss different styles of cross-examination because they can affect the witness's specific plan of defense to them as well as help the witness identify the spectrum of possible stylistic approaches.

a. The friendly "I-just-want-to-understand-what-you-did" approach.
b. The polite "We-agree-on-a-lot" approach.
c. The "Few-areas-of-disagreement" approach.
d. Direct confrontation pointing out errors in the witness's analysis. (This one is the most difficult to withstand, and it should be. Hopefully, you don't have much exposure here.)
e. Pointing out that the witness has relied on information from others (other experts, lawyers, etc.) and, if that information is wrong, so is the witness's conclusion. (This one is easy: the expert should concede what she relied on and, if it is wrong—hypothetically—the conclusion is hypothetically wrong also.)
f. The boisterous, argumentative lawyer who disagrees with everything the witness says.

Finally, I will review a spectrum of the types of questions cross-examining lawyers ask and cover recommended responses to deal with somewhat "trick" questions asked of expert witnesses. It is extremely helpful to be aware of the structure of these different types of questions so appropriate responses can be crafted. Some lawyers have standard questions; experts sometimes need standard answers.

SURVIVING CROSS-EXAMINATION

Raising expert testimony to an art form requires the witness to do or consider the strategies set forth in the following paragraphs.

Stylistically, don't ever argue. An expert witness shouldn't be in the business of arguing; you are searching for the truth. The more the cross-examining lawyer argues or elevates the emotional tension of the interaction, the calmer the witness should attempt to be. In terms of pure emotional connection, the observer (fact finder) is more attracted to a pleasant personality than an argumentative or obnoxious one. Regardless of the substance of the discussion, you want to be on the winning side of the personality contest.

Be confident in your analysis and conclusion. You have critically evaluated the problem presented to you, focusing on both the strengths and weaknesses of the underlying argument.[79] You haven't ignored the weaknesses, but you have weighed their importance

79. I use the term "argument" in the judicial sense, not in the adversarial sense. It is a coherent set of reasons or reasoning supporting a scientific or technical conclusion. An "argument" is a well-reasoned analysis that considers supporting, objective rationale at every decision point in the investigation.

and determined that competent rationale supports your ultimate opinion. You don't deny the existence of weaknesses (of course they always exist), but you have established that the strengths of the argument outweigh its weaknesses. The weaknesses that go against your conclusion are less important than the strengths that support your conclusion. In the final analysis, you are comfortable with your opinion and you believe it to be true. You have every reason to be confident in the reasonable certainty of your opinion. Make the personal effort to quietly exude that confidence.

If the cross-examining lawyer catches you on a point, give it to him. Don't try to defend an indefensible position. You will look stupid and you will undermine your credibility on the other positive elements of your analysis. If every little point went your way, you probably wouldn't be in litigation, so you shouldn't act like your position is 100% certain—it isn't. Also, if you're asked a question you don't know the answer to, say so. Don't ever try to fake it.

If you're asked to hypothetically change a calculation or opinion based on an alternative factual assumption, don't be a jerk about it. If the alternative assumption is a reasonable interpretation of the facts of the case, the witness should give a changed, hypothetical conclusion while politely noting something like "Mr. Smith [my client] disagrees with that underlying assumption." If the alternative factual assumption is unreasonable, the witness should politely note the apparent unreasonableness. In this case, the changed answer should be qualified in detail and the changed conclusion should be given, but not without stating "hypothetically" or "based on an assumption that I find to be unreasonable." For example:

Question: I want you to assume that the plaintiff was able to return to his previous employment at $52,000 per year as of the end of this trial.... Can you assume that?
Answer: Yes, I can assume that.
Question: Under that circumstance, what would your calculation of Mr. Smith's lost future income be?
Answer: Based on everything I have been advised of, Mr. Attorney, that assumption is not reasonable, but if I were to hypothetically assume Mr. Smith could fully offset his lost income by returning to work at his previous employment, that hypothetical fact would offset his loss of future earnings.

Take advantage of "open" questions. Good cross-examining attorneys know the difference between closed questions and open questions. Closed questions are leading questions that usually seek only "yes" or "no" answers. (Example: "You didn't visit the offices of the business, did you, Mr. Black?" Or, "It was after midnight when you visited the scene of the accident for the first time, wasn't it?") Open questions are not as restrictive to the witness; they allow for an explanatory answer. Good cross-examining lawyers will not usually ask open questions because they allow an adverse expert witness to explain her position. If the door is opened with an open-ended question, an experienced expert will drive a truck through the opening. Now, be very mindful of not doing that too often—driving a truck through the opening—because that makes you look argumentative and biased for your side of the case, but be ready to take advantage of the opportunity occasionally. Expert Witness #101 teaches us to know the difference between closed and open questions; Expert Witness #401 teaches us to use the opening occasionally, and discreetly.

Incorporate all weaknesses and deflect them on direct exam. Every weakness in an expert's substantive inquiry must be considered and incorporated into the analysis. "Real" weaknesses include the inability to investigate important information; inaccuracy of information provided to the expert; lack of confirming, external data; choice of one technical method of analysis to the exclusion of others; and a specific error in the expert's calculations or application of a technical step of analysis.

"Asserted" weaknesses are argumentative weaknesses that will be argued by the other side under any circumstances. Examples of asserted weaknesses are imprecision of the expert's conclusions (meaning they include estimates); dismissing comparable data used in a study (i.e., "It is not comparable enough"); statistical impurity in any outside study; other methods that could have been used and weren't; the analysis could have been more thorough; and the conclusion could have been different (even if only slightly different).

Before you take the witness stand at trial, consider the weaknesses in your expert analysis and prepare the best brief explanation of your evaluation of the weaknesses and the reasons you have overcome each of them in reaching your final opinion. As previously noted, you want to structure deflection of your weaknesses into your direct examination. Don't leave yourself in the position of articulating your response to a weakness for the first time on cross-examination. Practice your responses to yourself (or anyone who will listen) in advance.

Be mindful of the pace. The pace of cross-examination is an important tactic used by the examining lawyer, and the expert must be aware of the pitfall of succumbing to its dangers. A good lawyer creates a back-and-forth tempo of questions and answers, and the listener is drawn into the regularity of the pace. The lawyer will press the witness into a speedy timing of the exchange and then insert a very difficult question into the mix. All eyes are on the witness at this moment, and it is critical to not break the pace of the exchange. Using a tennis match analogy, when your opponent makes a great shot, be sure you quickly lob the ball back to him. In the courtroom, don't pause when all eyes are on you; be sure to fill the silence with a brief answer, even if it's a somewhat defensive one, like "I didn't fully understand the question, Mr. Jones. Could you explain what you mean by X and Y in the question?" You may only be filling the silence with a "lob" return instead of an "ace," but a lob is much better than silence with everyone staring at you. Don't let a silence happen. And the best defense to this potential problem is not to get pulled into the pace of the cross-examining lawyer. Pause after every question and collect yourself for a well-thought-out answer.

Controlling the pace of cross-examination reminds me of a football story from many years ago. Growing up in Erie, Pennsylvania, I was a fan of the Cleveland Browns, a great team of the 1960s. No one from those days can forget the great running back, Jim Brown, arguably one of the greatest who ever played the game. I once saw an interview of Brown after he retired (at the ripe old age of 29!) when he described his technique of always getting up very slowly and deliberately after every tackle; he almost looked lazy. He said that early in his career he realized that if he got up quickly and energetically after a good run, and slowly after a run where he was slammed hard, his opponents could see what condition he was in after each play. He didn't want to telegraph his physical condition to anyone to his disadvantage, so he learned to always get up slowly. Loose as this analogy is to withstanding cross-examination, I think the witness should maintain a slow, deliberate pace in answering the lawyer's challenging questions, always pausing for a few seconds to collect her thoughts before plunging into the answer. The witness always looks composed, thoughtful, and scholarly. Don't allow yourself to be rushed by a staccato litany of questions being thrown at you.

Be calm, cool, and collected. From the witness's perspective, the most effective cross-examination testimony is a gentle, scholarly argument; it is not a high school debate. The objective is to convince the listener (finder of fact) of the reasonableness of your position and the fact that you are aware of, and have considered, weaknesses in your position. No intelligent listener expects there to be no weaknesses in any position. It is foolish to respond to the presentation of any weakness defensively or argumentatively. Concede the obvious. Good lawyers know how to elicit facts that go in their client's direction, and they will bring them up on cross. You should expect some level of aggression toward you on the witness stand; it shouldn't be viewed as offensive, it's just part of the professional situation. You're just doing your job.

Don't overstate your opinion. Frequently, your client and his lawyer are asking you to make arguments for them, and you need to know the difference between arguments and facts. Don't let your own client bully you to overstate your opinion; it will come back to haunt you. If you overstate your opinion, it is fertile ground for effective cross-examination. And, sometimes a throw-away comment that a witness thinks will help her position can be devastating. Knowing the difference between an argumentative characterization and a supportable fact is critical.

Here's an example from a case I testified in recently. My client, a plastic bottle manufacturer, alleged that the defendant (a large soda company) breached a supply contract for the purchase of plastic bottles from its manufacturing plant. Consequently, the financial statements of my client were in issue because we needed to know the profitability of the manufacturing of certain types and sizes of bottles. So the financial statements were admitted as evidence in the litigation. As is often the case, at the end of a year, there are different annual financial statements serially prepared as a company closes its books and refines its accounting adjustments to arrive at the final, fully adjusted financial statements. Upon seeing some different financial statements at a particular year end, the opposing accounting expert witness stated: "They have two sets of books!" a rather disparaging comment with negative ramifications to the credibility of my client.

On this general point, it's important to remember that any comment an expert makes on the record in deposition will be taken as expert testimony, and it can be used against him. When an accounting expert says, "They have two sets of books," that's an expert opinion, subject to cross-examination. In short, that expert better know what he's talking about—and be sure it is accurate—when the statement is made.

So, the cross-examination at trial of the "two-sets-of-books" expert goes something like this. "Mr. Green, do you ***know*** if Company X has two sets of books, or are you just assuming that fact?" "Is it possible, Mr. Green, that the two financial statements you were looking at were just part of the normal evolutionary process of closing the books and adjusting the financial statements?" "Now, 'two sets of books' implies significant accounting irregularity, doesn't it?" "And, it is clearly improper for a company to be running two sets of books, isn't it?" "And, you have suggested this accounting impropriety without really knowing or investigating this fact, haven't you?" "Aren't you required under Generally Accepted Accounting Principles to thoroughly investigate an accounting issue before you render an opinion on it?" With these types of questions, the lawyer on my side of the case was able to clearly show that Mr. Green didn't have any basis to claim there were two sets of books, and the derogatory nature of the comment, without any support, showed him to be biased against my clients. The message here is that the expert gets in serious trouble if he gets argumentative and uses his argument to overstate his opinion. Initially, his client and his client's lawyer loved the sound of "two sets of books" being alleged against my client, but everyone soon learned that an argumentative comment without full support is an unwise overstatement for an expert to make.

Be wary of absolute terms. Just as you shouldn't overstate your opinion, you shouldn't use absolute or extreme adjectives to characterize your analysis or opinion. These terms are very easy to cross-examine and, once they are used, it is difficult for the witness to retract them. Rather than saying something is "absolutely obvious" or "very clear," it's better to say something like "after I considered fact x, y, and z, it appears reasonable to me to conclude that [state your opinion]." Without watering down your opinion excessively, be mindful of tempering your statements down from the absolute, knowing that someone will be coming after you to criticize everything and anything you say.

Be mindful of precision and lack of precision. In my earlier years of practice, I was focused on precision: the precision of answering questions exactly as they were phrased, and not varying my answers from the specific matter that was asked. Over the years, I evolved that practice to—and now I will overstate it—answering what I want to say, regardless of the question. (This applies on both direct- and cross-exam.) Oftentimes, your examining lawyer will not ask the perfect—or even correct—question, and your answer needs to steer him to the important information. Of course, a non-responsive answer is subject to an objection or even a motion to strike the answer, but most of the time an experienced expert can evolve an answer to cover more ground than the narrow area of the question posed.

Taking a swipe at the opposition. Here is a high-level subtle point for the art of expert witness testimony. If you're going to take a little extra dig at the other side or opposing expert witness, you do it at great risk, but you certainly don't want or need to do it at deposition because you just educate the other side that you're going to do it and you allow them to prepare to attack your (possibly) overstated/exaggerated position. If you feel the need to take that great risk, I would only take it at trial where you might be able to blow it by an average cross-examiner.

The opposing lawyer. Do some research on the lawyer who will cross-examine you. Is he or she an experienced, highly regarded trial lawyer, or just another middle-of-the-road alternative? Find out what to expect. Good attorneys should know how to cross-examine experts, but the reality is many of your attorneys don't get to court as often as you do. The experienced expert needs to be aware of the opposition's tactics and be prepared to defend against them. It is also helpful to know when the cross-examining attorney isn't performing as well as he or she should, because this can factor into the expert's assessment of the risk of pushing the envelope on answering some questions that allow for expansion beyond the narrow answer required. Sometimes the witness can score a few extra points if the lawyer leaves the door open.

Finally, the witness should remember that not all cross-examinations will be undertaken by good lawyers; sometimes the witness gets lucky and the opposing lawyer isn't very sharp. (This is the "average" lawyer that I frequently refer to.) The witness may get the opportunity to remain calm while the cross-examiner becomes emotionally charged or hostile, or the witness may have the opportunity to re-explain points of direct examination because the lawyer has asked poor, open questions. The experienced expert will be ready for either approach to cross-examination.

TACTICS FOR DEFENDING THE EXPERT OPINION

I suggest the expert be armed with defensive tactics and some standard answers, although it is wise to use them discreetly and sparingly. Some of these tactics are redundant to previous explanations, but here are my suggestions:

a. Maintain a calm, scholarly attitude toward the cross-examining lawyer.
b. Maintain respect, but defend your opinion.
c. "Mr. Attorney, the characterization of the facts in your question is simply inaccurate…"
d. "A one-word answer would be misleading. May I have the opportunity to explain?"

e. "I will be glad to answer your hypothetical, but it doesn't seem to conform to my understanding of the facts."
f. Don't be drawn into a staccato pace of cross-examination. Use pauses before each answer to help control the pace (even though you are only defensively in control of the exchange).
g. If a brilliant question is "shot across your bow," don't hesitate to reply with an immediate "lob," like, "Could you repeat that question, Mr. Jones," or "I didn't exactly understand that question, Mr. Jones." Give yourself time to think, without feeding a long silence—or even a short one—in front of the jury.
h. A tactful cross-examination will build up gradually, seeking agreement on small, obvious points leading up to a seemingly logical conclusion that goes against your position. Without being argumentative, try to avoid agreeing with all the underlying points of the buildup as they are presented, in anticipation of the seemingly logical closing question.
i. If you have the opportunity to explain or re-explain an answer, try to do it in a calm, organized narrative that lays out high points of your argument.
j. Use the aggressive answer very judiciously. You may get an opportunity to take a "swipe" at opposing counsel, but do it very cautiously, and infrequently.
k. Don't be afraid to give ground or agree with opposing counsel during cross-examination.
l. Any question that starts with "Isn't it possible…," the answer has to be "yes." But the question is: Is it reasonable? Or is it likely?
m. Don't agree with a denigrating characterization of your analysis. ("So, you just *picked* a number, then?" Or, "After you *glanced* at the medical record, you *guessed* that enough time was not allowed for the procedure?") In your answer, politely

disagree with the inaccurate characterization in the question, and do it before you give the (possible) affirmation or denial.

n. If you are asked to recalculate or re-examine some aspect of your testimony, don't feel the need to do it on the fly. If you require time to reconsider something, simply tell the court that you can't do this immediately (in front of everybody). Ask to take a break and agree to return with the new information.

TYPES OF QUESTIONS AND "STANDARD" RESPONSES

One of the best books I have found on the subject of cross-examination is *Expert Testimony: A Guide for Expert Witnesses and the Lawyers Who Examine Them,* by professors Steven Lubet and Elizabeth Boals. The book is published by the National Institute for Trial Advocacy, and it is an excellent resource for all aspects of expert witness testimony. The book includes a particularly good chapter on "How to Cope with Cross-Examination," and within that chapter, the authors have beautifully identified a series of "types of questions" that lawyers tend to ask on cross-examination, with some suggested answers for expert witnesses. Because of the brilliant categories and descriptions of the types of questions, I have taken the liberty, with permission from the authors, to paraphrase liberally from their treatise. I recommend the book to any serious student of expert witness work.[80] Some of the comments/suggestions are redundant of others stated earlier, but we experts can't hear this advice too many times.

80. Lubet, Steven, & Boals, Elizabeth I., *Expert Testimony: A Guide for Expert Witnesses and the Lawyers Who Examine Them, Fourth Edition* (2020) is available from the National Institute for Trial Advocacy, https://www.nita.org/s/product/expert-testimony-a-guide-for-expert-witnesses-and-the-lawyers-who-examine-them-fourth-edition/01t4W00000DALuCQAX.

RESPONDING TO CROSS: TYPES OF QUESTIONS AND SUGGESTED RESPONSES

1. **Use full sentences.** The attorney's objective is to maintain control of the witness's testimony, while the witness would like to teach and explain. The lawyer's tactic is to ask for short answers, "yes and no." One simple way for the witness to "create some space" in which she can expand her answers when necessary is to answer questions with complete sentences—beginning at the very start of cross-examination. "By doing this, the witness can begin to establish the right to give full answers throughout the examination.... Once the pattern is in place, it is much less likely the witness will have to fight to be able to explain."[81]
2. **"Yes" or "No."** Attorneys will try, but witnesses are under no obligation to answer questions "yes" or "no." The safest responses are either "I'm sorry, but the way you phrased that question makes it impossible to answer 'yes' or 'no.'" Or, "A one-word answer would be misleading. May I have the opportunity to explain?" These answers throw the burden of the misleading question back to the attorney to either clarify or insist that you give a "misleading" answer.
3. **Predicate Questions.** The question includes an implicit predicate, which may be an inaccurate or misleading fact. Answering the question without contradicting the predicate tends to be misleading. The witness should not accept the assumption. For example:

81. Lubet & Boals, *Ibid.*, p. 151–152.

Question: Mr. Appraiser, a profitable business similar to Ace Manufacturing Company would sell for three to four times net income, wouldn't it? *[The question implies Ace is profitable, which it is not.]*

Answer: I don't agree that Ace is profitable, but would you still like me to answer the question?
Or,

Answer: Your question assumes that Ace is profitable, which it is not, so the assumption is inaccurate.
Or,

Answer: When a small manufacturing company is profitable, which Ace is not, it would tend to sell for some multiple of its profitability in the market.

4. **Explanations first (the "yes, but" dilemma).** The cross-examiner's objective is to prevent the witness from explaining the answer. The "yes, but…" response is inherently weak and it will often be cut off by the examining attorney. If the one-word answer requires a qualification or an explanation, offer the explanation before the affirmation.
5. **The unexpected negative.** Unreasonable questions can come in all formats. They all confine the expert's ability to explain. Frequently, the questions will come in a series, seeming to require continued affirmations (or denials). When the unexplained answers are a series of affirmatives, everyone in the courtroom expects the next answer to be nothing more than another affirmation. (Again, be aware of the forced pace.) When the series of questions is stretched to require an unexplained answer to be misleading or incomplete, the witness should ask for the opportunity to explain

the answer, before the next affirmation of the question. If the lawyer refuses and requires a simple "yes" or "no," the witness should say something like "In that case, my answer is that you are wrong." If the expert does this, Lubet and Boals suggest that most lawyers will take the bait and invite the witness to explain.

6. **Loaded question, or "negative pregnant."** These are questions with a mischaracterization of facts in the predicate to the question. "After you glanced at the doctor's notes, you then concluded that Mr. Smith couldn't work as a laborer any longer, didn't you?" The characterization of "glancing at the notes" is inaccurate because the witness thoroughly reviewed the doctor's notes and did a number of other things before concluding that Mr. Smith could no longer work. If the question contains a negative pregnant premise, politely disagree with the premise. Don't accept the lawyer's (mis) characterization of a fact, even if it's a preface in a question.
7. **The completeness fallacy.**[82] The fallacy begins with a broad overgeneralization, seeking the witness's logical agreement to the statement. "Once given, the cross-examiner can exploit that agreement, pointing out that the witness's own work is not in 'complete' accord. For example:

   "**Question**: Dr. Lipton, will you agree that profit projections should always be based on a full analysis of every relevant factor?

   "The statement in the question seems straightforward. Unpacking it, however, we see that it contains several sweeping generaliza-

82. The completeness fallacy is taken directly from Lubet & Boals, *Ibid.*, p. 158. It is an excellent explanation and example.

tions: projections should *always* be based on a *full* analysis of *every* relevant factor. A witness who, without qualification, agrees with this statement will soon find herself attempting to defend even the slightest deviation from this unrealistic norm:

> "**Question**: Dr. Lipton, you have agreed that you should always perform a full analysis of every factor, right?
>
> "**Question**: In projecting lost profits, you did not do a market study of consumer preferences, right?
>
> "**Question**: You did not evaluate the state's recent application for federal highway funding, did you?

"And there will be more. A talented lawyer will be able to identify an unlimited number of ways in which the expert failed to perform a full analysis of every factor. It will not even be that difficult, since no one can always do everything. The witness will even have trouble claiming that certain steps were not necessary, since her initial answer acknowledged that one should always do everything.

"The witness's mistake was answering without qualification. Consider the alternative:

> "**Question**: Dr. Lipton, will you agree that profit projections should always be based on a full analysis of every relevant factor?
>
> "**Answer**: Profit projections should be based on reliable data and should take the most important and reasonable factors into account.

"The lawyer may press the point, rejecting the witness's qualifying explanation:

> "**Question**: But my question is, will you agree that profit projections should always be based on a full analysis of every relevant factor? Please answer 'yes' or 'no.'

"In which case the witness might need to engage the unexpected negative.

> "**Answer**: Given the way you have phrased the question, I will have to answer 'no.'

"The lawyer will now have to choose between asking for an explanation and accepting the witness's answer as given."

8. **The perfection fallacy.** A foundational question establishes a "perfect" way to do an analysis. "Ms. Green, you would agree that the best way to do a comparative market analysis is to view a large number of similar transactions, wouldn't you?" Then the lawyer will show you that you didn't do that. Similar to the completeness fallacy, be careful of agreeing to the initial, perfect definition, without qualification. In this case, the more appropriate response to the "perfect" question is something like: "The best way to do a market analysis is to review the available relevant market-data transactions that are comparable to the subject property." The expert can then fall back on the notion that she did that in the present analysis.
9. **Partial truths.**[83] This question is the opposite of the negative pregnant question. The two-part question contains a true predicate, but a false conclusion. For example:

83. Partial truths example taken directly from Lubet & Boals, *Ibid.*, p. 160.

> "**Question:** Mr. Green, isn't it true that you had to rely on a technique called 'sampling' to arrive at your analysis because the plaintiff's financial records were so poor, correct?

"In fact, sampling is a reliable tool, whether or not the underlying records have been perfectly kept. But note how poorly a 'yes, but…' answer will convey this information:

> "**Answer:** Yes, but we would have used sampling anyhow.

"The partial truth has become part of the witness's answer. Now consider an answer that avoids partial truth:

> "**Answer:** Sampling is a reliable accounting tool that we use in virtually every engagement.

"If the lawyer wants to proceed, the question will now have to be uncoupled:

> "**Question**: But in this case you used sampling because the records were so poor?
>
> "**Answer**: That is wrong. We used sampling because it could give us an accurate result.

"The best response to a 'partial truth' question is simply to state the whole truth, rather than agree with half of it."

10. **Fees.**

> "**Question**: Isn't it true you are being paid $500 an hour to come and testify today?"

Answer: I am being paid my normal hourly rate for the time I have spent working on this matter, which includes coming to court today.

11. **"Your lawyer asked you to perform this analysis...."**

Answer: Mr. Brown is not my lawyer; he and his client retained me to perform analysis in this matter.

ADVISING YOUR ATTORNEY ON CROSS-EXAMINATION

Dealing with your own client's lawyer can be challenging. The average lawyer (on your side) will occasionally strongly suggest that you not give any ground—even conceding the smallest point—but that advice needs to be taken with a grain of salt. As I have already pointed out, not conceding the obvious is foolish. It makes you look like an advocate and discredits your entire testimony. It is possible that there is a major point or two in your position that you must defend against all attack, but it is illogical to take that position for every fact or weakness that goes against your position. The simple reality is that there are some things that go against your position, and you should acknowledge them. It is simply disingenuous to intractably deny any weakness in your work.

Here are a handful of cross-examination rules that attorneys should be aware of. Unfortunately, sometimes the experienced expert has to help her lawyer through the process.

a. The overarching rule for successful cross-examination is to use only leading questions and keep them very short. ***Only a minority of lawyers do this!*** A simple, single-phrase closed question can require a "yes" or "no" answer. The best questions are statements of fact that are undeniable.[84] The lawyer is in complete control, leading the witness through a number of points that are detrimental to the expert's position and favorable to the cross-examining lawyer's. If the expert has a weak substantive position, the short questions can directly attack the core of the expert's analysis. For example:

Question: Professor Green, you used an income approach to value Ace Manufacturing Company, didn't you?

Answer: That's correct, yes.

Question: Based on the audited financial statements, the business reported net losses in four out of the last five years, isn't that correct?

Answer: Yes.

Question: You made numerous adjustments to the audited financial statements, correct?

Answer: Yes.

Question: After your adjustments, the adjusted financial statements show that Ace was profitable every year, correct?

Answer: Yes, that's correct.

Question: Without your adjustments, Ace showed a loss, as reported on the audited financial statements, isn't that true?

Answer: Yes, that's true, but the adjustments needed to be made.

84. Lubet & Boals, *Ibid.*, p. 113.

Question: Objection: Motion to strike everything in the last answer after "that's true."

Court: Sustained. Motion granted.

Question: Professor Green, will you please just focus on my questions?

Answer: Yes, I will.

Question: Ace's audited financial statements showed a loss every single year, didn't they?

Answer: Yes.

Question: In your testimony to the jury this morning, you did not use a market approach to determine the value of Ace, correct?

Answer: That's correct.

Question: Thank you. I have no more questions.

Here, the lawyer has correctly pointed out that the witness adjusted the financial statements from losses to profitability (although the witness wanted to explain why, but was not able to) and the witness did not use an important method of valuation in the appraisal analysis. That's all. No allowance for explanation or education by the witness. This is good, tight cross-examination.

On the other hand, if the expert has a strong, substantive position, the cross-examining lawyer can use the same technique to simply ruffle the expert around the edges, creating some doubt about the analysis in the minds of the listener. Obviously, this cross-examination is not as good, but the expert's position doesn't have glaring weaknesses to exploit. For example:

Question: Professor Green, you visited the business for one hour on June 7, 2019, correct?

Answer: I'm not sure of the time or date, Mr. Attorney.

Question: Let me show you your billing (showing the document, maybe with a bit of drama, like searching for the billing and asking the judge if the lawyer may approach the witness).

Question: This is your billing summary, isn't it?

Answer: Yes.

Question: There is a charge for one hour for a premises visit, do you see that?

Answer: Yes.

Question: And the premises visit charge is on June 7, 2019, correct?

Answer: Yes, that's correct.

Question: You didn't visit the business any other time, did you?

Answer: That's correct. I did not.

Question: Looking at the calendar here, June 7 was a Tuesday, wasn't it?

Answer: That's correct.

Question: You didn't visit the business on a Monday, the day when the business receives raw materials, did you?

Answer: No, I did not.

Question: So you didn't see that on Monday the employees in the receiving department worked overtime to accommodate the large amount of materials received, did you?

Answer: [The answer almost doesn't matter: the witness didn't go there on Monday so he doesn't have any direct observation of the business on a Monday. Is that really a weakness? Who knows? But the lawyer is making it look like a weakness. And a good cross-examiner won't let Mr. Green say he "didn't think he ***needed*** to go there on Monday," only that he "didn't go there" on Monday.]

b. A question with several phrases and/or adjectives will allow the witness to either disagree with the premise of the question or have to explain the answer. The best cross-examination question is an unambiguous closed question consisting of one phrase. There should not be a complicated premise to the question that the witness can politely disagree with, taking the thrust out of the question.
c. Don't ask a question that you don't know the answer to. It opens the door to getting beaten up by the witness and, strategically, cross-examination isn't a good place for that.
d. Don't argue with the witness.
e. Seek agreement on any parts of the witness's direct examination that are helpful to your client.
f. The competent cross-examiner does not want to look for information on cross-examination. He wants to tell his story.
g. The last thing the cross-examiner wants to hear is an actual answer—other than a "yes" or "no"—from an expert witness.
h. A failed cross-examination is one in which the witness was given the opportunity to explain.
i. A lawyer's cross-examination strategy depends on the substance of the expert's opinion and direct testimony. If the expert opinion is very solid, the cross-examination should simply seek to obtain agreement with the witness on the "agreeable" facts and approaches, rather than any disagree-

ments. For example, "You relied on the same medical reports as Dr. Thomas (the opposing expert) as the basis of your evaluation, didn't you?" "Both you and Dr. Thomas agree that the surgery on Mr. Smith was necessary, right?" "And, both you and Dr. Thomas agree that Dr. Anderson (defendant) was properly trained and qualified to perform the surgery, right?" The point is that there is a benefit to the cross-examining lawyer to seek agreement on uncontroverted facts with the opposing expert.

j. Alternatively, if the cross-examining lawyer truly disagrees with the analysis and conclusion of the expert witness, the lawyer should challenge the witness. A good lawyer will narrow the challenge to the true points of disagreement and not attack every aspect of the expert's involvement in the case. In other words, if the expert is qualified, the lawyer shouldn't challenge that fact. If the expert has applied appropriate methodology, there's no need for challenge unless the lawyer disagrees with the methodology. Perhaps the expert has assumed particular facts that are disputed; if so, the lawyer should challenge the assumption of the correctness of those facts. If the expert's opinion turns on fact A, the lawyer should ask a narrow hypothetical question that asks the expert to assume fact B. Perhaps the expert has omitted steps that the opposition believes should have been considered; consequently the lawyer should challenge those omissions. But, good cross-examination should focus on aspects of legitimate disagreement with the opposing expert and attack only the disagreements.

k. Any weaknesses (errors, questionable assumptions, questionable substantive theory) should be pointed out or inquired about in very narrow questions, such as:

> **Question**: Your calculations assume that the plaintiff's vehicle was traveling at 45 miles per hour, correct?
>
> **Question:** You are aware that there is some evidence that the plaintiff's vehicle was traveling at 70 mph, correct?
>
> **Question:** Your calculations do not include an assumption that the vehicle was traveling at 70 mph, correct?
>
> **Question:** If your calculations were based on the assumption that the plaintiff's vehicle was traveling at 70 mph, your opinions and conclusions would be different, wouldn't they?
>
> [Now, if the lawyer is any good, he/she can grind on the witness a little bit (not too much, though). This is the skill of cross-examination.]

REDIRECT EXAMINATION

Before I leave the subject of cross-examination, I want to raise the issue of redirect examination. This is really a point of discussion for the lawyer, but I have to approach it from the perspective of the expert witness. In my discussion here, I will use some broad generalizations that don't apply in every case, but I make these blanket statements to make the point about the problem of redirect examination.

Let me begin by saying, if redirect examination is necessary, it should absolutely be undertaken. If the witness was beaten up on cross-examination and some important points need to be clarified or explained, then a focused redirect examination is appropriate. Whether to proceed with redirect is always a matter of judgment, but there should be no hesitation by the lawyer to redirect a damaged witness.

But, here's my biased opinion as an expert who has testified in about 300 trials: I hate redirect examination. I have sustained more damage as a result of redirect examination than any other part of expert testimony. The simple reason for the problem of redirect examination is that it's followed by recross-examination. At the risk of overgeneralizing, let me share what frequently happens.

So, I have given my direct examination and I've made it through cross-examination. As happens in almost every case, there are a few weaknesses in my analysis and, hopefully, I have finessed those weaknesses on cross-examination. Candidly, if I'm lucky, I have even blown some of them past the cross-examining lawyer. He is a little nervous and he's thinking on his feet; we're dealing in my area of technical expertise, and I might get lucky and not get grilled on a point or two that I should be grilled on—and it might even be a significant point. I'm finished. It's time to walk out of the courtroom with my head held high, radiating the look of success.

Now, here's the problem. Many lawyers just don't know when to shut up. If they can get one more bite at the apple, they will usually take it, regardless of the necessity to do so. This is particularly true of the lawyer who doesn't get to trial very often, and because he is so excited to be there, he just can't keep his mouth shut. So, here's what happens at the end of my cross-examination. The judge looks at my lawyer inquisitively, saying, "Mr. Attorney…?" And my lawyer says, "Oh, just a couple of questions, Your Honor." Then he proceeds to ask one or two meaningless questions on redirect examination that don't really do anything in the grand scheme of things.

But this tactical mistake gives the opposing lawyer the chance to sit down for a minute and rethink the thing that I blew by him that he didn't catch on cross-examination the first time. And then, on recross, he proceeds to stand up and kick my ass on one or two points that I beat him on the first time around. Now a good lawyer will tell you—correctly—that recross-examination is limited to the issues that are raised on redirect examination. That is technically correct, but it rarely happens that way. In my experience, most judges will allow the floodgates to be opened on recross, allowing the cross-examining lawyer one more bite at the apple. And that's where I get killed.

What should the lawyer do in the situation where his expert has successfully gotten through cross-examination? If nothing of great significance occurred, the lawyer on the expert's side should just casually say, "Hmmm... no further questions, Your Honor." Or, "I don't have any questions, Your Honor." [Implying that there's nothing to talk about. The cross-examining lawyer didn't do anything to my guy. Let the lack of drama make the point that cross-examination was ineffective.]

In summary, the expert witness is not in charge of the proceeding, so this is really advice for the examining lawyer. But as the expert witness, I always admonish my lawyer to proceed very cautiously with redirect examination and only do it for a very good reason. If the expert witness is meaningfully damaged on cross-examination, then by all means redirect is appropriate. But don't do redirect examination just to make a couple of little points. There is too much exposure to the witness by giving a few minutes to the cross-examining lawyer to rethink his examination.

CONCLUSION

Cross-examination is probably the most feared aspect of the expert witness's role in litigation services engagements. Ironically, the best defense to this aspect of trial testimony is a thorough, competent analysis supporting the basis of the expert's opinion. If the expert's direct examination proceeds to adequately describe the underlying investigation and it also acknowledges any weaknesses that have been considered, the stage is set for minimal impact against the expert on cross-examination. Of course, awareness of the strategies and tactics to defend oneself on cross-examination increases the chance of overcoming this threatening litigation procedure.

CHAPTER 14

LEGAL PRIVILEGES RELATING TO EXPERT WITNESSES

Perhaps the most important point to note about the subject of legal privileges relating to expert witnesses is that, historically, virtually none applied. A significant exception to the general rule was adopted in 2010 with the amendment of FRCP Rule 26, allowing expert report drafts and communications between counsel and witnesses relating to those reports to be shielded from discovery. Other than that exception, once an individual is designated as an expert witness, everything that he or she considered, reviewed, discussed, or rejected in arriving at the expert opinion is discoverable by the opposing party to the litigation. Some lawyers and many experts either don't know this fact or forget it, and the results can be devastating to a client's position in a litigated matter. Under the pre-2010 common law, and in many states presently, it is critical to realize that anything that is said or transmitted to a designated expert is fully discoverable by the other side of the litigation, unless the matter is within federal jurisdiction or a state that follows the 2010 amendment to the Federal Rules.

About 35 states have adopted the Federal Rules of Civil Procedure in part, at least. It is critically important that the forensic consultant be familiar with the law of the jurisdiction in which he is operating because it controls the discoverability of the expert's file. California, the state where I have practiced my entire career, has not adopted the Federal Rules and I have always operated under the assumption that nothing in my file is protected from discovery. The safest practice, regardless of the location of the case you're involved in, is to follow careful rules of file documentation and operate as though all of your notes, drafts, communications, and preliminary analyses will be seen by the opposition. The message is: document your files carefully.

The remainder of this chapter is written following the common law, not the Federal Rules of Civil Procedure. And, in my experience, most small cases are venued in state courts, and your state may not follow the FRCP.

ATTORNEY WORK PRODUCT RULE

An attorney can hire a consultant to assist him or her in the preparation of a case, and the work product and knowledge of the consultant can be privileged under the attorney work product rule. The attorney work product rule is the legal doctrine that provides that materials prepared by an attorney in preparation for litigation are protected from discovery by the opposing side to the litigation. The rule has been extended to agents of the lawyer working at the lawyer's direction, although the privilege is not absolute. Generally, however, a lawyer can retain a consultant to assist in the preparation of a matter, and the work of the consultant is privileged from discovery.

The attorney work product rule has given rise to the term "consulting expert," meaning a consultant who performs services for the lawyer related to the litigation who will not be designated as an expert witness in the matter. The consultant's work is protected from discovery in the same way that the work of the lawyer's secretary or paralegal is protected. In many cases, an attorney will initially hire a technical professional as a consultant to investigate an issue relevant to the litigation. Frequently, the consultant will perform some initial research and/or investigation and report preliminary findings to the attorney. The attorney may then designate the consultant as an expert witness in the case. If that occurs, the trend of authority indicates there is no privilege shielding the consultant-turned-expert from discovery. Some lawyers would suggest there is a "line in the sand" that exists before the expert designation, but there seems to be no authority supporting that argument. In reality, there is no protection from the discovery of all of the designated expert's work in the case, both before and after the formal expert designation.

This problem is mitigated by the fact that a consulting expert who provides a "negative" opinion to an attorney early in a case will probably not be designated as an expert witness, so the concern about the consultant's discoverability is moot. The attorney is free to try to find another expert who evaluates the substantive issue more favorably to the client. And, unfortunately, attorneys generally believe they can find an expert to render just about any opinion their case needs. Even more unfortunately, there seems to be some truth to that belief.

THE EXCEPTION FOR DRAFT REPORTS AND PRETRIAL PREPARATION

In 2010, the Federal Rules of Civil Procedure were amended to protect certain communications between forensic experts and their attorney-clients, including the exchange of draft expert reports between these two parties. FRCP 26(b)(4)(B), *Trial Preparation Protection for Draft Reports or Disclosures*, states: "Rules 26(b)(3)(A) and (B) protect drafts of any report or disclosure required under Rule 26(a)(2), regardless of the form in which the draft is recorded." Rule 26(b)(4)(C) protects communications between "a Party's Attorney and Expert Witnesses." Specifically, the Rule states: "Rules 26(b)(3)(A) and (B) protect communications between the party's attorney and any witness required to provide a report under Rule 26(a)(2)(B), regardless of the form of the communications, except to the extent that the communications [relate to the expert's compensation; identify facts or data provided by the attorney and considered by the expert; identify assumptions provided by the attorney and relied on by the expert]."

"The 2010 amendments seem to provide complete protection for drafts regardless of to whom the expert provides a copy, including the attorney-client, ultimate client personnel, other experts, or other consultants; however, this interpretation of protection beyond the attorney-client is too liberal given further provisions about 'communications' in the revised Rules. In short, communications with other than the attorney-client are not protected: therefore, providing a draft report to someone other than the attorney-client as a 'communication' would not be protected from disclosure."[85]

As a practical matter, in matters governed by the Federal Rules of Civil Procedure, the expert and the attorney may exchange preliminary drafts of reports and share comments with each other without exposure to discovery of the communications by the opposition. If the attorney chooses to share the draft(s) with the client or another consultant, that can be beyond the expert's knowledge, and therefore shielded from discovery. Of course, none of this protection from discovery applies to state jurisdiction matters.

ATTORNEY-CLIENT PRIVILEGE

The attorney-client privilege is the privilege that protects certain communications between a client and his or her attorney and keeps those communications confidential. Although there are minor variations, the elements necessary to establish the privilege are: the asserted holder of the privilege is a client; the person to whom the communication is made is a member of the bar (or subordinate) and is acting as an attorney; and the communication was for the purpose of securing legal advice. There are a number of exceptions to the privilege; most noteworthy relating to expert witnesses is the exception that the communication was made in the presence of individuals who were neither the attorney nor the client. Although some lawyers and experts think the attor-

85. Rosenthal, R. Christopher, "The Expert Report," *Lost Profits Damages: Principles, Methods, and Applications*, Harry, E.P. and Kinrich, J.H. eds., Valuation Products and Services, LLC, Ventnor City, NJ, p. 705.

ney-client privilege insulates expert witnesses from discovery, that position does not seem to be supportable. The only privilege that has anything to do with the use of experts is the attorney work product rule, and it is only applicable if the expert is not designated as an expert witness to testify in the matter.

CONFIDENTIAL COMMUNICATIONS AND RELATIONSHIPS

Many professions have codes of conduct that include confidentiality of client communications and client information, but it is important to understand that confidentiality does not equate to a legal privilege. Within the context of forensic consulting, a communication is either legally privileged or it isn't. There is no such thing as "confidential."

One place where this issue presents itself is the subscript at the bottom of email communications. Most professionals' emails have some type of legend saying something like "the contents of this email communication are privileged and confidential and will not be disclosed…." The problem is that this representation is false, or at least misleading. It implies that a client can write something to the forensic consultant and it will be shielded from disclosure, and that is simply wrong. And, the unknowledgeable client could later say, "You told me it was confidential (or privileged), and it wasn't."

Practice Tip. Consider the following legend at the bottom of your email communications: "Written communications to Forensic Consultants Inc. are ***not privileged*** under the attorney-client priv-

> ilege or the attorney work product rule. All written communications to Forensic Consultants Inc. are subject to discovery by parties to litigation matters in which Forensic Consultants Inc. is designated as an expert witness."

CONCLUSION

As a practical matter, the forensic consultant should assume that no legal privileges apply to the research, analysis, writings or communications of a consultant who is designated as an expert witness in a litigation matter. Everything the consultant does is discoverable, except for draft reports and related communications in jurisdictions following the federal rules. Awareness of this fact will inform your internal practices for note-taking, file documentation, billing descriptions, internal communications, and external communications. You should expect that every scribble of writing will be shown to the other side and may end up as Exhibit 1 in the trial of the case.

CHAPTER 14 APPENDIX

FEDERAL RULES OF CIVIL PROCEDURE
RELEVANT PORTION OF FRCP 26 REGARDING EXPERT WITNESSES AND PRIVILEGES
(RULES IN EFFECT AS OF JULY 2022)

RULE 26. DUTY TO DISCLOSE; GENERAL PROVISIONS GOVERNING DISCOVERY

(a) Required Disclosures.

(1) *Initial Disclosure.*

(A) *In General.* Except as exempted by Rule 26(a)(1)(B) or as otherwise stipulated or ordered by the court, a party must, without awaiting a discovery request, provide to the other parties:

(i) the name and, if known, the address and telephone number of each individual likely to have discoverable information—along with the subjects of that information—that the disclosing party may use to support its claims or defenses, unless the use would be solely for impeachment;

(ii) a copy—or a description by category and location—of all documents, electronically stored information, and tangible things that the disclosing party has in its possession, custody, or control and may use to support its claims or defenses, unless the use would be solely for impeachment;

(iii) a computation of each category of damages claimed by the disclosing party—who must also make available for inspection and copying as under Rule 34 the documents or other evidentiary material, unless privileged or protected from disclosure, on which each computation is based, including materials bearing on the nature and extent of injuries suffered; and

(iv) for inspection and copying as under Rule 34, any insurance agreement under which an insurance business may be liable to satisfy all or part of a possible judgment in the action or to indemnify or reimburse for payments made to satisfy the judgment.

(B) *Proceedings Exempt from Initial Disclosure.* ...[omitted]...

(C) *Time for Initial Disclosures—In General.* ...[omitted]...

(D) *Time for Initial Disclosures—For Parties Served or Joined Later.* ...[omitted]...

(E) *Basis for Initial Disclosure; Unacceptable Excuses.* ...[omitted]...

(2) *Disclosure of Expert Testimony.*

(A) *In General.* In addition to the disclosures required by Rule 26(a)(1), a party must disclose to the other parties the identity of any witness it may use at trial to present evidence under Federal Rule of Evidence 702, 703, or 705.

(B) *Witnesses Who Must Provide a Written Report.* Unless otherwise stipulated or ordered by the court, this disclosure must be accompanied by a written report—prepared and signed by the witness—if the witness is one retained or specially employed to provide expert testimony in the case or one whose duties as the party's employee regularly involve giving expert testimony. The report must contain:

(i) a complete statement of all opinions the witness will express and the basis and reasons for them;
(ii) the facts or data considered by the witness in forming them;
(iii) any exhibits that will be used to summarize or support them;
(iv) the witness's qualifications, including a list of all publications authored in the previous 10 years;
(v) a list of all other cases in which, during the previous 4 years, the witness testified as an expert at trial or by deposition; and
(vi) a statement of the compensation to be paid for the study and testimony in the case.

(C) *Witnesses Who Do Not Provide a Written Report*... [omitted]...

(D) *Time to Disclose Expert Testimony.* ...[omitted]...

(E) *Supplementing the Disclosure.* ...[omitted]...

(3) *Pretrial Disclosures.*

(A) *In General.* ...[omitted]...

(B) *Time for Pretrial Disclosures; Objections*...[omitted]....

(4) *Form of Disclosures.* ...[omitted]...

(b) DISCOVERY SCOPE AND LIMITS.

(1) *Scope in General.* Unless otherwise limited by court order, the scope of discovery is as follows: Parties may obtain discovery regarding any nonprivileged matter that is relevant to any party's claim or defense and proportional to the needs of the case, considering the importance of the issues at stake in the action, the amount in controversy, the parties' relative access to relevant information, the parties' resources, the importance of

the discovery in resolving the issues, and whether the burden or expense of the proposed discovery outweighs its likely benefit. Information within this scope of discovery need not be admissible in evidence to be discoverable.

(2) *Limitations on Frequency and Extent.*

(A) *When Permitted.* ...[omitted]...

(B) *Specific Limitations on Electronically Stored Information.* ...[omitted]...

(C) *When Required.* ...[omitted]...

(3) *Trial Preparation: Materials.*

(A) *Documents and Tangible Things.* Ordinarily, a party may not discover documents and tangible things that are prepared in anticipation of litigation or for trial by or for another party or its representative (including the other party's attorney, consultant, surety, indemnitor, insurer, or agent). But, subject to Rule 26(b)(4), those materials may be discovered if:

(i) they are otherwise discoverable under Rule 26(b)(1); and

(ii) the party shows that it has substantial need for the materials to prepare its case and cannot, without undue hardship, obtain their substantial equivalent by other means.

(B) *Protection Against Disclosure.* If the court orders discovery of those materials, it must protect against disclosure of the mental impressions, conclusions, opinions, or legal theories of a party's attorney or other representative concerning the litigation.

(C) *Previous Statement.* Any party or other person may, on request and without the required showing, obtain the person's own previous statement about the action or its subject matter. If the request is refused, the person may move for a court order, and Rule 37(a)(5) applies to the award of expenses. A previous statement is either:

(i) a written statement that the person has signed or otherwise adopted or approved; or

(ii) a contemporaneous stenographic, mechanical, electrical, or other recording—or a transcription of it—that recites substantially verbatim the person's oral statement.

(4) *Trial Preparation: Experts.*

(A) *Deposition of an Expert Who May Testify.* A party may depose any person who has been identified as an expert whose opinions may be presented at trial. If Rule 26(a)(2)(B) requires a report from the expert, the deposition may be conducted only after the report is provided.

(B) *Trial-Preparation Protection for Draft Reports or Disclosures.* Rules 26(b)(3)(A) and (B) protect drafts of any report or disclosure required under Rule 26(a)(2), regardless of the form in which the draft is recorded.

(C) *Trial-Preparation Protection for Communications Between a Party's Attorney and Expert Witnesses.* Rules 26(b)(3)(A) and (B) protect communications between the party's attorney and any witness required to provide a report under Rule 26(a)(2)(B), regardless of the form of the communications, except to the extent that the communications:

(i) relate to compensation for the expert's study or testimony;

(ii) identify facts or data that the party's attorney provided and that the expert considered in forming the opinions to be expressed; or

(iii) identify assumptions that the party's attorney provided and that the expert relied on in forming the opinions to be expressed.

(D) *Expert Employed Only for Trial Preparation.* Ordinarily, a party may not, by interrogatories or deposition, discover facts known or opinions held by an expert who has been retained or specially employed by another party in anticipation of litigation or to prepare for trial and who is not expected to be called as a witness at trial. But a party may do so only:

(i) as provided in Rule 35(b); or

(ii) on showing exceptional circumstances under which it is impracticable for the party to obtain facts or opinions on the same subject by other means.

(E) *Payment.* Unless manifest injustice would result, the court must require that the party seeking discovery:

(i) pay the expert a reasonable fee for time spent in responding to discovery under Rule 26(b)(4)(A) or (D); and

(ii) for discovery under (D), also pay the other party a fair portion of the fees and expenses it reasonably incurred in obtaining the expert's facts and opinions.

(5) *Claiming Privilege or Protecting Trial-Preparation Materials.*

...[omitted]...

(B) *Information Produced.* If information produced in discovery is subject to a claim of privilege or of protection as trial-preparation material, the party making the claim may notify any party that received the information of the claim and the basis for it. After being notified, a party must promptly return, sequester, or destroy the specified information and any copies it has; must not use or disclose the information until the claim is resolved; must take reasonable steps to retrieve the information if the party disclosed it before being notified; and may promptly present the information to the court under seal for a determination of the claim. The producing party must preserve the information until the claim is resolved.

(C) PROTECTIVE ORDERS… [OMITTED]….

(D) TIMING AND SEQUENCE OF DISCOVERY… [OMITTED]….

(E) SUPPLEMENTING DISCLOSURES AND RESPONSES… [OMITTED]….

(F) CONFERENCE OF THE PARTIES; PLANNING FOR DISCOVERY… [OMITTED]….

(G) SIGNING DISCLOSURES AND DISCOVERY REQUESTS, RESPONSES, AND OBJECTIVES…[OMITTED]….

CHAPTER 15

WRITTEN REPORT OF EXPERT TESTIMONY

I specifically call this chapter "Written Report of Expert Testimony" because that's exactly what a written report is. It is a document that may be used in the courtroom in place of expert testimony, and the forensic consultant should be aware of its importance in that regard. In fact, the 1993 Notes from the Advisory Committee on Rule 26 of the Federal Rules of Civil Procedure elaborate on the expert report's requirements:

> The report, which is intended to set forth the substance of the direct examination, should be written in a manner that reflects the testimony to be given by the witness, and it must be signed by the witness. The report is to disclose the data and other information considered by the expert and any exhibits of charts that summarize or support the expert's opinions.[86]

Most discussions of report writing focus on the requirements for inclusion in a proper expert report, often based on the requirements of FRCP 26. There may be additional requirements for expert reports based on state law as well as requirements for inclusion in professional reports in various disciplines. For instance,

86. Advisory Committee Notes, 146 F.R.D. at 634.

the Uniform Standards of Professional Appraisal Practice contain reporting requirements for appraisals, and the American Institute of Certified Public Accountants has reporting requirements for accounting reports. Your profession and/or the professional organizations to which you belong may have reporting requirements that experts should be mindful of, because lawyers will obtain lists of those requirements and cross-examine experts to make sure all the rules have been followed. Meeting the legal requirements for report writing is essential because the expert report will not pass initial muster if those requirements have not been met. If the expert's profession requires other inclusions in reports, the omission of those items will give rise to the argument that the expert is not in compliance with professional standards governing his work.

The Federal Rules of Civil Procedure mandate the following requirements for written reports of expert testimony. FRCP 26(a)(2)(B) requires:

(i) a complete statement of all opinions the witness will express and the basis and reasons for them;
(ii) the facts or data considered by the witness in forming them;
(iii) any exhibits that will be used to summarize or support them;
(iv) the witness's qualifications, including a list of all publications authored in the previous 10 years;
(v) a list of all other cases in which, during the previous 4 years, the witness testified as an expert at trial or by deposition;[87] and
(vi) a statement of the compensation to be paid for the study and testimony in the case.

---

87. See comment in Chapter 10, page 163, about what is required under this provision, and what is not required.

These requirements must be met at a minimum for the report to be acceptable as the underlying basis allowing the witness to provide an expert opinion.

A written report is not simply a document that has to include the routine list of items set forth in FRCP 26(a)(2)(B); it is a writing that requires the expert to consider the intellectual basis of her analysis. The beauty of a written report—as it's being developed, before it is finalized—is that it compels the thinking process of the expert's substantive analysis. Forcing the logic of your substantive analysis into sentences and paragraphs obliges you to think through the application of the reliable principles and methods you have applied in deriving your conclusion.

This general discussion of report writing can't enumerate the steps of rationale that must be undertaken in different technical areas of expertise; that principled reasoning falls within each substantive area. But the discussion can emphasize the intellectual rigor of the process of reducing a scientific or technical analysis to a cogent written summary.

A written report demands that the consultant lay out the facts, assumptions, rationale and conclusions of the points of the analysis in a way that can be followed by an objective, rational reader (or thinker). The report's development is somewhat circular in that the very writing of it makes the writer think through the rationale of the analysis. In the same way that a lawyer's trial brief sets up the issues and arguments for the court, the expert's written report lays out convincing logic for each step of the expert's analysis and conclusion. The mere process of writing introductory sentences to paragraphs sets up the organization of the paragraphs (steps of the analysis). A paragraph's concluding sentence summarizes the four or five steps that the paragraph explains. The written explanation of the expert's work expresses the logic (or lack of logic) of the analysis.

In my opinion, there is something more important about creating a written report than meeting the detailed requirements for inclusion under the federal rules or other professions' mandates for reports. If the logic of the expert's analysis doesn't make sense, that fact will show up in the writing of it. So the very process of reducing the analysis to written form supports the intellectual rigor needed to successfully meet the requirements of FRE 702, those being that "the expert has reliably applied the principles and methods [of the substantive field] to the facts of the case."[88] Report writing logically follows the steps of logic explained in Chapter 9, Developing the Expert Opinion.

The benefit of the written report to the fact finder is that it explains what the expert did, what the expert relied on, what was assumed, and why it was done this way, and it sets forth the expert's conclusion. And, to be effective, the report has to be well-written and "read" well. The detriment to the forensic consultant is that the report can be used as a map to cross-examination. A poorly written report—even if it's attempting to explain a good analysis—will be used as a sword against the expert. You have to think both argumentatively and defensively in preparing the report because often the reader is looking for anything in the report that can be used as an argument against the expert.

Two important considerations in writing a report are that (1) the writing of a poorly-thought-out opinion will expose the expert to a strong cross-examination (and it should!), and (2) a poor

88. Federal Rule of Evidence 702.

choice of wording (absolute terms, overstated conclusions, dogmatic conclusions) are fertile ground for easy cross-examination.

Examples of good choices of wording are statements like:

a. "based on this analysis, it is reasonable to conclude that..."
b. "a review of the facts indicates that..."
c. "it appears that..."
d. "it is logical to conclude that..."

Examples of poor choices of wording are:

a. Conclusive or absolute statements, like:
   1. "the plaintiff will find work as a machinist within six months of the date of trial..."
   2. "There is no way that Ms. Jones can recover from the emotional devastation caused by the defendant's actions."
   3. "I conclude that the plaintiff will obtain employment in fields similar to _____, ____ and _____ within four to twelve months after he begins a diligent employment search."

Over the years, I've heard commentators talking about the Supreme Court's deliberations on important issues and discussing how justices have changed their minds because the opinion "won't write." The reality is that if the analysis and conclusion don't make sense, you can't convincingly write them. In the past, I have certainly found myself in that situation, trying to explain my analysis in writing, and concluding that parts of it don't make as much sense as I thought they did, and learning that fact when I tried to explain the analysis in writing. In those situations, I have often changed my analysis in response to trying to write the report.

Report writing may be viewed as a necessary evil of forensic consulting, but it more importantly is a reconciling of the intellectual thinking process that is the foundation of the expert's final opinion. If you have developed a well-thought-out opinion that you believe in, you should have no concerns about writing a report that lays out the rationale for your conclusion. If the underlying rationale for your opinion is faulty, however, you should be reluctant to put it in writing, or you will have difficulty putting it in writing.

So, I believe the primary benefit of writing a report is confirming the well-reasoned rationale that supports the expert's opinions and conclusions. The secondary reason is to conform to the requirements of FRCP 26(a)(2)(B), which mandates the inclusion of six categories of information, the most significant of which is including "a complete statement of all opinions the witness will express and the basis and reasons for them."[89] The benefit of the written report is to present the logic and rationale that the expert has considered when understanding and interpreting the facts, adopting assumptions that are reasonable in the analysis, applying reasonable scientific or technical procedures to the facts and assumptions, and deriving a logically based conclusion.

Finally, don't forget the lack of privilege in your report-drafting procedures. Even if you are working within the Federal Rules of Civil Procedure (and most jurisdictions do not follow them with respect to expert reports), the earlier iterations of an expert report are not protected from discovery, only the copies exchanged between the expert and the attorney-client (under the FRCP). In non-litigation practice, many professionals follow a drafting procedure of saving Version 1, Version 2, Version 3, etc.,

89. FRCP 26(a)(2)(B)(i).

of an evolving document. A non-privileged forensic expert will be required to produce these superseded documents if they exist in the expert's computer network. The sophisticated forensic consultant will overwrite or delete these earlier drafts as they evolve, without maintaining earlier versions. The existence of these earlier versions is fertile ground for a distorted cross-examination of the expert's evolving, preliminary thinking process. Their existence is not helpful to the forensic expert. Have a formal practice of iterating over earlier versions as they are superseded.

CHAPTER 15 APPENDIX

FEDERAL RULES OF CIVIL PROCEDURE (PARTIAL INCLUSION) RELEVANT PORTION OF FRCP 26 REGARDING WRITTEN REPORTS (IN EFFECT AS OF JULY 2022)

DUTY TO DISCLOSE; GENERAL PROVISIONS GOVERNING DISCOVERY

(a) Required Disclosures.

(1) *Initial Disclosure..........*

(2) *Disclosure of Expert Testimony.*

(A) *In General.* In addition to the disclosures required by Rule 26(a)(1), a party must disclose to the other parties the identity of any witness it may use at trial to present evidence under Federal Rule of Evidence 702, 703, or 705.

(B) Witnesses Who Must Provide a Written Report. Unless otherwise stipulated or ordered by the court, this disclosure must be accompanied by a written report—prepared and signed by the witness—if the witness is one retained or specially employed to provide expert testimony in the case or one whose duties as the party's employee regularly involve giving expert testimony. The report must contain:

(i) a complete statement of all opinions the witness will express and the basis and reasons for them;

(ii) the facts or data considered by the witness in forming them;

(iii) any exhibits that will be used to summarize or support them;

(iv) the witness's qualifications, including a list of all publications authored in the previous 10 years;

(v) a list of all other cases in which, during the previous 4 years, the witness testified as an expert at trial or by deposition; and

(vi) a statement of the compensation to be paid for the study and testimony in the case.

(C) *Witnesses Who Do Not Provide a Written Report.* Unless otherwise stipulated or ordered by the court, if the witness is not required to provide a written report, this disclosure must state:

(i) the subject matter on which the witness is expected to present evidence under Federal Rule of Evidence 702, 703, or 705; and

(ii) a summary of the facts and opinions to which the witness is expected to testify.

(D) *Time to Disclose Expert Testimony.* A party must make these disclosures at the times and in the sequence that the court orders. Absent a stipulation or a court order, the disclosures must be made:

(i) at least 90 days before the date set for trial or for the case to be ready for trial; or

(ii) if the evidence is intended solely to contradict or rebut evidence on the same subject matter identified by another party under Rule 26(a)(2)(B) or (C), within 30 days after the other party's disclosure.

(E) *Supplementing the Disclosure.* The parties must supplement these disclosures when required under Rule 26(e)....

CHAPTER 16

ENGAGEMENT LETTERS

This chapter discusses the contractual agreement between the forensic consultant and the client(s). I try to identify issues that should be considered when preparing a litigation services engagement letter, but this chapter does not offer legal advice to the reader. The practice tips in this chapter cannot be relied on as conclusive contractual provisions for your engagement letters. You should consult legal counsel in your jurisdiction to develop a legally enforceable contract.

The engagement letter is the contract memorializing your retention by either the lawyer or the client in the present matter. It has two consequences that the retained expert should be mindful of, one intended and the other unintended. First, it is a contract that establishes the duties and responsibilities of each party to the agreement and, second and unfortunately, it will also serve as a road map to the expert's cross-examination in both deposition and trial. Both of these purposes must be considered when drafting an artful expert witness engagement letter.

Sound principles of contract law would dictate that the engagement letter contract should be specific as to its terms. Many professions' standards recommend or require the professional to reach an understanding with clients concerning engagements and communicate this understanding orally or in writing. However, there is no legal requirement for written engagement letters in litigation services assignments, but common sense dictates their usage.

The discoverability of the engagement letter in litigation matters requires a different spin on the tight application of contract principles to the document. Discoverability by the opposition means the engagement letter can be used as a guide to the intricacies of the analysis conducted by the forensic consultant as well as the details of the business relationship between the parties. Consequently, you should sacrifice a detailed description of the anticipated services in favor of a more general description of the steps of the analysis expected to be undertaken in the assignment. This issue will be more completely addressed in this chapter.

ADDRESSEE OF THE ENGAGEMENT LETTER AND LIMITATION OF THE ENGAGEMENT

Who is the forensic consultant's client in a litigation services matter? Is it the lawyer, the lawyer's client, or both? And, in most cases, does it really matter who the client is?[90] And, is there a good reason to limit the letter to one, the other, or both? Some attorneys believe that addressing the engagement letter to the attorney may provide some privilege or confidentiality to the communication, although the clear trend is to the contrary. The test of privilege is based on expert designation, not the addressee of the engagement contract.[91] Nevertheless,

90. Many would suggest that the precise definition of the client is always important, but I have never found it to be that significant. In many depositions, I have easily identified either the lawyer or ultimate client or both as "the client" without any adverse ramifications.
91. See Chapter 14. Throughout this treatise, I have explained that virtually no legal priv-

the forensic consultant should deal with the question of the addressee with the attorney.

At the very least, the lawyer is the agent of the client and, even if the lawyer retains the expert, the ultimate client is the principal in the relationship. It is logical to conclude that the forensic consultant has responsibilities to both, regardless of the precise identification of the "client" in the engagement letter.

There does seem to be one instance when the lawyer should be formally identified as the client, however. In the case where the forensic is only being retained as a consultant and not as a designated expert witness, the attorney work product privilege clearly applies to the services rendered by the consultant to the lawyer. In that situation, it makes sense to have the lawyer be the identified client. The lawyer owns the work product privilege, and it is probably cleaner if the lawyer has the direct relationship in retaining the forensic consultant, rather than retention by the ultimate client.

In situations in which the expert will be a designated expert witness, I have adopted the practice of addressing my engagement letter directly to the client's lawyer and identifying the retention agreement to him or her "as to the assignment." Because I (almost) never expect the lawyer to be responsible for my professional fees, I make it clear in the engagement letter that the lawyer is not responsible for my fees as follows: "It is clearly understood that my professional fees are the responsibility of your client, John Doe, and not the responsibility of your law firm." I ask both the lawyer and the ultimate client to

ileges apply to communications between anyone and a designated expert witness who proceeds to the deposition stage of a case, so the addressee (lawyer or ultimate client) of the engagement letter is likely irrelevant to the question of privilege. The possible exception to this statement is a (nontestifying) consulting expert's engagement letter addressed to the retaining lawyer, as opposed to the ultimate client.

execute a copy of the engagement letter, the lawyer "as to the assignment" and the client "as to the fee agreement."

My rationale for having the lawyer be the retaining party "as to the assignment" is my general belief that the lawyer is the more sophisticated person to understand the subtleties of my expert witness services, as opposed to the client's understanding of them. I don't like to think negatively about any client relationship, but my feeling is if the relationship sours later on, there is a better meeting of the minds between the lawyer and me as to the services I performed rather than the ultimate client's understanding of those services. I believe the potential alignment between the two professionals is stronger than the alignment between the ultimate client and the forensic consultant. I don't suggest that this is a foolproof strategy, but if any of the parties in the client relationship ever become adverse to each other, I think it is more likely that the ultimate client would be the more adverse party, as opposed to the client's lawyer.

The engagement letter should initially reference the case name and case number so the present assignment is clearly related to the pending litigation matter, and not a general consulting agreement for professional services unrelated to the litigation matter.

Practice Tip. Sample engagement letter heading and salutation:

John L. Lawyer, Esq.
Ace Lawyers, LLP
123 Broadway, Suite 400
Phoenix, AZ 85002
Re: Brown v. Greene, et al.
Case No.: L3279841 – CV – 2020
Arizona Superior Court

Dear Mr. Lawyer:...

The introductory paragraph(s) of the engagement letter should identify the letter as an agreement for consulting services related to the litigation matter in question. It may be addressed to the lawyer, the ultimate client, or both. If considered important, the initial paragraph may precisely identify the "client" in the relationship.

Practice Tips. Sample engagement letter introductory paragraphs:

> ***To lawyer:*** "This letter is the written agreement by which you are retaining Forensic Consultants Inc. as [*financial, appraisal, engineering, vocational rehabilitation, medical, life care plan, construction, etc.*] consultants in connection with the above-referenced litigation. It is my understanding that you represent the {plaintiff/defendant}, [*Client*]."
>
> ***To lawyer:*** "This letter confirms our [*recent telephone conversation?*] in which we have been retained to furnish [*substantive area*] consulting services for your client, [*Client*], in connection with the course of [*case name*], Case Number _____."
>
> ***To lawyer with report:*** "This letter confirms our [*recent telephone conversation?*] in which we have been retained to furnish [substantive area] consulting services for your client, [*Client*], in connection with the course of [*case name*], Case Number _____. Our written report will be submitted to you in draft form upon the completion of our assignment. **OR)** We will report to you orally prior to preparing a written report, if one is required."
>
> ***To client:*** "This letter is the written agreement by which you are retaining Forensic Consultants Inc. as [*financial, appraisal, engineering, vocational rehabilitation, medical, life care, construction, etc.*] consultants in connection with the above-referenced litigation. It is my understanding that you are the Plaintiff in the matter and you are represented by [*Lawyer*]."

> ***Detailed introduction:*** "This Consulting Fee Agreement ("Agreement") will serve to confirm our agreement whereby [*Client name*] ("you" or "your") have engaged Forensic Consultants Inc. ("FCI," "we," "our," or "us") as [*substantive area*] consultants in connection with the above-referenced matter."

The engagement letter should include a sentence (somewhere) that restricts the use of the consultant's work to the present matter. The consultant would like to limit the use of his or her work as much as possible, and the engagement letter is the place to start. A restriction of use in any written reports is also recommended. Following is a provision that should be considered:

Practice Tip. Sample restriction of work:

> "Our work in this matter (including any reports that we might prepare) is to be used only for the purpose of this litigation and may not be published or used for any other purpose without our prior written consent."

SCOPE OF SERVICES

At the outset of a forensic consulting assignment, the detailed steps are often both unknown and unknowable. Neither the consultant nor the lawyer knows the twists and turns that the case may take over the months leading to trial in the matter. Facts change, strategies change, causes of action emerge and disappear; there is no way to anticipate these changes at the outset, and there is no good reason to articulate the anticipated detailed steps in the first inning of the engagement that the lawyer and the forensic think they might be undertaking later on.

In addition to the uncertainty of the stages of the assignment, given the discoverability of the engagement letter, it is simply unwise to detail the anticipated steps of the project. There is downside risk later on from disclosing steps that were preliminarily thought to be needed, but subsequently abandoned for any one of a number of reasons. Why should your engagement letter list these preliminary, somewhat unfounded steps, only to be raised in cross-examination in deposition or trial months down the road? "Why didn't you do X that you said you were planning to do in the engagement letter?" It seems that the balance of the considerations weighs in favor of a generalized scope of services, broad enough to cover all expected areas of the expert's possible testimony. If substantial details are included in the scope paragraph, the details will almost invariably be wrong and a list of the details will be fodder for strong cross-examination.

Practice Tip. Consider the following scope of services paragraphs:

> ***Economic services engagement:*** "The scope of our services is not completely determined as of the date of this writing. In general, our services will relate to an analysis of the possible economic losses that the [*plaintiff/defendant*] may have experienced in connection with [*the general claim in the matter*]."
>
> ***Other substantive engagement:*** "As of the date of this writing, the scope of our services has not been completely determined. In general, our services will relate to [*financial and economic aspects; construction defect aspects; engineering design aspects; medical evaluation aspects; vocational rehabilitation aspects; etc.*] of the case."

> ***Vocational rehabilitation engagement:*** "As of the date of this writing, the scope of our services has not been completely determined. In general, our services will relate to an evaluation of potential employment opportunities for [*plaintiff/defendant*] at the present time."

> ***Medical expert engagement:*** "The scope of our services includes a review of the medical records of Plaintiff John Doe to determine the level of care provided to Mr. Doe."

> ***Appraisal engagement:*** "Our services will relate to an evaluation of the fair market value of the residence at 234 Oak Street, Phoenix, Arizona, at December 31, 2020."

> ***General statement:*** "We will assist you with analysis and consultation regarding the ABC litigation matter as you may direct."

> ***General statement:*** "We are available to assist you with your representation of [*plaintiff/defendant*] in the matter of the ABC litigation. We will consult with you regularly as to the specifics of the services you wish us to perform."

Practice Tip. Using the same examples from the previous practice tip, the following would ***not*** be advisable statements of the scope of services in an engagement letter:

> ***Economic services engagement:*** "The scope of our services will include the determination of Mr. Doe's lost earnings and benefits from the date of his injury until his anticipated work life expectancy and his lost household services from the date of injury to his anticipated life expectancy. Future losses will be discounted to present value according to present value tables in the Arizona Jury instructions."

> ***Other substantive engagement:*** "The scope of our services will include a detailed analysis of the construction defects

experienced on the project at 1220 State Street, Phoenix, Arizona, including, but not limited to roof leakage, improper sub-flooring preparation, __________, and _________. We will also include an analysis of lost rents and profits during the anticipated period of repair from January 15, 2022, to November 15, 2022."

Vocational rehabilitation engagement: "The scope of our services will include an evaluation of potential employment opportunities for [*plaintiff/defendant*] based on our review of the medical reports of Drs. Jones and Smith as well as our research related to the employment market in the greater Phoenix area in the third quarter of 2021, the anticipated date of trial in this matter."

Medical expert engagement: "The scope of our services will be a review of the medical records of John Doe, specifically the records from Dr. Jones and St. Vincent's Hospital with a view toward determining whether the care provided was below the community standard."

Appraisal engagement: "Our services will include a determination of the fair market value of the residence at 234 Oak Street, Phoenix, Arizona, at December 31, 2020 based on market data available to us at that time. We will also analyze the fair market value based on the income and cost approaches as required by the Uniform Standards of Professional Appraisal Practice (USPAP)."

The examples of what ***not*** to include are more precise contract language describing what the forensic consultant might do in the assignment, but these specific descriptions are not helpful to the consultant expert in litigation. More general descriptions of the anticipated project are suggested, even though general descriptions may not be the best specifics under contract law.

In summary, the engagement letter must adequately identify the general scope of the expert's assignment in the litigation matter, but it should not provide information to the opposing side that can be used to undermine the expert's opinion and conclusions. The strategy of this general description of the anticipated assignment protects the ultimate client in the long run. A detailed contract gives the other side a guide to what the expert ***might*** plan on doing and the notion that the expert obviously thinks these detailed steps might or will be important. Disclosing this information gives the opposition the opportunity to question whether the expert undertook each of the steps enumerated, and why or why not. There is more potential harm than benefit to this level of detail in the engagement letter; it will only damage the expert's ability to present his or her opinion in litigation.

LIMITATIONS OF ASSIGNMENT

If there are any limitations or exclusions from the assignment, they should be specifically identified in the engagement letter. Following are some examples of exclusions:

Practice Tip. Exclusions from forensic consulting assignment:

> ***Accountant's general limitation:*** "It is to be clearly understood that our financial consulting services do not constitute an audit or verification of any party's underlying financial records. We do not render legal, tax, or accounting advice; our services relate to financial and economic aspects of the case."

From business appraisal assignment: "To clarify our assignment, we will not be appraising any real property which may be owned by ABC Company or any related entities. The scope of our engagement excludes this real estate, although we are able to assist in obtaining a competent real estate appraisal for the property."

From real property appraisal assignment: "To clarify our assignment, we will not be evaluating or opining on the construction cost estimates to complete the commercial building located at 1234 Broadway, Costa Mesa, California."

Other substantive experts: There may be other aspects of professional consulting that should be identified and specifically excluded from forensic consulting assignments. The substantive expert should be aware of the requirements of his or her profession to make certain that no aspect of services is assumed to be included, based on professional standards. For example (and these are only possibilities because I am not expert in these other areas):

- The forensic architect who is rendering limited consulting services and is not responsible for larger design services;
- The reviewing physician is not providing complete medical services and is not responsible for fully investigating the health of the client;
- The rebuttal expert who is only responding to the opposition expert witness and whose work is strictly limited to that rebuttal.

DOCUMENTS REQUESTED

It is certainly reasonable to provide a document request list in an engagement letter (or as an attachment to the letter). Again, though, because the engagement letter will ultimately be used to cross-examine the expert, it is important to NOT state that the requested documents are "necessary" or "required" to perform the expert analysis. The document request should be identified as "the following documents would be helpful in our analysis of _________." Obviously, if documents are "required" and not every document is provided (which will often occur), the logical extension of that request is that the expert could not have competently completed his analysis without receiving all of the "required" documents.

Practice Tip. Obviously, the document request will conform to the substantive area of the forensic consultant's analysis and be different for every case. Examples follow:

"In order for us to proceed with our [substantive] analysis, it would be helpful for us to obtain copies of the following documents to be retained in our files:

1. A copy of the complaint in the litigation matter;
2. Relevant deposition transcripts and/or interrogatory responses;
3. [*medical records; employment and earnings records; a summary of medical expenses incurred; a summary of repair costs incurred; financial statements; architectural drawings; accident reports; reports of other experts; etc.*]
4. As our analysis proceeds, it may be necessary for us to request additional documents."

The expert should consider two types of deadlines in a document request: one for the date by which the documents should be provided, and another to clearly point out that the forensic consultant needs a minimum amount of time between document production and report preparation (or expert testimony). The consultant may not have the power to require that documents be provided by a certain date, so the language can be adjusted accordingly, but some date should be included to at least establish an expectation as to when documents will be provided.

Practice Tip.

> ***Minimum language:*** "It would be most beneficial for us to receive the requested documents prior to arranging a [*premises visit, meeting with client, etc.*] and it is imperative that we receive documents at least 30 (45?, 60?, 90?) days prior to the date the analysis is expected to be completed."
>
> ***Stronger language:*** "It is imperative that requested documents be provided at least 30 (?) days prior to the anticipated deposition date or other date that we are expected to render a [*substantive*] opinion. Forensic Consultants Inc. must be given adequate time to perform our analysis, and a minimum of 30 (?) days is required. Forensic Consultants Inc. cannot and will not assume responsibility to provide services in cases where we are advised of deposition dates or report due dates less than 30 (?) days before documents are provided."

Many forensic consultants include a statement about document retention or disposition in their engagement letters. While not necessarily critical information at the outset of the engagement, there seems to be no downside to including this provision in the initial written agreement with the client.

Practice Tip.

> "At the conclusion of the engagement, it is our practice to retain a complete copy of our file (excluding our expert depo-

sition transcripts), including client-provided documents, for a period of five years. Unless directed to the contrary by you, we will follow this practice in this engagement."

FEE PROVISIONS

This is a small point to start this important section, but I have always thought it was tacky to begin the engagement letter with paragraphs relating to fees. Yes, we all know how important fees are, but do you really want fees to be the first substantive paragraph of your engagement letter after the salutation? Aren't there more important things to address, or at least make look like they are more important? It's up to you, but I like to deal with fees a little later in the letter.

When you do cover fees in the engagement letter, the provisions should include:

i. A clear statement of who is responsible for payment (and who isn't—perhaps the lawyer—they like to see that in writing!);
ii. A clear statement that your fees are hourly and not contingent on the outcome of the matter, and a statement of your hourly rate;
iii. The terms of required ongoing payment of fees (i.e., statements will be sent monthly and outstanding balances are payable within 30 days);
iv. That there are points during the process at which all outstanding balances must be cleared (i.e., prior to report delivery or expert testimony in either deposition or trial);

v. That you cannot predict with any degree of certainty the total amount of fees that will be incurred in the case because of x, y, z (the unforeseen complexities of litigation, the difficulties raised by the other side, the degree to which your analysis and opinions will be challenged, etc.);
vi. The requirement of a retainer (if you can't get a retainer, what is your first clue?);
vii. If the fees are not paid as agreed, you have the right to withdraw from the case, and;
viii. Although not directly a fee issue, you should include a provision that if the client changes lawyers, you have the right to withdraw from the case.

I have been teaching Finance & Accounting for Lawyers at the University of San Diego School of Law for twenty-five years. In my first class every semester, I propose a set of damages facts from a new client walking into the fledgling lawyer's office, and I close my hypothetical with the following question to the class: "What is the first question you ask this client after hearing his factual situation?" Invariably, I get a stream of responses like: "Does the opposition have deep pockets?" or "Were there clear misrepresentations made to the client?" "Are there other defendants to be considered?" The creative responses of law students are limitless.

After milking the hypothetical for a few minutes and after a dramatic pause, I give them ***my*** answer to the question I posed to them. The first question to ask the client is "Do you have a retainer?" I then apologize profusely for my cynicism, but I carefully advise them that if they don't provide their professional services for a respectable fee and demand payment of it, they won't be in business long enough to practice the profession they aspire to.

I need not dwell on the reality of the importance of professional fees with readers of this book. Everyone understands their importance.

Practice Tip. Following are sample paragraphs relating to professional fees.

Fee paragraph with no estimate: "The services of this firm are billed on an hourly basis at rates ranging from $xxx to $yyy per hour. It is not possible to estimate with precision the total amount of time that will be required in this matter. Litigation services (pretrial conferences, depositions, and expert testimony) are billed at $yyy per hour. In addition to fees for services, out-of-pocket expenses relating to the consulting engagement are also billed directly to the client."

Fee paragraph with fee estimate: "The services of this firm are billed on an hourly basis at rates ranging from $xxx to $yyy per hour. Based on information that has been provided to us, it is our preliminary estimate that fees in this engagement should range from $____ to $_____, although this estimate does not affect the hourly basis of our billing. Litigation services (pretrial conferences, depositions, and expert testimony) are billed at $yyy per hour. In addition to fees for services, out-of-pocket expenses relating to the appraisal engagement are also billed directly to the client."

Retainer request; right to withdraw: "The services of this firm are provided on a retainer basis, and we request a retainer of $________. Fees in excess of the retainer will be billed a) at each month end during the course of the engagement. b) at the completion of the engagement. Our consulting fees are due upon presentation of statements, and a 1% per month interest charge is assessed on balances outstanding beyond thirty (30) days. The account balance is due prior to delivery of the appraisal report. Forensic Consultants Inc. reserves the right to withdraw from this engagement if fees have not been paid as agreed."

No retainer; right to withdraw: "In this matter, no retainer is being requested. During the course of this engagement, statements will be issued on a monthly basis to [*Client*], the responsible billing party. Fees for our services are due within 15 days of the receipt of statements and all professional fees are due prior to the time that expert testimony is rendered. A 1% per month interest charge is assessed on balances outstanding beyond 30 days. Forensic Consultants Inc. reserves the right to withdraw from this engagement if fees have not been paid as agreed."

Fees not contingent: "It is to be clearly understood that the fees for our services are in no way contingent on the outcome of the matter."

I have learned over the years that the more demanding you are about your professional fees, the more commanding is your reputation. Fees are only a problem if you let them be a problem. There's no point working for free, and you don't want to do it. The sad truth is that some clients are not happy at the end of their cases. One of the sad realities of litigation is that it is a very inefficient way to resolve problems, and clients learn that fact going through the process. Divorce cases are a good example of that, but so is civil litigation. At the end of the day, a client who has fully paid his bill is less likely to complain about the quality of your services than the client who owes you $15,000.

Fee estimates are problematic. I have been giving them for years, and I shoot myself in the foot regularly when I do it. I am wrong about 85% of the time, so why I continue to do it, I don't know. It always takes longer than you predict to figure out a complicated problem and break it down to a simple, objective, defensible solution.

As long as we're discussing expert witness fees, I will remind you of my admonition against charging a premium hourly rate for expert testimony (see Chapter 6, Billing Rates section). It's not a good idea for the reasons I stated there.

CONFLICTS OF INTEREST

Conflicts of interest are discussed in Chapter 6. Some forensic experts believe it is necessary to inform the client in writing that they have determined there are no conflicts that would prevent them from acting as a consultant or expert witness for the attorney and/or the attorney's client. Although this representation can be made in the engagement letter, the necessity of doing so is unclear. Of course, the forensic consultant will check conflicts and clear them, satisfying himself or herself that no significant conflicts exist. Arguably, a direct representation to the client that none exist is not necessary, and can only be used to the detriment of the forensic expert later. For this reason, I don't recommend having a "no conflict" paragraph in the engagement letter, but if you insist:

Practice Tip. Sample paragraph for having checked conflicts.

> ***No conflict representation:*** "We have endeavored to check conflicts, and as of the time of this letter, no conflicts exist of which we are aware..."

LIMITATION OF LIABILITY

Some forensic experts include a provision to attempt to hold them harmless from any liability resulting from their involvement in this matter. Although the enforceability of such a provision is always uncertain, a provision like the following is a good safeguard:

Practice Tip. Limitation of liability.

> ***Limitation of liability:*** "You and your client agree to hold our firm, its partners, and employees harmless from any and all liabilities, costs, and expenses relating to this engagement, and expenses (and those of our legal counsel) incurred by any reason of any action taken or committed to be taken by us in good faith. In no event will our firm be liable for incidental or consequential damages even if we have been advised of the possibility of such damages."

RIGHT TO WITHDRAW FROM ENGAGEMENT

Consideration should be given to including a provision that allows you to withdraw from and terminate the engagement if certain things occur. It is possible that facts may be uncovered that lead you to arrive at conclusions adverse to the client party's position. It is also possible that the client or attorney may exert unreasonable pressure for the forensic expert to provide an opinion with which he or she may disagree. The following is an example of such a clause:

Practice Tip. Right to withdraw.

> ***Right to Withdraw:*** "Should information become known that would make our continued involvement in this engagement inappropriate or should attorneys or parties involved in this litigation change, we reserve the right to withdraw from the engagement."

ARBITRATION CLAUSE

Consideration should be given to the inclusion of an arbitration provision in the consultant's engagement letter. An arbitration clause is a clause in a contract that requires the parties to resolve any dispute under the contract through the arbitration process as opposed to a judicial process. States have different requirements for arbitration clauses to have enforceability, and consideration must be given to state law to determine the enforceability of a clause in the forensic consultant's engagement letter.

Practice Tip.

> ***Sample arbitration clause:*** "Any dispute arising out of or relating to this agreement shall be finally resolved by arbitration in accordance with the rules of the American Arbitration Association then currently in effect, and judgment upon award rendered by the arbitrator(s) may be entered by any court having jurisdiction thereof." [THIS CLAUSE MAY NOT BE VALID IN YOUR STATE. LEGAL ADVICE SHOULD BE OBTAINED TO DRAFT A QUALIFYING ARBITRATION CLAUSE IN YOUR STATE.]

OTHER PROVISIONS

I have always been concerned that I would have an immovable scheduling conflict with a required expert testimony, but it hasn't happened to me in forty years. Yes, I have canceled vacations (or come home sooner) to testify in cases, but I have always managed to show up. But, since it isn't safe to assume that you can always solve the problem with good luck, I sometimes have included a "substitution of expert" clause in my engagement letters. Now, a substitution is easier to talk about than to actually accomplish, but it is possible to arrange it. And, it simply puts your client on notice that there may possibly be a scheduling problem.

Practice Tip.

> ***Sample substitution clause:*** "As a precautionary measure in the event of a scheduling conflict, we recommend that you co-designate either [*primary expert*] or [*secondary expert*], both qualified [*accountants, architects, physicians, life care planners, etc.*] and principals of Forensic Consultants Inc. to render expert testimony as to the analysis performed in this matter."

JOINT RETENTION ENGAGEMENTS

Many forensic consultants provide services jointly to both sides of a dispute. The practice is common for accountants and appraisers trying to help parties resolve their financial disputes. Joint retentions require special attention to the contract of engagement, client communications, production of documents, report preparation and expert testimony. If you choose to render services jointly to clients on opposing sides of a dispute, you should consider requiring a court appointment as opposed to a simple contractual stipulation between the parties as the basis for your retention. Performing services by order of a court probably provides an additional layer of insulation from being directly liable to the clients for the performance of your services.

Joint retentions require more complicated case management than one-party retentions. The parties are usually involved in a legal dispute, so there are issues of confidentiality of information being shared with the consultant, transparency of communications, and possible required sharing of information provided to the consultant. The handling of these issues should be discussed and understood by all parties to the retention agreement.

Fee issues are particularly sensitive in joint retentions because one side may advance its one-half of the fees when the other side doesn't. The paying side will logically expect to receive a copy of the work product upon payment, but it is inappropriate to provide a report to one party to a joint retention without providing it to the other side. Over the years, I have concluded that jointly retained work should only be done on a retainer basis, with both sides being required to deposit their share of the required fees in advance. When the work is nearing completion, if an unpaid balance remains, the consultant should advise the parties to complete their respective payments. At the end of the matter, the forensic consultant should not release a report until complete payment is made. Another reality of jointly retained work is that one side is frequently disappointed with the work product. This possible outcome doesn't make collecting an unpaid balance any easier.

Practice Tip.

Sample joint retention paragraph: "In this engagement, we are being retained by stipulation of both parties, although the parties are not stipulating to the conclusions that we may reach. We would appreciate your acknowledging the fact of this stipulation. For the record, the source of our engagement does not affect the conclusions that we reach."

ENGAGEMENT ACCEPTANCE AND TIME LIMITATION

Practice Tip.

Acceptance of agreement: "If this letter accurately sets forth the terms of our agreement in this matter, please sign and return the enclosed copy indicating your acceptance. We require receipt of the requested retainer prior to the time we are expected to begin our financial analysis."

"The proposed terms of our engagement are subject to review if not accepted within 60 days of the date of this letter."

Very truly yours,

Name
Forensic Consultants Inc.

ACCEPTED AS TO ASSIGNMENT:

________________ ________________________________

Date Attorney

ACCEPTED AS TO FEE AGREEMENT:

________________ ________________________________

Date Client

OTHER INCLUSIONS TO CONSIDER

Time limitation for disputing fees. The engagement letter can have a limitation on the time allowed to dispute the amount or characterization of fees.

Practice Tip.

> "It is agreed that any and all disputes or disagreements regarding the form, presentation, substance, amount, or any other aspect of a periodic invoice that we issue in connection with our services must be communicated to us in writing by you within 30 days of our delivery of such invoice, as defined in this Agreement. Absent this written communication to us by you, it is understood and agreed that you waive any and all disputes or disagreements pertaining to the form, presentation, substance, amount, and any other aspect of such periodic invoice and that the invoice will be paid in full in accordance with the terms of this Agreement."

Limitation on the amount of damages. Although there may be legal restrictions in some jurisdictions limiting the effect of a damage limitation, the consultant should consider a limitation on the amount of damages in the event of a dispute with the client. The engagement letter can have a limitation on the time allowed to dispute the amount or characterization of fees.

Practice Tip.

> "Unless otherwise prohibited by law or applicable professional standard, you agree that Forensic Consultants Inc., any of its affiliates, and any personnel of Forensic Consultants Inc. shall

> not be liable to you for any claims, liabilities, or expenses relating to this engagement for an aggregate amount in excess of the fees paid to us pursuant to this Agreement, except to the extent determined by the court to have resulted from the bad faith or intentional misconduct of Forensic Consultants Inc. Unless otherwise prohibited by law or applicable professional standard, in no event shall Forensic Consultants Inc. be liable for consequential, special, indirect, incidental, punitive, or exemplary losses or damages relating to this Agreement. This limitation on liability provision shall apply to the fullest extent of the law, whether in contract, statute, tort, professional standard, or otherwise."

CONCLUSION

Every engagement should have a contract memorializing the rights and responsibilities of the forensic consultant and the client. In the majority of cases, the engagement letter will be initially signed, then filed and forgotten. When something goes wrong in a case, however, the expert will fall back on the provisions of the agreement as the guideline for the resolution of the problem. Don't be caught in a difficult situation without a clear understanding of what the expert's and the client's respective responsibilities are.

CHAPTER 17

CONCLUSION

Nothing in *Mastering the Art of Expert Witness Testimony* is intended to subvert the forensic expert witness's ethical responsibility to provide objective, truthful analysis and opinions to clients in the environment of dispute resolution. This professional responsibility overrides any practice management considerations or strategies of expert witness testimony.

With the understanding of the expert's professional responsibilities, there are two overarching concerns in operating a successful forensic consulting practice. The first is the need to do very smart, high-level substantive work in the field of the forensic consultant's area of expertise. The work will be examined by other experts and challenged by the opposition. To prevail, the expert's work must be substantively first-rate.

The second concern in a forensic consulting practice is the reality that every part of the development of the opinion is exposed to scrutiny and, because of the adversarial nature of litigation, the scrutiny is not necessarily fair. I have repeatedly pointed out that there is (almost) no privilege that protects the expert's work product and that the opposing side of a disputed matter is trying to contradict the expert's analysis in every way. This argumentative aggression against the expert's work colors the procedures the expert must employ in planning the analysis, developing the opinion, documenting the work, and presenting his or her answers in litigation (depositions and trial). I have tried to cover those bases in this book.

In addition to being highly technically proficient, the successful expert witness must be aware of the strategies and tactics of litigation to successfully advance her substantive opinion in a dispute resolution forum.

The methods and suggested practices in *Mastering the Art of Expert Witness Testimony* are intended to help the forensic consultant elevate the process to an art form. I hope I have helped you get closer to it.

ACKNOWLEDGMENTS

Everything I have accomplished in my professional career has benefited from the support of others, including *Mastering the Art of Expert Witness Testimony*. Here, I will acknowledge the contributions of my colleagues currently and over the years.

My professional associate, Elena Gladson, CPA, coauthored *Developing and Managing a Litigation Services Practice* with me in 1999, and that book is the outline for this one. More recently, my professional coach, Jill Thiry, has helped motivate me to continue to be persistent in finishing this work. My editors at Publishing Partner, Bethany Kelly and Frank Steele, have significantly enhanced the quality of this book.

My partners and colleagues at Brinig & Company Inc. and CBIZ Forensic Consulting Group include Chris Summers, Paul Zimmer, Bob Taylor, Cheryl Kessler, Joe Baldonado, Yesenia Lozoya, Kate Kowaleski, Amy Pillersdorf, Jamie Haven, Marilyn Weber, Diana Wroblewski, Megan O'Neill, Joni Deiters, Sarah Ross, Marie Ebersbacher, Jeff Bussell, Alejandro Lopez, and others who have helped build a successful professional firm that we are extremely proud of.

Professional colleagues who have given their time and thought to various chapters of this book include Paul Regan, Michael Ueltzen, Bob Taylor, Robert Hall, Tony Yip, Scott Metzger, Dirk Metzger, Denny Webb, Jim McCafferty, Steve Roach, Jack Young, Benni Mortimer, Annette Stalker, Craig Enos, Paul Marchegiani, Professor Steven Lubet, Professor Elizabeth Boals, and one anonymous federal judge.

Finally, the one for whom I do it all: my wonderful wife of twenty years, Lisa Brinig.

ABOUT THE AUTHOR

Brian Peter Brinig is a certified public accountant and non-practicing lawyer who has specialized in forensic accounting and business valuation for more than forty years in Southern California. He is a managing director at CBIZ Forensic Consulting Group LLC, the publicly traded company that acquired the forensic accounting firm he founded and operated since 1983.

Mr. Brinig holds accreditations in business valuation from the American Institute of CPAs and the American Society of Appraisers, and he has qualified as an expert witness in federal and state courts more than 300 times on financial issues. He has been the state chairman of the California Society of CPA's Business Valuation Committee, and he has served on the board of directors of the San Diego Society of CPAs. He holds a degree in business from Georgetown University and a law degree from the University of San Diego School of Law.

Mr. Brinig has been an adjunct professor of law at the University of San Diego School of Law for twenty-five years and previously taught both graduate and undergraduate accounting and finance. He is the past president of the Financial Analysts Society of San Diego, and he has written three other books and many articles on the subjects of forensic accounting, business valuation, and techniques of expert witness testimony. He is also the author of *Mastering Self-Discipline: A Thoughtful Approach Gets Better Results* (New York, NY: Burlington Business Press, 2020).

www.ingramcontent.com/pod-product-compliance
Lightning Source LLC
LaVergne TN
LVHW022023310725
817594LV00001B/7
9798218067465